T0063510

MY RACIAL GROUP'S PURPOSE ON EARTH

MY RACIAL GROUP'S PURPOSE ON EARTH

EVERY RACIAL GROUP AROUND THE GLOBE HAS A SPECIAL PURPOSE TO FULFILL

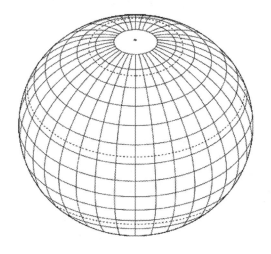

Know your racial group's purpose if you were born on the continent of Europe, Africa, Asia, Australia, North America, South America, Antarctica or anywhere else such as on an Island, aircraft or water vessel.

Dr. Franklin T. Gibbs

iUniverse LLC
Bloomington

MY RACIAL GROUP'S PURPOSE ON EARTH
EVERY RACIAL GROUP AROUND THE GLOBE
HAS A SPECIAL PURPOSE TO FULFILL

Copyright © 2013 Dr. Franklin T. Gibbs.

All rights reserved. No part of this book may be used or reproduced by any means, graphic, electronic, or mechanical, including photocopying, recording, taping or by any information storage retrieval system without the written permission of the publisher except in the case of brief quotations embodied in critical articles and reviews.

iUniverse books may be ordered through booksellers or by contacting:

iUniverse LLC
1663 Liberty Drive
Bloomington, IN 47403
www.iuniverse.com
1-800-Authors (1-800-288-4677)

Because of the dynamic nature of the Internet, any web addresses or links contained in this book may have changed since publication and may no longer be valid. The views expressed in this work are solely those of the author and do not necessarily reflect the views of the publisher, and the publisher hereby disclaims any responsibility for them.

Any people depicted in stock imagery provided by Thinkstock are models, and such images are being used for illustrative purposes only. Certain stock imagery © Thinkstock.

ISBN: 978-1-4917-0824-8 (sc)
ISBN: 978-1-4917-0825-5 (e)

Printed in the United States of America.

iUniverse rev. date: 11/07/2013

CONTENTS

INTRODUCTION

As you read this book from cover to cover, you'll breath a breath of fresh air as you discover the purpose for which God created your racial group to fulfill here on earth (and in heaven for that matter). For God's callings (i.e., His purposes for all racial groups) will never end. (Romans 11:29).

This book is the greatest source of enlightenment that you'll find on the subject of God's purpose for creating a variety of colorful racial groups. This book also enlightens you about the purpose (calling) that God gave **your** racial group (in particular) to fulfill here on earth. Hence, above all things, you must know your racial group's purpose so that you can serve God completely.

In this book, we're going to take a journey. As we begin, the great flood of (Gen 6:11-19) has ceased, Noah and his family are descending from the Ark, and we will continue our journey through the millennium (Christ's 1,000 year reign).

Except for Noah's family, the flood killed all humans and animals that were on the earth. God chose Noah's 3 sons (Shem, Ham and Japheth) to preserve life on earth. (Gen 9:1, 7, 10, 18-19). So, just as God filled the earth with a variety of colorful racial groups before the flood, He used Shem, Ham and Japheth to refill (replenish) the earth with the same variety of racial groups after the flood. So, Shem, Ham and Japheth were the progenitors of three different family lines.

So, all people are (1) direct descendants of Shem's family line, Ham's family line or Japheth's family line or, (2) descendants by the mixing and blending of their gene pools. Thus, Shem, Ham and Japheth were the progenitors of all racial groups on earth today: Israelites, East Indians, Spaniards, Indonesians, Germans, Chinese, Afro Americans, American Indians, South Americans and Vietnamese.

Likewise, they were the progenitors of the Australians, Hawaiians, Africans, Hispanics, Frenchmen, Japanese, Koreans, Arabs, Greeks, Mexicans, Russians, British, Italians, Eskimos, Filipinos, Samoans, Austrians, Canadians, Cubans, Polynesians, Panamanians, Egyptians, Turks, Swedes, Pakistanis, Malaysians, Yugoslavians, Armenians, Caribbean people, the Irish, and the list goes on. All of these racial groups trace back to the family line of Shem, the family line of Ham or the family line of Japheth.

Today, far too many people from different racial groups are walking contrary to the purpose for which God created their racial groups to fulfill here on earth. In other words, there are far too many people from different racial groups who don't dwell in peace with other racial groups as God has called them to do. Consider the following passages of Scripture.

"Follow peace and holiness with all men, without which no man shall see the Lord." (Heb 12:14). "Let God's peace rule in your hearts, to which also you are called in one body (i.e., peace is one of your racial group's primary purposes for being here) . . ." (Col 3:15)). ". . . God is the God of peace and not the author of confusion (strife, disorder, disturbance, etc) . . ." (1 Cor 14:33). "For, He is our peace who reconciled man and God unto peace. He broke down the middle wall of partition between us (i.e., Jesus made peace between God and man). (Eph 2:14).

That said, not only are people from different racial groups not following peace as God desires, but they're not in line with their God given purpose for being here. As we go along, you'll gain a wealth of knowledge and benefits from studying the biblical doctrines that this book shares about the purpose for which God created all racial groups. That is, in this book you'll gain the following wealth of knowledge:

(1) To begin with, this book clearly shows why God created His colorful racial groups with different skin tones, nose sizes, lip shapes and hair textures. This divine truth will increase your knowledge and understanding of God's intended design in all of its beauty and glory. You'll not only gain a tremendous appreciation for what God was up to when He created your specific racial group, but you'll be able to see His ingenious creation through His eyes. For, He knew exactly what He was doing.

You'll appreciate the enlightenment that you'll gain by knowing why some people propagate myths, stereo types, prejudices and negative energy about different racial groups. For centuries, these people (with bitter hearts) have caused serious misunderstandings between different racial groups.

Their unfounded propaganda has been running amuck for centuries (i.e., it has gone too far). But, once you know the origin of this negative energy and the course of action that God designed for you and your racial group to take in overcoming this negativity, you'll definitely be able to breathe a breath of fresh air.

(2) Your eyes will be opened as you realize that God intended for mixed children of color from interracial marriages (between men and women) to serve a special purpose both on earth and in Paradise. That is, mixed children of color are God's intended design. As such, the parents of mixed children of color are tremendously blessed for procreating or adopting mixed children of color who are created for a special purpose on earth and in Paradise. You'll gain great comfort in knowing God's intended and eternal purpose for mixed children of color.

(3) You'll be relieved and greatly benefited to know your racial group's purpose for being here. In this light, we'll study God's cherubim (special angelic beings) in great detail. For God patterned His cherubim's behavior after man's expected behavior. (Eze 1:5).

Since God's cherubim behave like we're supposed to behave, we study them to see what we're supposed to do. Hence, cherubim act like, imitate and exhibit the behavior that God expects of us—i.e., they act like humans are supposed to act, for they have the likeness of a man. (Eze 1:5).

Thus, cherubim are pivotal in (i.e., the keys to) unlocking the purpose for which God created His colorful racial groups. So, God uses cherubim to show us our racial group's calling. We can pinpoint the specific cherub function that identifies with our particular racial group. We can then serve God completely. The bottom line is that the callings that God gave Ham, Shem and Japheth can be identified (pinpointed) by studying the calling (functions) that God gave His cherubim.

(4) You'll be pleased to know the multiple blessings that God will bestow upon you if you choose to be His bride (i.e., His wife) by getting saved through Christ. God's blood covenant can be grouped into four major components: His eternal life blessing, His peace blessing, His word blessing and His wealth blessing.

As for His wife, God's purpose is to dwell with her for eternity in a spiritual marriage union. God offers you a marriage proposal. You'll gain valuable knowledge as we study Christ's spiritual marriage with His church and God's spiritual marriage with Jewish people. The marriage ceremony and supper for Christ's wife (i.e., His church) will be held in heaven. God will have a marriage supper on earth for Jews who're not part of the church. You'll be delighted to know how you and your racial group fit into God's wedding plans.

One of the most crucial issues of life is that there are serious consequences for those who reject God's proposal. These consequences pertain to (1) Old Testament sinners who looked forward to Christ's death but yet rejected God's marriage proposal, (2) people who dwelled in Christ's day but rejected His marriage proposal, and (3) people who look back on Christ's death and reject God's marriage proposal (i.e., they reject His sacrificial death for their sins).

Those who reject God's marriage union will suffer eternal punishment in hell. (Rev 20:10-15). So, it's a must that you know what Satan is up to. He strives to (1) divide the people of God's racial groups, (2) keep them in the dark about their racial group's purpose, and (3) destroy them by any means necessary. (Jn 10:10).

One of Satan's key strategies to divide and conquer is to influence society to dictate beauty in man's eyes. Some people (heavily influence by Satan) propagate that the large noses, full lips, dark skins and hair textures of some of Ham's offspring are ugly. But, you'll have a rude awakening as you gaze upon their creative beauty through God's eyes. You'll be amazed at the wealth of knowledge that Solomon's Song provides on the beauty of Ham's descendants.

God created beauty in the first place and revealed that His creation was very good (i.e., His creation was His masterpiece that could not be improved upon). (Gen 1:31). Who is man to dare dispute with God about His creative beauty? That is, you haven't seen beauty until you see it through God's eyes. That said, this book shows the beauty of Ham's offspring through God's eyes.

So, sit back, get comfortable and enjoy to the fullest extent the ingenious purpose for which God created your racial group and the amazing treasures and benefits that He has in store for you and your fearfully and wonderfully made racial group. (Ps 139:14).

ACKNOWLEDGMENTS

I thank my Lord for being my guiding light during the writing of this book. Day by day He gave me my daily bread (His words of knowledge) to use in writing this book. He supplied all of my needs. I couldn't have done it without Him. For He was indeed my vine (i.e., He was my source of knowledge). (John 15:4-5). I give Christ, my Lord and Savior, all the glory!

I thank my wife Joan for her prayers and support. I love the way that she sticks by my side through my stormy days (down times) and sunny days (up times). As my loving help mate, she happily contributed her artistic skills in creating the design for the cover of this book. She is indeed my breath of fresh air.

I thank my wonderful children (Deborah, Everett, Stephen and Terry) for supporting me during the writing this book. I also thank my other close family members and friends for supporting me during the writing of this book.

CHAPTER 1

Your Racial Group Has A Purpose To Fulfill On Earth—Session 1

Fulfilling your racial groups' purpose

You were born. Therefore, you exist. God has sworn. Therefore, you can be on heaven's list.

From birth, you were in God's hands. From birth, you were in God's plans. You have a purpose to fulfill. Your purpose Satan wants to kill.

From birth you were given everything you need. From birth, your racial group was born to succeed.

Every racial group has a purpose to fulfill on earth and in Paradise. You were born. Therefore, you exist. This means that you're in God's plans. God has a divine plan for His creation, which includes every racial group on earth.

As God told Jeremiah, "Before I formed thee in the belly, I knew thee; and before you were born, I ordained thee as prophet." (Jer 1:5). Just as God gave Jeremiah a purpose, He also gave you and your racial group a purpose to fulfill.

First you must discover your individual calling so that you can operate it within the framework of your racial groups' calling. This book discusses God's divine purpose for your racial group so that you can serve and worship God completely.

Satan strives to keep us in the dark about our racial group's purpose. He doesn't want us to worship God completely. He wants to keep all racial groups clawing at one another. He not only comes to steal, kill and destroy, but he also knows that a house divided against itself cannot stand. (John 10:10, Mark 3:25).

Noah's three sons: Shem, Ham and Japheth

We'll study Gen 9:25-27. These verses provide knowledge about God's purpose for each racial group. We'll study Noah's three sons. After the flood (Gen 6:5-7, 17), they refilled the earth with all racial groups of today. (Gen 9:1, 18-19).

By studying Gen 9:25-27 and Noah's 3 sons, we can know each racial group's purpose. We must use the gifts of our personal calling as we operate within the framework of our racial groups' calling. Far too many people are so busy harming, hating and discriminating against other groups that they're going to die before they even get a chance to learn their racial group's purpose. If we follow our racial group's purpose, our racial problems would be solved—i.e., they would go away.

We need to know that we're God's little gods (we're not equal to God, but we're His magistrates on earth). (Jn 10:34). In fulfilling our purpose, God meant for heaven to be His domain and earth to be our domain. "The heavens are the Lord's: but the earth hath He given to the children of men." (Ps 115:16, Matt 5:5).

Believers are those who believe that (1) Christ died for us, (2) He was raised from the dead, and (3) if they confess this truth aloud, they'll not perish in hell. (Rom 10:9-10). Believers inherit God's covenant promises. (John 3:16). God's covenant promises can be grouped into four major components, which are:

1. God's eternal life blessing (raised from the dead to live forevermore);
2. God's peace blessing (eternal peace, joy and bliss);
3. God's word blessing (eternal knowledge, wisdom and truth); and
4. God's wealth blessing (living an abundant life forevermore).

If you're a saved offspring of Shem, Ham or Japheth, you have inherited God's birthright blessing (God's covenant). And, you have to fulfill (here on earth) both your personal calling and your racial group's calling. So, God has some important things on earth to do. We need to know what racial group is supposed to do what?

The bottom line is that all people on earth are descendants of Noah's three sons: Shem, Ham and Japheth. After the great flood (Gen 6:5-7, 17), the earth was repopulated by these 3 family lines. (Gen 9:1, 7, 18-19). The divine callings that God gave Noah's three sons directly pertain to you and your racial group. So, your personal and racial group's calling are important to God's purpose for man.

That said, we need to know God's divine purpose for our respective racial groups. In no way does Satan want us to know that God has given our racial group a divine purpose to fulfill both in this world and in the world to come (i.e., our racial group's purpose will continue in the new world to come). (Rom 11:29).

Prelude to God's racial callings—Part I (Satan's strategies)

Let us now discuss—in 9 parts—a foundational prelude to God's racial callings. God created many racial groups with a variety of skin tones like unto a beautiful flower garden. God wanted all people of His colorful racial groups to accept Christ as their Savior so that they could be His spiritual wife for eternity.

God would give each racial group a purpose to fulfill. These groups would glorify and reflect God's divine being. He would bless them with the four components of His birthright blessing. In time, He would gather them to dwell with them forevermore. (Eze 37:21-28, Zech 2:10-11, Rev 19:7-9, Hos 2:19-23).

There are many indicators in the creation of how God is mindful of us and that He has a purpose for us. But, what God intends for good, Satan (His Archenemy) strives to destroy (i.e., Satan is a negative indicator of God's good intentions).

That said, Satan devised some evil strategies to destroy God's good intentions for His colorful racial groups. One of his strategies is to keep our racial group's purpose hidden from us. So, Satan is the culprit behind people's blindness about their racial group's purpose. Another one of his strategies is to divide and conquer. A house divided against itself cannot stand. (Matt 12:25, Mark 3:24-25).

Satan uses many demonic strategies to derail God's plans for us. In order be aware of what he's up to, we need to know all we can about his evil schemes to disrupt God's salvation plans for us. I don't care if we're saved or unsaved; we're at war with Satan in the battle between good and evil. There's nothing he wouldn't do to get us to join him in the eternal lake of fire. For, as a roaring lion, he roams about seeking whom he may devour (destroy) if we allow him. (1 Pet 5:8).

Satan is out to get everybody to defame or bring shame to God's holy name. He doesn't care who we are, his objective is to bring us down any way he can. He hates God and every man, woman or child that God created. So, we have to be aware of his strategies to know what he's up to.

In one of his most evil strategies, Satan made a vile attempt to contaminate Shem's family line, Ham's family line and Japheth's family line (i.e., he sought to contaminate the entire human race). Satan sought to do this so that God would not be able to use them to fulfill His purpose. Let's take a closer look.

God created some angels with the power to enter the earth in human form to carry out missions. (Heb 13:2). Even though a third of the angels rebelled against God and were cast out of heaven (Rev 12:4), some of them retained their power to enter the earth in human form. (Gen 6:1-4, Jude 1:6-8). Satan had these angels, who could enter the earth in human form, marry and impregnate human women. (Gen 6:1-4). These angels had the physical features and emotions of human males.

An angel having sex with women was an unnatural act of strange flesh. In those days, angels and human women produced giants who were mixed with angelic genes and human genes. (Gen 6:4). Unnatural acts of strange flesh also pertain to humans having sex with animals, men having sex with men and women having sex with women. (Rom 1:26-28).

Satan wanted to mix humans with a hybrid of angelic and human offspring. He wanted to contaminate the human race, which would (1) destroy the identities of humans, (2) derail their racial group's calling, and (3) ruin God's plans for them.

In time, Satan would have contaminated the human race. In order to protect the human race and His purpose for it, God chained these fallen angels in Tartarus (an area of the bottomless pit of hell). The people of Sodom and Gomorrah who fornicated and went after strange flesh are examples of what happens to those who do this. They're suffering in the fires of Hades as I speak. (Jude 1:6-7).

These fallen angels and their human wives were a stench to God as well as the rest of the world that was full of wickedness. It is written, "Go d saw that man's wickedness was great on earth. Every imagination and thought of man's heart was evil continually." (Gen 6:5). Fed up with the wide spread wickedness on earth, God brought a great flood upon the earth to destroy all flesh. (Gen 6:5-7, 17).

After the flood, God would use Noah's three sons (Shem, Ham and Japheth) to repopulate the earth so that He could start all over again with colorful racial groups that would fulfill His purpose here on earth.

Even so, Satan is still around today trying to disrupt God's purpose for His racial groups. Because of Satan, racial groups have been bickering and clawing at one another for centuries. But, once we become aware of and follow our racial group's purpose (as shown in this book), our racial problems will be solved—i.e., they'll go away. That said, in this book, you'll enjoy to the fullest extent the ingenious purpose for which God created you and your racial group and the amazing treasures and benefits that He has in store for you and your racial group.

Prelude to God's racial callings—Part II (The Prayer of Salvation)

As noted, there are many indicators in creation of how God is so mindful of His colorful racial groups. For example, many Scriptures in the Bible are indicators of God's good plans for salvation and the consequences of rejecting God's salvation plans. Hence, the most important truth that people of all racial groups should know is that the Prayer of Salvation is their key to eternal life. Once we accept salvation through Christ, God translates us into the safest place in the universe: God's kingdom of righteousness and peace.

In order to be safe from the horrors of hell, we must accept Christ as our Savior through the Prayer of Salvation. The good news is that Christ came to earth to save us and translate us into God's kingdom. God loves us so much that He gave His only begotten Son, Jesus so that if we believe in Him we'll not perish, but have everlasting life. (John 3:16). Hence, God was always mindful of us.

Jesus died on the cross to pay for our sins. God raised Him from the dead on the third day with a heavenly body. If we believe in our hearts and confess with our mouths that Jesus died for us and that God raised Him from the dead, God will also raise our bodies from the dead with new bodies. (Rom 8:11).

So then, to secure your safe place, simply recite, aloud, the following Prayer of Salvation to the Lord God Almighty, "Lord, I confess with my mouth that Jesus Christ died on the cross to pay for all of my sins. Forgive me of my sins. I believe in my heart that God raised Jesus from the dead. Lord Jesus, please come into my life and be my Lord and Savior." (Rom 10:9). Say this simple prayer aloud and you'll be translated into God's kingdom immediately! It's just that easy to be translated to the safest place in the universe. (Rom 10:10).

Prelude to God's racial callings—Part III (The color of my skin)

Noah's three sons had three different gene pools (i.e., family lines). This fact is another indicator of how God is mindful of His colorful racial groups. Their three different gene pools shows that God had in mind (from the foundation of the world) to fill the earth with a variety of colorful racial groups.

After the great flood that killed all flesh (except for Noah and his family), God resumed His plan to create a variety of colorful racial groups. God chose Noah to preserve life on earth. He saved Noah and his family from the flood (8 people). (Gen 6:17-22, 7:12-13, 1 Pet 3:20, 2 Pet 2:5,).

Like Adam and Eve, Noah and his wife could produce children of any color in God's spectrum of skin tones (explained later). Ham had dark skin. Japheth had pinkish skin. Shem had olive skin—a blend of Japheth's and Ham's skin tones. So, just as God filled the earth before the flood, He repopulated (refilled) the earth after the flood with an array of skin tones: very dark, golden brown, copper, tan, cream, olive, yellowish, pinkish, etc. These facts are indicators in God's creation of how God is mindful of His colorful racial groups.

So, by the mixing the gene pools of Noah's 3 sons, all racial groups (Germans, Hawaiians, South Americans, Israelites, Spaniards, Indonesians, Chinese, British, Africans, Afro Americans, American Indians, East Indians, Vietnamese, Koreans, Japanese, Frenchmen, Australians, Hispanics, Arabs, Greeks, Mexicans, Russians, Italians, etc.) trace back to Noah's 3 sons. God gave each of Noah's sons a special purpose to fulfill on earth and in Paradise. (Gen 9:1, 7, 18-19).

Prelude to God's racial callings—Part IV (Mixed children of color)

We're examining the numerous indicators in the creation of how God is mindful of His colorful racial groups. From His colorful racial groups many mixed children of color were born. We need to know that God created mixed children of color for a special purpose in this world and in Paradise. They're created as a special blend of Ham's, Shem's and Japheth's gene pools.

Satan strives to derail God's purpose for mixed children of color from interracial marriages. He strives to keep them in the dark about their racial group's purpose. Far too many of them suffer mental or physical abuse because of their skin color. Many of them suffer from an identity crisis. They constantly ask, "Do I go by my mother's side or father's side? Do I go by my features or my culture? Who am I?

Uninformed people call them mixed breeds with no identity. They neither know God nor understand Him. They're ever learning and unable to come to the truth. (2 Tim 3:7). Mixed children of color should not allow them to dissuade them.

God's plan is to have peace on earth; not strife. Racial groups are of one blood (Adam's blood). God determines their times and habitations. Mixed children of color should seek God for the truth. In Him they live, move and have their being. (Acts 17:24-28). Furthermore, if God did not have a special purpose for mixed children of color, He would not have told Noah's sons—who have different gene pools—to repopulate the earth. (Gen 9:1, 7, 18-19).

Mixed children of color resulted from mixing the gene pools of Noah's 3 sons. The mixing of their gene pools through interracial unions is the only way that the earth could have been repopulated after the flood with mixed children of color.

As we go along, you'll find out how wrong these ridiculers are (in God's eyes) for harassing mixed children of color from interracial marriages who are born with a special purpose on earth and in heaven. So, gene mixing is indeed an indicator of how God is mindful of His mixed children of color from His colorful racial groups.

Prelude to God's racial callings—Part V (Who am I?)

A racial identity crisis is a painful experience. If you're a mixed person of color, have you ever asked yourself, "Who am I?" Allow me to ease your mind. As we study the many indicators in the creation of how God is mindful of His racial groups, we'll find that God always had His mixed children of color in mind to serve a special purpose on earth and in heaven.

As noted, after the flood, God used Ham, Shem and Japheth to refill the earth (Gen 9:1, 7, 18-19). Hence, all racial groups descended from one of Noah's sons. That is, Eskimos, Filipinos, Samoans, Austrians, Canadians, Cubans, Polynesians, Turks, Egyptians, Swedes, Pakistanis, Malaysians, Yugoslavians, Armenians, Caribbean people, the Irish, Panamanians, and so forth trace back to Shem's family line, Ham's family line or Japheth's family line.

Thus, since Noah's three sons repopulated the earth, people have a mixture of their gene pools. Because of mixed marriages and sexual unions in our ancestry, we're all mixed. There are, however, people who only have Ham's, Japheth's or Shem's genes. They're of pure descent. But, for the most part, we're all mixed children. As you can see, the three different gene pools of Noah's three sons are indicators in the creation of how God is mindful of His colorful racial groups.

So, all mixed children need to do is trace their father's bloodline back to Shem, Ham or Japheth and they'll not only know their true identity, but they'll also know their racial group's calling. Just like that, their identity crisis would be over.

Why is your racial group's purpose traced through your father's bloodline? God gave your racial group's calling to the male progenitors (i.e., Shem, Ham and Japheth). Hence, your racial group's purpose is determined by your paternal side. Not only that, but scientifically, it is your father's blood that flows through your body. Not an ounce of your mother's blood flows through your body.

You inherited ½ of your genes from your father and ½ from your mother, but your blood came only from your father. So, your father's blood traces back to Japheth, Ham or Shem so that you can determine your true identity and racial group's purpose. Therefore, your paternal side determines your racial group's purpose (calling). That is, you are whoever your father is.

All racial groups lived in the land of Shinar and spoke the same language. Instead of being obedient, they chose to be their own gods by building the tower of Babel to get to heaven in their own power, which—unto this day—is humanism.

God scattered them over the earth and gave them different languages. (Gen 10:8-19, 11:1-2). They didn't acquire their skin tones by being in new climates. God created them (in the beginning) with different skin tones. (Gen 1:27, 2:7).

So, neither mixed children of color nor any other people on earth really have an identity crisis. All they have to do is trace their father's bloodline back to the original land areas where Shem's, Ham's and Japheth's descendants migrated to and settled and they'll know their true identities and their racial group's purpose.

For ages couples have been having children. Your father may have very dark skin, but he may really be in Shem's family line. He may have highly pinkish skin, but he may really be in Ham's family line. Hence, your father's color or features may not always reveal your true identity and racial group's calling. That's why you must trace your father's ancestry back to Shem, Ham or Japheth to be certain.

For more accuracy of your father's family line, males can use Y-chromosome DNA testing to trace back to the land areas where Ham's, Japheth's and Shem's offspring settled. Fathers pass Y-chromosomes to their sons; not their daughters. So, Y-chromosome DNA testing is vital in tracing the ancestry of males.

Females can trace their biological father's ancestry through the Y-chromosome DNA testing of their biological father, father's biological brother, male cousins or male grandparents in their biological father's bloodline. You also need to trace your mother's roots. Mothers pass mitochondrial DNA data to their sons and daughters. Tracing your father's and mother's roots determine your racial mix.

Armed with this data, as well as historical, anthropological, and archeological data of your ancestry, you can determine (pretty accurately) whether you trace back to the geographic area of Japheth's, Ham's or Shem's descendants. You must make sure that the professionals who do your tests use statistical precision. DNA testing can help determine your racial mix. You could trace your parent's genes and find that your racial mix is 60% African, 30% European, and 10% Asian.

Prelude to God's racial callings—Part VI (The coat of many colors)

The coat of many colors is an indicator in the creation of how God is mindful of His racial groups. The coat of many colors is an indicator of how believers from all racial groups will (through Christ) win the battle of good and evil. So, if you're a believer, you're blessed by the coat of many colors. Let's examine this truth.

Jacob made a special coat of many colors for his favorite son, Joseph. (Gen 37:3). The coat of many colors portrays all colorful racial groups over which Christ rules in His kingdom of righteousness and peace that'll never end. (Dan 7:14, Rev 12:5, 15:4).

Joseph's coat of many colors is also symbolic of a covering. The coat of many colors speaks of being covered by the blood of Christ. For Christ is our Savior who washes away our sins with His blood. (Rom 4:7, Matt 26:28). Those covered by His blood are covered because of their choice to serve and worship Christ.

Serving Christ means that each racial group under the sun has a unique purpose (calling) to fulfill here on earth. Satan strives to derail God's purpose, His callings and the four components of His birthright blessing. But, Satan will not succeed.

Satan's defeat is portrayed by Joseph's brothers who took his coat of many colors and threw him into a pit. This shows how Satan tried to defeat Christ. Satan crucified Christ and His soul descended into Hades. Satan thought that he had defeated Christ. But, lo and behold, by God's divine providence and omnipotent power, Christ was raised (resurrected) from the dead and lived.

Joseph (who had the coat of many colors) was raised out of the pit and (like Christ) he lived. For, he was thrown into the pit, but yet he lived. (Gen 37:18-28). This event shows that Christ and His believers will be the ultimate victors of the battle between good and evil. So, these events in God's creation are indicators of how God is mindful of His colorful racial groups. Hallelujah, to God be the glory!

Prelude to God's racial callings—Part VII (The anointing)

The anointing is another indicator in the creation of how God is mindful of His colorful racial groups. Consider the verses of Scripture that follow.

". . . God sent His word to Israel to preach peace through Christ . . . and how God anointed Jesus with the Holy Ghost and with power: who went about doing good and healing all who were oppressed of the devil: God was with Him . . . God raised Him the third day and showed Him openly." (Acts 10:36-40).

"God's Spirit is upon Christ, because He has anointed Him to preach the gospel to the poor. God sent Him to heal the brokenhearted, to preach deliverance to the captives and recovering of sight to the blind . . ." (Luke 4:18-19, Isa 61:1). God also establishes, strengthens and anoints us in Christ. (2 Cor 1:21).

The Hebrew word for anointed (Ps 20:6) is mashiyach (maw-shee´-akh). It refers to the smearing of oil (symbolic of the Holy Spirit) upon someone who is set aside, sanctified and consecrated for a special purpose, office, function or service. The anointing authorizes and empowers a person to use all the power of the Godhead to fulfill God's purpose for him and his racial group. (Matt 28:18-20).

When God anoints you for a holy purpose, He equips you with everything you'll need to succeed. God's anointing teaches you about Him, His truths and your purpose (calling). The anointing prevents you from being deluded by Satan.

Your anointing abides in you. It teaches you truth. (1 John 2:27). So, you can't fail your calling unless you set your will against God's purpose for your life.

Prelude to God's racial callings—Part VIII (Focusing on the anointing)

A person's will is an indicator of how God is mindful of His racial groups. The only force that can stop us from focusing on our anointing and our racial group's purpose is our wills. Satan uses a three pronged attack to disrupt our wills.

Satan's knows that if people find out their racial group's purpose and set their minds to obey, nothing will be restrain from them. (Gen 11:6). That said, the world is filled with so much violence and discrimination because far too many people don't have a clue about their racial group's purpose.

Prelude to God's racial callings—Part IX (Principle of spiritual adoption)

The principle of spiritual adoption is another indicator that shows how God is mindful of us. Your racial group's purpose is determined by your biological father's ancestry. But, what if you don't know who he is? You may be adopted or conceived by donor sperm and you don't know who he is. What then?

Fret not. When a man becomes your father (1) by adoption, (2) by becoming your step father, or (3) by becoming your father figure who's your spiritual overseer, you're to trace your racial group's purpose through his ancestry.

Jacob said to his son Joseph, "And now thy two sons (Ephraim and Manasseh) which were born unto thee in the land of Egypt before I came unto thee in Egypt are mine; as Reuben and Simeon, they shall be mine." (Gen 48:5).

Genesis 48:5 shows God's principle of spiritual adoption—i.e., Ephraim and Manasseh took on the name and rights of Jacob's sons. Jacob adopted them as his sons. When God adopts us, we take on His name as His sons. Jacob said, ". . . Ephraim and Manasseh . . . are mine . . . bless the lads and let my name be named on them, and the name of my fathers, Abraham and Isaac . . ." (Gen 48:5, 16).

Joseph was Ephraim's and Manasseh's biological father. When Jacob stepped in as their spiritual father, the boys not only took on Jacob's name, but they also took on the name of Jacob's ancestors, Abraham and Isaac. This is how God's principle of spiritual adoption works.

God's principle of spiritual adoption shows that if our biological father is unknown, we can trace our racial group's purpose through the ancestry of our adopting father, step father or father figure who gives us spiritual oversight. So, God was mindful of (thought of) everything when He created us.

Before God made us, He knew through whom we would trace our racial group's purpose—i.e., before He formed us, He knew us. (Jer 1:5). So, God's principle of adoption is an indicator of how He's mindful of us. Even though some traces of our true biological father's purpose may be evident in us, God providentially saw to it that we would trace our purpose through our current (known) father figure.

Hence, there is no force in the universe that can stop believers from fulfilling their personal and racial group's calling. This concludes our foundational prelude to God's purpose for all of His colorful racial groups on the face of the earth.

Your individual and racial group's calling are important to God's purpose for your life. Having said that, let's go to the next chapter and take a journey back in time to the day that the flood ceased. This is the day that Noah, his wife, his three sons and their wives (8 people) left the ark. God made a faith based blood covenant with them and their descendants (which includes you). (Gen 9:8-17).

CHAPTER 2

God's Faith Based Blood Covenant—Session 2

God's faith based blood covenant for believers—Part I

Your racial group was given a divine purpose on earth. Your group has a right to His blood covenant from birth.

Christ makes all things possible for He is our potential. His help in fully developing it is essential.

Your group has a home in Paradise to enjoy forevermore. It's your utopia where life, wealth, word and peace blessings pour.

Our goal is to reveal God's purpose for each racial group on the face of the earth. God wants us to fulfill our purposes and receive His blessing that's far beyond anything we could ever hope for, dream of, or imagine. This blessing is God's faith based blood covenant which we'll study in 9 parts.

To exist is potential. To move on potential is the fear that moves unto wisdom and knowledge. To believe the potential set forth is utopia eternal.

Allow me to elaborate. First, you exist—i.e., you were born. You're fearfully and wonderfully made. (Ps 139:14). God created you with full potential to fulfill your purpose both on earth and in the new world to come (Paradise).

Second, when you move on (walk in) the potential that God put in you, it shows that you fear (i.e., reverence) God. This is wisdom (i.e., the reverential fear of God is the beginning of wisdom). Knowledge of His holiness leads to understanding. (Prov 9:10).

Third and finally, when you believe in God and the potential that He created in you—i.e., when you believe in Christ (who is your potential for all things) and accept Him as your Savior, God will bestow His heavenly blessings upon you as your utopia to enjoy in Paradise forevermore. Stay with me as we delve deeper into what God reveals to us about His heavenly blessings.

You definitely cannot afford to miss the information in the paragraphs that follow. Relative to what God reveals about His heavenly blessings, listing all of God's birthright (heavenly) blessings is beyond the scope of this book. Nevertheless, God's numerous covenant promises can all be grouped into four major categories or four major components, which are:

1. His eternal life blessing;
2. His peace blessing;
3. His word blessing; and
4. His wealth blessing.

God wants you to fulfill your purpose and receive these blessings. So, in fulfilling your racial group's purpose, you have to know the wonderful blessings that God will bestow upon you. Let us now take a look at how God's numerous birthright blessings can be grouped into four major components.

God promised believers long days on earth if they honor their parents. (Exod 20:12). God said, "Forget not my law . . . length of days and long life . . . shall they add to thee." (Prov3:1-2). God says, "I am the Lord that heals you." (Exod 15:26). God said, "Believe in Christ and you'll not perish, but have everlasting life." (John 3:16). These promises can all be grouped under God's eternal life blessing.

Peace I leave with you . . . not as the world giveth. Let not your heart be troubled, neither let it be afraid. (John 14:27). The angel of the Lord encamps around them that fear Him and delivers them—i.e., they protect them and keep them in peace. (Ps 34:7). Submit yourselves to God. Resist the devil and he'll flee from you (this brings you peace). (James 4:7). These covenant promises can all be grouped under the peace component of God's birthright blessing.

The word of God is the sword of the spirit that fights your foes. (Eph 6:17). I will neither break my covenant nor alter what I've spoken. (Ps 89:34). If ye keep my word, you'll abide in my love; even as I have kept my Father's word, and abide in His love. (John 15:10). The Lord gives wisdom: out of His mouth comes knowledge and understanding. (Prov 2: 6). These covenant promises can all be grouped under the word component of God's birthright blessing.

Remember the Lord who gives you power to get wealth . . . (Deut 8:18). Christ came that you might have life more abundantly. (John 10:10). In the house of the righteous is much treasure . . . (Prov 15:6, Ps 112:2-3). Store up treasures in heaven where neither moth nor dust doth corrupt . . . (Matt 6:20). God will supply all of your needs. (Phil 4:19). These covenant promises can all be grouped under the wealth component of God's birthright blessing.

So, all of God's covenant promises in the Bible fall under (i.e., are categorized under) one of the four major components of God's birthright blessing: His eternal life blessing, His peace blessing, His word blessing and His wealth blessing.

God's faith based blood covenant for believers—Part II

Recall that our goal is to reveal God's purpose for each racial group. God also wants us to receive His covenant promises. As such, each racial group's purpose is centered on God's faith based blood covenant. That is, our purpose cannot be fulfilled unless we've accepted God's blood covenant of eternal life, which is by faith in Christ's blood sacrifice on the cross that paid for all of our sins (past, present and future). (1 Pet 1:18-19, Matt 26:28, Rev 1:5).

In Gen 9:25-27, God shows the purpose that He gave our respective racial groups. After the flood, God resumed His plans for us. He told Noah and his sons to be fruitful, multiply, and replenish the earth. (Gen 9:1). The same as God blessed Adam and told him how to live a fruitful life (Gen 1:28, 2:15-17), He also blessed Noah and his sons and told them how to live fruitful lives. (Gen 9:1, 4-17).

That is, God told them what He expects. (Gen 9:1-3). Through Noah, God gave them their callings. God made them little gods in His image and gave them dominion over the earth and the works of His hands—i.e., we're not equal to God, for God is God alone. (Isa 43:10, 44:6). But, we're little gods in the sense that we're God's magistrates in the earth. (Ps 8:6, 82:6, Jn 10:34, Gen 1:26-27). So, the heavens are the Lord's: but He has given unto us the earth. (Ps 115:16).

God wants us to know that even though He cleansed the earth with a flood (an outward cleansing), we still need an inward cleansing by Christ's blood that washes away our sins (this is God's **faith based blood covenant**). So, even after the flood, sin is still with us. God's ideal purpose was to bless us with His **faith based blood covenant** and for us to fulfill our purpose on earth. Having blessed us with His blood covenant, God's purpose was to also bless all of our seeds (descendants) with His **faith based blood covenant**.

"God blessed Noah and his sons and said unto them, Be fruitful, and multiply, and replenish (fill) the earth." (Gen 9:1). "God spoke to Noah and his sons, saying, Behold, I establish my covenant with you and with your seed after you." (Gen 9:9).

So, God has a plan and purpose for all racial groups on earth. The offspring of Noah's sons are to accept God's faith based blood covenant—this is God's plan for all racial groups. God's caution to the seeds of Noah's sons is that there are serious consequences for those who reject God's blood covenant (i.e., birthright blessing).

God cautions Shem's descendants (the Jewish race), in particular, that they're to accept Christ as their Messiah. There'll be serious consequences for Jews who do not accept Christ as their Messiah before they die. God cautions Japheth's offspring (in particular), that they're to accept Christ and not try to work their way to heaven in their own strength, which is the curse of the law. Japheth's offspring are also cautioned to watch over Shem's offspring (explained later).

God cautions Ham's offspring that they must accept Christ. They must not serve Satan. They're to serve their neighbors and not commit crimes against them. They're to help Japheth's offspring protect the Jews. Nevertheless, the above cautions for Japheth, Shem and Ham apply to all racial groups in general.

Now, after the great flood ceased, Noah's three sons repopulated the earth with the different racial groups that God created. Noah and his sons were the only men left on earth after the flood. Noah and his wife didn't have any more children.

So, that left only Shem, Ham, Japheth and their wives to repopulate the earth with colorful racial groups to fulfill God's purpose. (Gen 9:1). Thus, we all (no matter what racial group we belong to), descended from Noah's sons or a mixture of their gene pools. Every racial group on earth, therefore, can trace its genes back to one of Noah's sons, for they were the only progenitors on earth after the flood.

In conclusion, God promised that He would not send another flood to destroy the earth. He guaranteed it by setting a rainbow in the clouds. (Gen 9:8-17). Since the imagination of man's heart is evil from his youth (i.e., he's hopeless: Gen 8:21), Christ would have to die for man's sins Himself. So, through Christ, God gave us a **faith based blood covenant**. (Gen 9:11, 15).

God's faith based blood covenant for believers—Part III

Gen 9:18-22 sets the stage for Noah's prophecy over his sons. Noah planted a vineyard, drank its wine, became drunk and was naked in his tent. (Gen 9:20-21). Ham looked on his nakedness and drunkenness. Noah's nakedness shows how our sins are exposed to God. His sin also shows that even after the flood that cleansed the earth, we still need to be cleansed by Christ's blood (an inner cleansing).

Ham looked on Noah's nude, drunken body, but he did not cover Noah's body in its drunken state. (Gen 9:20-22). Ham's actions symbolize the law (i.e., his actions symbolize those under the law).

The law looks on sin, but it doesn't cover it or wash it away. Jesus' blood washes away our sins. (Rev 1:5, Matt 26:28, 1 Pet 1:18-19, Eph 1:7). Nobody can be justified (i.e., saved) by the law. It is written, "No man is justified (saved) by the law in God's eyes: for THE JUST SHALL LIVE BY FAITH. (Gal 2:16, 3:11).

Those under the law (i.e., those who are unsaved) need Jesus Christ to save them from eternal punishment. If they don't accept Jesus Christ as their Savior before they die, they'll suffer eternal punishment in hell. (John 3:16).

Having said that, let us now consider what Ham's brothers did. Ham's brothers (Shem and Japheth) covered Noah's nude, drunken body, but they did not look upon his drunkenness and naked body. They put a garment on their shoulders and went backward to cover him without looking upon his sin. (Gen 9:23).

Shem's and Japheth's actions portray how Christ covers (washes away) our sins (past, present and future) with His blood. God doesn't look on saints' sins. He puts them behind Him, washes them away, doesn't remember them and removes them from them as far as the east is from the west. (Ps 51:2, 103:12, Isa 38:17, 43:25). Jesus was cursed for our sins. He was our substitute. His death freed us from the curse of the law and placed us under grace. (Gal 3:13, Rom 6:14).

Thus, our focus should be on fulfilling our personal and racial group's purpose and preparing for the eternal joys that God's faith based blood covenant will bring us in heaven. Now, consider the phrase "Ham is the father of Canaan" (cited in Gen 9:18). This phrase refers to God's **faith based blood covenant**. For this phrase teaches us a great spiritual truth about Christ's sacrificial curse for our sins.

Canaan was cursed (substituted) for Ham's sin. (Gen 9:25). Since he was substituted for Ham's sin, it reflects how Christ was cursed (substituted) for our sins which is the faith based blood covenant that God made with us. So, Canaan's curse in Ham's place symbolizes God's **faith based blood covenant** wherein Christ was cursed in our place. This is the true meaning of "Cursed be Canaan".

Some scholars have been misinterpreting this truth for years by teaching that Canaan's curse means that Ham's descendants were called to be lowly slaves unto men. God forbid! This is not the proper interpretation of Gen 9:18, 25.

These scholars are clearly misguided and couldn't be further from the truth. Canaan's curse in Ham's place symbolizes Christ's curse (substitutionary death) in our place. That is, Canaan's curse in Ham's place symbolizes Christ's **faith based blood covenant** wherein Chist was cursed in our place. (Gal 3:13, Rom 6:14).

God's faith based blood covenant for believers—Part IV

While Noah was asleep, God gave him a vision. When he woke up, he knew that Ham's actions symbolized being under the curse of the Law—i.e., he knew what Ham had done. He also knew that it was time to prophesy unto Ham, Shem, and Japheth about their respective purposes (callings) on earth. (Gen 9:24). God revealed Ham's, Shem's and Japheth's purposes to Noah while he was asleep.

God gave each son a component blessing to minister. (Gen 9:24-27). As we'll see, Ham's offspring are to minister the peace blessing. Japheth's offspring are to minister the eternal life blessing. Shem's offspring are to minister the word blessing. All of Noah's sons are to minister the wealth blessing. God has a tremendous blessing stored up for them for fulfilling their purposes on earth.

God's faith based blood covenant for believers—Part V (cherubs' four faces)

It's vital that we know all we can about God's cherubim (a special order of angels). They play a pivotal role in helping us to identify our racial group's purpose. Each cherub has four faces. God uses their four faces to confirm the reality and importance of the four components of His birthright blessing. Their four faces also show us the importance of incorporating the four components of God's birthright blessing into our personal and racial group's calling.

It is written, "As for the likeness of the cherubim's faces, they had the face of a man (in front), the face of a lion on the right side, the face of an ox on the left and the face of an eagle (in the rear)." (Eze 1:10). Let us now study each of their faces.

God's faith based blood covenant for believers—Part VI (the lion's face)

The cherub's four faces represent God's entire creation. Each face speaks of the crowned or the chief member of its species. Their faces also speak of the reality of the 4 components of the birthright blessing. Let's study the lion's face first.

The lion is called the king of his species. His face is on the right side of the cherubim, which means that he sits in a position of honor and authority over the animal kingdom. God wants us to know the reality of His word blessing and the importance of incorporating it into our personal and racial group's calling. The lion's face represents the word component of God's birthright blessing.

How does the lion's face portray God's word blessing? The lion's face portrays Christ, the Lion of Judah. (Rev 5:5). Christ (the lion of Judah) is the living word of God. (Rev 19:13). Christ sits on God's right side. God's right side is symbolic of His power, sovereignty, and highest position of honor. (1 Peter 3:22).

Christ has all power and occupies the highest position of honor and authority in the kingdom. He's the word of God and King of the creation. (Rev 19:16). He's God's living Word. For His name is The Word of God. (Rev 19:13). KING OF KINGS AND LORD OF LORDS is written on His vesture and thigh. (Rev 19:16).

So, the lion's face portrays the Lion of Judah who is the King of kings. The cherubim's lion faces portray God's word blessing who is Christ; the living word.

"In the beginning was the Word (Christ); the Word was with God, and the Word was God." (John 1:1). "The Word was made flesh and dwelt with us. We beheld His glory; the glory as of the only begotten Son of God . . . He's full of grace and truth." (Jn 1:14). ". . . He's the mighty God, the everlasting Father . . ." (Isa 9:6).

God uses the cherubim's lion like faces to confirm that His word blessing is just as real as we are. It's our instruction manual on living right. His word gives us the victory. His word is our prayer warrior and the medium through which we invoke the power of God's Spirit. His word gives us the authority to go to God's throne for help, mercy and grace. (Heb 4:16). We need God's word blessing in our lives.

God's Word is our authority to handle God's sacred things. It's our source of health, strength, and help. (Ps 107:20). It's our battle sword that gives us victory. (1 Jn 2:14, Rev 12:10-11). It's our life fountain that keeps us out of Satan's traps. God's word is our path to rewards for obediently fulfilling our purposes on earth.

These truths confirm (undoubtedly) that the cherubim's lion like faces (on their right sides) speak of God's Word (Jesus Christ). That is, the cherubim's lion like faces speak of the word component of God's birthright blessing which is just as real as we are. Let's go to the next chapter and study the man's face on each cherub. These truths are vital in helping us to gain a clearer understanding of our racial group's purpose and God's treasures that are stored up for us in Paradise.

CHAPTER 3

God's Faith Based Blood Covenant—Session 3

God's faith based blood covenant for believers—Part VII (the man's face)

> Cherubim, sweet cherubim tend to our heavenly nesting. And their faces, four faces portray our eternal blessing.
>
> The man's face on each cherub portrays a true blessing that's as precious as gold. For the man's face on each cherub portrays eternal wealth which is a blessing to behold

If we fulfill God's purpose, He has a tremendous inheritance in store for us. He reveals His wondrous blessing through the four faces of His cherubim. We've studied the lion's face. We'll now study the man's, the eagle's and the ox's face.

The man's face in the front of each cherub represents the wealth component of God's birthright blessing. For God has stored up in heaven all the riches you could ever hope for, dream of, or imagine. God also blesses man with wealth on earth. (Deut 8:18). How does the man's face portray God's wealth blessing?

Man is the head of the human species and the crown and glory of God's creation. (Gen 1:27, Ps 8:5-6). God gave man and woman dominion over the heavens, the earth, and the waters, which comprise God's great storehouse of wealth and abundance for man's benefit, sustenance and enjoyment. (Gen 1:26-28).

So, the man's face represents God's wealth blessing. For the earth is teeming with precious jewels and stones (rubies, diamonds, etc). God deposited minerals, ores and elements in the earth that are waiting to be tapped: gold, silver, bronze, etc. There is plant life on earth for man's health and pleasure: herbs, fruit, rich vegetables, vines and a multitude of botanical splendors. (Gen 1:11-12, 29).

Earth's waters are teeming with wealth and abundance. The oceans, seas, rivers, etc., are teeming with the treasures of the deep: pearls, corals, plants, marine life, etc. Man has oxygen to breathe and sun rays for his warmth. He has birds for his service and pleasure. God who owns all the wealth that exists, ever existed, or ever will exist gave it all to man for his benefit, sustenance and enjoyment.

Made in God's image and blessed with the treasures of heaven, earth and the waters, God also gave man dominion over the works of His hands. (Ps 8:6, Gen 1:26-28). The bottom line is that, in giving man dominion over the works of His hands, God put all of the above wealth, riches and treasures in man's hands.

So, the man's face portrays God's wealth blessing. The man's face speaks of man's inheritance as an heir of God. (Rom 8:16-17). All things in heaven and earth are God's, whether visible, invisible, thrones, dominions, principalities, or powers. (Col 1:16). And God put all of His wealth and works in man's hands. (Ps 8:6).

God not only wants us to know the importance of incorporating His wealth blessing into our personal and racial group's calling, but He also wants us to know that His wealth blessing is just as real as we are. God's wealth blessing plays a key role in helping us to be successful in carrying out our callings.

This means that believers have at their disposal all the wealth and riches they could ever hope for, dream of, or imagine. Even though many believers check their bank balances and their balances are nowhere near all the wealth and riches they could ever hope for, dream of, or imagine, they must still continue to cast their bread upon the waters. (Eccl 11:1)

That is, believers must continue to sow good seeds to reap God's blessings (financial and otherwise). In order to reap plentifully, they must sow plentifully. They must plant their seeds wisely and never give up.

That said, God not only teaches believers how to profit by leading them by the way that they should go (Isa 48:17), but He also gave them power to get wealth. (Deut 8:18). God not only sent Christ so that believers might have life more abundantly (John 10:10), but He also sent Christ so that He (God) might supply all of their needs according to His riches in glory through Christ. (Phil 4:19).

At all costs, Satan wants to derail our racial group's calling. If he can keep us scratching, clawing and climbing up the rough side of the financial mountain, he'll have us right where he wants us: in no financial shape to carry out our personal and racial group's calling.

Satan knows that without God's wealth blessing, we (as believers) may run into serious financial difficulties in trying to carry out our personal and racial group's calling. Nevertheless, we have a serious calling on our lives. And we need money to accomplish our God given purposes. As noted, God will supply all of our needs according to His riches in glory through Christ. (Phil 4:19).

God's wealth blessing is very important in our lives. We need God's wealth blessing to support our families and churches. We need wealth to carry out the visions that God gave us such as building churches, building homes for the needy, feeding the hungry, spreading the gospel and the list goes on.

God's wealth blessing is indeed a real and vital birthright component that we need to incorporate into our lives. In conclusion, the man's face on each cherub not only represents the wealth component of God's birthright blessing, but it also confirms that God's wealth blessing is just as real as we are.

Furthermore, the man's face on each cherub shows us that, from the spirit realm, cherubim coax us on how to live holy before God and incorporate God's wealth blessing into our callings.

God's faith based blood covenant for believers—Part VIII (the eagle's face)

The eagle's face (in the rear) portrays the eternal life component of God's birthright blessing. God wants us to know the reality of His eternal life blessing and the importance of using it in carrying out our callings. How does the eagle's face on the cherubim portray God's eternal life blessing?

The eagle sits in a position of honor among the bird species. His face speaks for its species. He soars high in the air. His wings are mightier, his tolerance of the sun is greater, and his nest is loftier than all others. His magnificent splendor crowns him as a royal bird of heaven with extremely sharp eyesight.

That is, the eagle is not only the acclaimed chief of the bird species, but much like Christ, he is high and lifted up above all others. Just as Christ is the crown and glory of God's creation, the eagle is the crown and glory of its species. The eagle, therefore, portrays Christ in His exalted position of glory, power and majesty.

For example, high above the earth, the eagle—like Christ—moves to and fro about the heavenly firmament. As the heavens consider the grace and elegance of his flight, they proclaim, "Oh, how high and lofty are the wings of an eagle."

Symbolic of Christ, the eagle mounts up with wings and soars above the storm clouds. As the winds press upon his breast, he rises above them and glides upon the strength of his wings. So, the eagle portrays Christ in His exalted position.

Let us now consider the turtledove—a bird of a lower order. It portrays Christ who—motivated by unconditional love—left His exalted position in heaven, came to earth, humbled Himself by taking on the form of man, bled and died on the cross, and wrought eternal life for us. So, the eagle portrays Christ in His exalted state. The turtledove (a bird of a lower order) portrays Christ in His humbled state.

Christ's death in His humbled state guarantees that Japheth's, Ham's and Shem's offspring who believe in Christ's death and resurrection, will be resurrected with heavenly bodies like unto Christ's glorious body. (Phil 3:21).

The symbolism associated with the eagle and the turtledove shows that it was the turtledove (a bird of lower order than the eagle) that died. The eagle and the turtledove portray Christ's sacrificial death that wrought eternal life for us. For Christ left His exalted position in heaven (the eagle) humbled Himself and came to earth (the turtledove) and died on the cross so that we might have eternal life.

This great spiritual truth is confirmed by the sacrifice of Gen 15:7-18. God told Abraham to sacrifice 5 animals: a heifer, a goat, a ram, a turtledove and a pigeon. Since the turtledoves and pigeons were easily obtainable, both the rich and the poor could use them to make sacrifices unto the Lord. (Gen 15:8-9).

Abraham split the animals in half and laid their pieces on the altar. But, he was not to split the turtledove or the pigeon (i.e., their bones were never broken). Their blood was poured out on the altar, but their bones were never broken. (Gen 15:10).

Now, recall for a moment how a Roman soldier thrust his spear into Christ's side. Blood and water flowed out of His wound and trickled down to the ground, but Christ's bones were never broken. (John 19:33-34). When birds were sacrificed, God allowed their blood to pour out unto death, but He never allowed their bones to be broken. Their bones were protected by divine order. Christ's bones speak of His covenant of protection over us if we belong to Christ.

God said, "For no man ever yet hated his own flesh; but nourishes and cherishes it, even as the Lord cherishes His church. For, we are members of His body, of His flesh and of His bones." (Eph 5:29-30). In other words, Christ protects His bones (His believers) from ever going into hell's fury (i.e., saints will never experience punishment in the eternal lake of fire). For their bones are divinely protected.

Simply stated, these verses reveal that as believers, our flesh and bones will never be hurt by hell's fury. Our bones belong to Christ—i.e., He protects saints (His beloved bones). (Ps 34:20, Jn 10:28-30). This spiritual truth is portrayed by the fact that Christ's bones were never broken. (Jn 19:33-36, Num 9:12, Ex 12:46).

So, the turtledove portrays Christ's death and His guarantee of eternal life. For the turtledove's bones (like Christ's bones) were never broken. Praise God!

As further proof that the eagle and the turtledove portray God's eternal life blessing, consider what God told Moses about leprosy. God told Moses to have the priests use two birds to cleanse a leper (who portrays sin and impurity). One bird was killed in an earthen vessel under running water (symbolic of our spirits being cleansed). The other bird was dipped in the slain bird's blood (symbolic of the washing away of our sins by Christ's blood) and set free. (Lev 14:1-8).

The sacrificed bird speaks of Christ's sacrificial death. The other bird that was set free speaks of Christ's resurrection and return to His exalted position (as portrayed by the eagle). The bird that was set free also speaks of how believers are dipped in Christ's blood and their sins are washed away—i.e., they're set free from death to fly away to bask in peace and ecstasy in God's kingdom forevermore.

So, the eagle and the turtledove are divinely linked in their portrayal of God's eternal life blessing. Hence, through the bird species in which the eagle sits in an exalted position like unto Christ, God confirms the reality of His free gift of eternal life. The cherubim's eagle faces, therefore, represent and confirm the reality of the eternal life component of God's birthright blessing with a heavenly body.

These truths teach us that in everything we do, we are not only to glorify, reflect and imitate God's eternal life blessing, but we are to help Christ seek and save the lost. (Luke 19:10). God is counting on Ham's, Shem's and Japheth's offspring (which includes you) to follow in the footsteps of Christ. (1 Peter 2:21).

Following in Christ's footsteps means that you are to walk worthy of your calling. (Eph 4:1, 1 Thess 2:12). Moreover, once you become a child of God, the cherubim take over and help you to walk holy and upright before the Lord. They stand guard over the four components of your birthright blessing to keep you informed of any evil that may interfere with your covenant blessings.

As believers, cherubim guide us (from the spirit realm) into paths of righteousness. For, as God is holy, so are we to be holy. (1 Peter 1:15-16). So, cherubim impress upon us (as believers) the importance of being holy in carrying out our personal and racial group's calling. Having been cleansed by Christ's blood and given God's gift of eternal life (Rev 1:5, Heb 9:14), we (as believers) are to speak life to everyone, everything and every situation that comes into our sphere of influence.

In summary, the cherubim's eagle like faces not only speak of God's eternal life blessing, but their eagle like faces also confirm that God's eternal life blessing is just as real as we are. Their eagle like faces speak of how vitally important it is to incorporate God's eternal life blessing into our personal and racial group's calling.

It is crucial, therefore, that Ham's, Japheth's and Shem's descendants know about, believe in, and receive the vitally important eternal life component of God's birthright blessing as portrayed by the eagle's face on each cherub.

God's faith based blood covenant for believers—Part IX (the ox's face)

The ox's face of each cherub portrays the peace component of God's birthright blessing. God wants us to know the reality of His eternal peace blessing and the importance of incorporating it into our personal and racial group's calling. How does the ox's face portray the peace component of God's birthright blessing?

To begin with, the ox is the chief of the domesticated animals. The ox speaks for the domesticated animals and its species. As a peaceful creature, the ox speaks for the peace component of God's birthright blessing. The ox carries our burdens. So, the ox portrays Christ, the Prince of peace (Isa 9:6), who carries our burdens. For Jesus said, "Come unto me all ye that labor and are heavy laden (i.e., all ye that have problems, burdens and worries), and I will give you rest—i.e., Christ will give us peace that passes all understanding." (Matt 11:28, Phil 4:6-7).

"Take my yoke (i.e., the ox's yoke) upon you and lean on me; for I am meek and lowly in heart: and ye shall find rest (peace) unto your souls. For, my yoke is easy and my burden is light." (Matt 11:29-30). Notice that the ox is not only a peaceful creature, but he's also a patient servant.

Christ gives rest to all who labor and are laden. We're to take His yoke and learn of Him. He's meek and His burden is light. (Matt 11:28-30). These verses show that the ox's face portrays Christ who bears our burdens and gives us peace. (Rom 15:33, 1 Peter 5:7). So, the ox's face represents God's peace blessing.

Like the ox, cherubim are also peaceful creatures. How is this so? Notice that in Ezekiel's vision, a cherub's face appeared instead of the ox's face. (Eze 1:10, 10:14). This means that God equates cherubim with the peaceful nature of an ox. So, like unto the oxen, cherubim are also creatures of peace. As such, the cherubim also portray the peace component of God's birthright blessing.

The soles of their feet are like calves' feet. (Eze 1:7). A calf is peaceful. A one year old calf was sacrificed for sins. As one of the firstlings (firstborn) of one's best cattle (new births), the calf is young, innocent and peaceful. This shows their peaceful nature. So, the calf portrays Christ and His peaceful nature.

For, Christ was innocent and peaceful, but yet He died to pay for our sins. By His death, He reconciled us unto God in peace. (1 Peter 2:22, Matt 27:3-4, Eph 2:15-16). Hence the calf like feet of God's cherubim shows that they're peaceful. As such, they also portray God's peace blessing. That is, they minister peace by coaxing and guiding us from the spirit realm. They reveal unto us the importance, and reality of God's peace blessing.

Since we (as descendants of Japheth, Ham or Shem) are made in God's image, we're to keep peace with everyone that comes into the sphere of our influence. We're to keep peace in our homes, relationships, churches, work places; racial group's calling, etc. Abiding in God's peace (John 14:27), we're to touch people in such a way that these people are made more peaceful by crossing our paths.

In summary, God not only confirms—through the ox's face—the reality of His peace blessing, but He emphasizes the importance of incorporating the peace component of God's birthright blessing into our personal and racial group's calling. Thus, we've shown (without a doubt) that the four faces of the cherubim (the lion's face, the man's face, the eagle's face and the ox's face) confirm the reality and importance of the four components of God's birthright blessing.

Not only that, but the cherubim also play a pivotal role in showing us how to identify (pinpoint) our racial group's calling. So, we must study God's cherubim in great detail. God thought of everything to help us learn about the four components of His birthright blessing. For God's utmost desire is that we fulfill our racial group's purpose and dwell with Him in a heavenly Paradise of peace, joy and happiness forevermore.

CHAPTER 4

He Rode Upon A Cherub—Session 4

He rode upon a cherub and did fly—Part I

> You're the God of knowledge, God of mercy and owner of all
> things. You're the God of love, God peace and they rest upon
> your wings.
>
> Creator of creation your sovereignty is divine. Maker of
> generations we're created to be thine.
>
> Your reign is from everlasting to everlasting; a pure sanctuary. In
> your reign the cherubim, sweet cherubim are divinely necessary.

Now, please let me have your undivided attention. The information in this
chapter about God's cherubim will open the eyes of our understanding
relative to our racial group's purpose both on earth and in the new world
to come (Paradise).

What I'm saying is that in order to embrace the reality and true knowledge
of our racial group's purpose, it's absolutely crucial that we know the
divine connection between God's cherubim and our racial group. For God's
cherubim provide the keys that unlock the doors that lead to our racial
group's purpose. That is, in order to pinpoint our racial group's purpose
(calling) on earth, we have to study God's cherubim in detail (we have to
know all that we can about them).

We cannot afford to miss out on studying the cherubim's duties and
behavior patterns. They're vital in knowing our racial group's purpose.
Without studying the cherubim in detail, it might prove to be a little difficult
for us to recognize, grasp or realize that both our personal and racial
group's calling work together to serve God completely. Satan (our staunch

enemy) strives to keep us in the dark about our racial group's purpose. He doesn't want us to serve God completely.

Before we study the cherubs (in 12 parts), let's first review God's Sovereignty. For, He's the source and foundation of all that we're talking about. Without Him as the center of our universe, nothing could live, move or have being. (Acts 17:28)

"He rode upon a cherub, and did fly: yea, He flew upon the wings of the wind." (Ps 18:10, 2 Sam 22:11). This shows that God reigns. (Rev 19:6). He rides on His throne-chariot supported by cherubs who turn not as they go. He moves about the universe as cherubim support and obey His commands. (Eze 1:22-28, 10:11).

This shows that God is the sovereign ruler over the universe. Nothing can alter His course. He rules in the affairs of men. As He moves about the heavens and the earth upon the wings of the winds, He watches over His people to deliver them.

He is God from everlasting to everlasting. (Ps 90:2). He's the ruler, judge, and sovereign God over the creation, for He owns all things and is exalted as head above all. (1 Chron 29:11-12). He's the God of all knowledge and mercies as well as the God of love, peace and comfort. (1 Jn 3:20, 2 Cor 1:3, 13:11, Dan 9:9). So, He's the Lord God omnipotent who reigns. (Rev 19:6). This is what the phrase "He rode upon a cherub and did fly" means.

He rode upon a cherub and did fly—Part II

As noted, in order to pinpoint our racial group's purpose, we have to study God's cherubim in detail. We need to know everything about them and everything that they do. Why is it so vital for us to know them in such great detail?

The key is that cherubim have the likeness of a man (i.e., their behavior is patterned after the behavior that God expects of us). (Eze 1:5). So, our racial group's purpose can be accurately pinpointed by studying their purpose. Once we know their purpose, we'll know our racial group's purpose. That's why we study them so closely. So, let us get on with studying their functions, duties and purpose.

God's angels are God's servants. (Ps 103:20-22). They serve the heirs of salvation (who're also God's servants—believers). (Heb 1:14). So, angels are servants of servants—i.e., they serve God's servants. But, Christ is God's special servant of servants. (Isa 52:13, Mk 10:35-45). For, He sacrificed His life because of His undying love for us. (Heb 9:24-26).

And, like unto Christ, cherubim are God's special servants of servants. For they guard the very throne room of God (God's dwelling places in heaven and on earth). They're humbled under God's throne-chariot (under His authority). (Eze 1:22-26, 10:1). Humbled under God's throne-chariot, they're special servants of servants unto God as His throne-chariot flies upon the wings of the winds. (Eze 1:12). Hence, His cherubim are God's special servants of servants like unto Christ.

Herein, we've identified one of the cherubs' key purposes (duties). That is, they're God's **special servants of servants**. Since cherubs act like God expects us to act, some racial group was created to be God's **special servants of servants** like unto the cherubim. One of Noah's sons and his offspring identify with this purpose. Our goal is to identify that son and his offspring. We'll do this shortly.

He rode upon a cherub and did fly—Part III

God rides upon His throne-chariot that speaks of God moving about the universe overseeing and judging the affairs of His creation. (Eze 1:25-26). As the God who judges the universe and metes out His divine providence, God created Lucifer (His anointed cherub) to guard His throne and the Ark of the Covenant on (1) His holy mountain in heaven, and (2) His holy mountain in Jerusalem.

Hence, as God's anointed cherub, Lucifer was created to stand guard over God's kingdom and everything that pertains thereto. God's confirms this divine truth. As it is written, "Thou (Lucifer) art the anointed cherub that covers (guards). I have set thee so: you were on my holy mountain (God's home in the 3rd heaven). Thou hast walked up and down in the midst of the stones of fire." (Eze 28:14).

Thus, as the guardian of everything that pertains to God's kingdom, Lucifer was created to stand guard over God's throne, His throne room, His eternal kingdom, His saints, His Ark of the Covenant and the tree of eternal life.

Guarding the eternal tree of life is extremely important. For when Adam and Eve sinned, they had to be banned from the Garden of Eden. Had they remained in the Garden to freely eat of the tree of eternal life, they would have lived throughout eternity in a state of sin. That's why the cherubim were created to guard the way of the tree of eternal life. (Gen 3:22-24).

In other words, cherubim prevent entry into the way of the tree of life for those who are unworthy. But, they allow access unto the way of the tree of life for those who are worthy. So, they help God convert the unworthy to be accepted as worthy (through Christ). Hence, cherubim are not only called to **guard God's throne**, but they're also called to **minister God's etetrnal life blessing** unto all people.

Cherubim also support, uphold and backup God's every move. "And there was a voice from the firmament that was over the heads of the cherubim . . . And above the firmament that was over their heads was the likeness of a throne as the appearance of a sapphire stone . . ." (Eze 1:25-26).

These verses show that God's cherubim are humbled below His throne-chariot. They go straight ahead and turn not as they go. (Eze 1:19). They cannot change God's course. By being humbled below God's throne-chariot, it shows that they support, uphold and backup all matters that pertain to God's throne and kingdom. For His throne and kingdom are the very sources of eternal life and peace.

We've now shown a second purpose of God's cherubim. They not only **guard God's throne**, but they support, uphold and backup God's every move as they **minister God's eternal life blessing**. Since they act like us, some racial group was created to **guard God's throne** and **minister His eternal life blessing** like the cherubim. One of Noah's sons and his descendants identify with this purpose. Our goal is to identify that son and his descendants. We'll do this shortly.

He rode upon a cherub and did fly—Part IV

Ezekiel saw God's cherubim in a vision. A wheel was beside each cherub. The wheel's height was dreadful. Its rims were full of eyes. The cherubim's bodies (backs, hands, wings, etc.) were full of eyes." (Eze 1:15-18, 10:12).

The exceedingly high wheels speak of God's Spirit that's everywhere. The wheels are so high that Eze 1:5 shows them in the clouds while Eze 1:15 shows them as also touching the earth. The wheels were full of eyes. This means that God sees all and knows all. (1 John 3:20). The cherubim covered with eyes and the wheels covered with eyes refer to God's Spirit who has the eyes of full knowledge relative to God's holy words. (1 Cor 2:11).

The eyes covering the cherubim's bodies symbolize God's knowledge and wisdom. This shows that cherubim know God's word verbatim. God verified it when He created His anointed cherub Lucifer to be the embodiment of knowledge and wisdom—i.e., the embodiment of God's word. Consider the following verse.

"Son of man, take up a lamentation upon the king of Tyrus (herein, God is also referring to Satan the evil culprit behind the king). Say unto him, Thus saith the Lord God; Thou sealest up the sum (i.e., you are the epitome of angelic beings), **full of wisdom**." ". . . Thou wast perfect in thy ways . . ." (Eze 28:12, 15). So, Lucifer was endowed with **perfect wisdom**—he knew God's word verbatim.

Herein, we've shown a third purpose (function) of God's cherubim. That is, they're the very **embodiment of God's words of wisdom**. Since cherubim act like God expects us to act, some racial group was created to be the **embodiment of God's words of wisdom** like unto the cherubim. One of Noah's sons and his descendants identify with this purpose. Our goal is to identify whether it's Ham's, Shem's or Japheth's offspring that identify with this purpose (calling).

Shortly I'll show whose offspring are called (like the cherubim) to be the embodiment of God's holy words—i.e., called to be the embodiment of God's knowledge, wisdom and understanding.

He rode upon a cherub and did fly—Part V

As special servants of servants, God called His cherubim to be the embodiment of praise and worship. They're His praise and worship leaders over His creation. We know that angels are servants of servants (Heb 1:14), but cherubim are God's special servants of servants. They guard God's throne. (Ezk 28:14). God gave the ministry of praise and worship to His special servants of servants, the cherubim.

God confirmed this truth when He created Lucifer (His anointed cherub) with perfect voice pipes, pitch, music tones, rhythms, percussions, beats, etc. That is, Lucifer was created as a walking symphony (the epitome of praise and worship).

It is written, "Thou (Lucifer) hast been in Eden, the garden of God; every precious stone was thy covering . . . the workmanship of thy tabrets (rhythms, beats, percussions, etc.,) and of thy pipes (voice pipes, vocal chords, ear for music, music tones, etc.,) was prepared in thee when thou wast created." (Ezk 28:13).

Herein, we've shown a fourth purpose (duty) of God's cherubim. They're the very **embodiment of praise and worship over God's creation**. Since cherubim act like God expects us to act, some racial group was created to be God's **praise and worship leaders over His creation** like unto the cherubim. One of Noah's sons and his descendants identify with this purpose. Our goal is to identify that son and his offspring who're called to be God's **praise and worship leaders** like the cherubim. Shortly, I'll show which racial group was created for that purpose.

He rode upon a cherub and did fly—Part VI

As noted, we're in the process of studying the calling (i.e., the functions and duties) of God's cherubim. For God's cherubim provide the spiritual key that unlocks the door that leads to the understanding our of racial groups' purpose that must be fulfilled here on earth. That is, cherubim are very crucial in helping us to determine (i.e., pinpoint) our God given racial group's purpose.

What I'm saying is that God patterned His cherubim's behavior after our expected behavior. (Eze 1:5). So, once we know the cherubim's functions and behavior patterns, we can accurately determine God's divine purpose for our particular racial group (i.e., our racial groups' purpose for being here on earth).

The inner walls of Ezekiel's temple were carved with cherubim positioned between a man's face looking toward a palm tree on one side and a lion's face (symbolic of Christ, the Lion of Judah: Rev 5:5) looking toward a palm tree on the other side. Palm trees portray victory and peace. (Eze 41:18-19). So, the fact that the man's face is looking toward a palm tree of victory and peace while the lion's face is also looking toward a palm tree of victory and peace reveals that God and man are reconciled unto peace by Christ's victory on the cross.

The fact that the cherub's body is positioned between a man's face and a lion's face reveals that cherubs have a special ministry of reconciliation between God and man unto the victory of peace. (Eph 2:13-16). So, cherubs are God's special peacekeepers. As noted, cherubim act like God expects us to act for they have the likeness of a man. (Eze 1:5). So, we study their calling to identify our racial group's calling.

In this light, Ezekiel's millennial temple with figures of cherubim and palm trees inscribed on the walls around the temple portray the walls of protection surrounding those who've been reconciled unto peace with God in His kingdom of righteousness and peace

Ezekiel saw a cherub's face in place of the ox's face. (Eze 10:14). So, God equates cherubim with the peaceful nature of oxen. Thus, cherubim are creatures of peace who serve as God's special peacekeepers. Although all saints are called to a ministry of reconciliation (2 Cor 5:18), God's cherubim are called to a special ministry of reconciliation between God and man unto peace.

Herein, we've shown a fifth purpose of the cherubim. They have a special ministry of reconciliation between God and man unto peace. Since they act like God expects us to act, some racial group is called unto a special ministry of reconciliation between God and man unto peace like the cherubim. One of Noah's sons and his offspring identify with this purpose. Our goal is to identify which one of Noah's sons (as well as his descendants) is called to fulfill this purpose (calling).

Shortly, I'll show which racial group is called to fulfill a special ministry of reconciliation between God and man unto peace—i.e., I'll show which racial group of people are created to be God's special peacekeepers.

He rode upon a cherub and did fly—Part VII

God blessed us with the 4 components of His birthright blessing: the eternal life blessing, the peace blessing, the word blessing and the wealth blessing. In this section, we'll focus on God's wealth blessing. Christ knew we would need wealth to fulfill His great commission. He purposed for us to help Him seek and save the lost. As believers, He gives us enough power and wealth to fulfill His mission.

He said, "All power is given to me in heaven and earth. Go ye and teach all nations baptizing them in the name of the Father, the Son and the Holy Spirit; teaching them to do all things that I have commanded: and, I am with you always, even unto the end of the world, Amen." (Matt 28:18-20).

In carrying out Christ's great commission, we need money to feed the needy and care for the sick. We need money to build churches, hospitals and Christian schools. We need money to finance gospel crusades, Christian films, outreach ministries, radio stations, satellite TV stations and other projects that spread God's gospel. So (as believers), we need wealth to fulfill Christ's great commission.

We (as believers) also need enough wealth to pay our tithes and offerings. We need enough wealth to pay our bills, give alms to the poor, provide a prosperous life for our families, invest in future benefits and save up for unexpected events. For these reasons, God gave us (as believers) power to get wealth. (Deut 8:18). He doesn't want us climbing up the rough side of the financial mountain.

In this light, Lucifer (God's anointed cherub) was called to minister God's wealth blessing. It is written, "Thou hast been in Eden, God's Garden (i.e., he was in heaven); every precious stone was thy covering: the sardius, topaz, diamond, beryl, onyx, jasper, sapphire, emerald, carbuncle and gold . . ." (Eze 28:13).

This divine truth shows that Lucifer's covering (clothing) glowed, sparkled and shown like a brilliant rainbow. You can surmise a person's wealth status by what that person wears and what that person owns. So, Lucifer dwelled in the midst of the lap of luxury. For, he was covered with all sorts of precious stones: the topaz, diamond, beryl, emerald and gold to name a few. Now, God owns everything.

It is written, "Thine, O Lord, is the greatness and the power and the glory and the victory and the majesty: for all that is in heaven and in the earth is thine. Thine is the kingdom O Lord and thou art exalted as head above all." (1 Chron 29:11; also see Ps 24:1, 50:10, 89:11, Col 1:16-17).

So, in heaven where God dwells, Lucifer had access to all of God's wealth and abundance. That is, he had access to all of the wealth he could ever hope for, dream of or imagine. For, as noted, he was indeed covered with every precious stone. (Eze 28:13). What was Lucifer supposed to do with God's wealth? He was supposed to distribute it to Ham, Shem, Japheth and their descendants.

For it is written, "Are they (i.e., the angels) not all ministering spirits, sent forth to minister to believers who'll be heirs of salvation?" (Heb 1:14). So, Lucifer (God's anointed cherub) was indeed created to serve believers.

The bottom line is that in order to minister financial blessings to God's people, Lucifer was entrusted with all of the wealth and riches of heaven and earth. As such, he was responsible for ministering God's wealth blessing to God's people.

But, lifted up in pride, Lucifer wanted to be like God. (Eze 28:2). Instead of serving God with his wealth, he wanted to enrich himself and be like God. (Isa 14:12-14). God spoke directly to king Tyrus (and indirectly to Lucifer: now called Satan) about being lifted up in pride and trying to be your own God. (Eze 28:1-2).

God's word came to Ezekiel saying, ". . . Say to the Prince of Tyrus . . . Because thine heart is lifted up and thou hast said I am God . . . thou art a man and not God (Herein, God is also speaking to Satan the culprit behind Tyrus)." (Eze 28:1-2).

"With thy wisdom and understanding thou hast gotten riches, gold and silver into thy treasures. By thy wisdom . . . thou has increased thy riches and thine heart is lifted up . . ." (Eze 28:5) ". . . I will cast thee as profane out of my mountain and destroy the O covering cherub from the midst of the stones of fire. (Eze 28:4-5, 16). As noted, God is talking to Tyrus and indirectly to Lucifer.

So, Lucifer was responsible for ministering God's wealth blessing to us. This is a sixth function of God's cherubim. They minister God's wealth blessing to saints. Since they act like God expects us to act, a racial group was created to minister God's wealth blessing, like the cherubim. One of Noah's sons and his offspring identify with this purpose. Our goal is to identify which son and his offspring are called to minister God's wealth blessing like the cherubim. We'll do this shortly.

CHAPTER 5

He Rode Upon A Cherub—Session 5

He rode upon a cherub and did fly—Part VIII

His throne is surrounded by His Shekinah glory and purity. The color blue portrays His throne and words of security.

The color blue portrays His abundant heavenly attributes. The color blue pays to the righteous judge many divine tributes.

Under His feet is the paved work of a blue sapphire stone. Like the clear blue sky, its brightness is beautifully shone. They sewed blue ribbons on every hem. Of His words the ribbons reminded them.

Let us study the spiritual meaning of the color blue. Blue not only refers to God's attributes, Shekinah glory and righteous judgments, but it also leads us to the seventh function that we're going to study relative to God's cherubim.

That said, we'll study (1) how the intensity of God's Shekinah glory is like a consuming fire, (2) how walking in God's Shekinah glory is like walking on stones of fire (symbolic of being in His presence), and (3) how the ***color blue*** refers to His divine attributes and His authority as the righteous judge of the universe. (Ps 9:8, Jn 5:26-27). For, He is indeed the Lord God omnipotent who reigns. (Rev 19:6).

Also, the truths associated with the ***color blue*** gives us a clear picture of this cherub duty that we're about to study—i.e., they oversee the execution of God's judgments against unruly saints. Let's study the significance of the ***color blue***.

Not only is the atmosphere around God's throne like a consuming fire, but the *__color blue__* portrays God's heavenly attributes and the fact that He's the righteous judge of the universe. As He judges the universe, His cherubim oversee the execution of His judgments against disobedient believers. Our objective in this chapter is to show that this is indeed a function (purpose) of God's cherubim.

How does the *__color blue__* portray God's heavenly attributes and that He's the righteous judge who gives His cherubim the duty of overseeing His judgments against unruly saints? In Exod 24:12, God told Moses to come up to the mountain and that He (God) would give him tables of stone with the Ten Commandments written thereon. God would write them with His own fingers. (Exod 31:18).

Moses and some of the Israelites had already seen the paved work of a blue sapphire stone under God's feet. (Exod 24:10). Hence, the tables of stone that God gave Moses had to have come from the blue sapphire stone under God's feet. For the blue sapphire stone under His feet is the only stone referred to in these verses.

The sapphire stone in Exodus 24:10 is of a sky-blue color. (Eze 1:26, 10:1). The sapphire stone may come in a variety of colors (blue, white, red, yellow, etc.), but the sapphire stone referred to in our study is of a sky-blue color. For Exodus 24:10 describes the sapphire stone as the clearness of the body of heaven (i.e., the sapphire stone under God's feet was as clear as the blue sky). (Exod 24:10).

These verses show that the *__color blue__* refers to God's throne, His aura, His attributes, His righteousness, His laws, His Ten Commandments, His holy words and the surface upon which His throne sits.

For example, God told Moses to tell the people to make fringes in the borders of their garments and put *__blue ribbons__* in the fringes of their borders. They were to look upon the *__blue ribbons__* to remember God's words and obey them. They were to be holy unto God. (Num 15:37-40). Having discussed the color blue, it leads us to the consuming fire around God's throne in which the cherubim operate.

He rode upon a cherub and did fly—Part IX

His glory, Shekinah glory is like fire around His throne. A consuming fire more intense than anyone has known. The throne's surface mingled with fire looks like a sea of glass. His cherubim are even portrayed as burnished brass.

Cherubim walk in His presence on stones of fire. Their protection of the commandments is His desire. They walk upon the throne's blue expanse in His name. As they walk the atmosphere around them is like a flame.

The atmosphere (in which cherubim operate) around God's throne is like a consuming fire (i.e., God's Shekinah glory is like a devouring fire: Exod 24:17).

Ezekiel saw the following vision. "Above the firmament over the cherubim's heads (i.e., above the **_blue colored_** expanse where God's throne sits) was the likeness of a throne that looked like a blue sapphire stone. On the throne was the likeness of a man (Christ). Ezekiel saw the color of amber that looked like fire around Him. From His waist upward and downward, Ezekiel saw the appearance of fire that was extremely bright around Him." (Eze 1:26-27).

Daniel also saw God's Shekinah glory in a vision. He saw God's throne and it was like a fiery flame with wheels like burning fire. A fiery stream issued forth from God's throne. (Dan7:9-10). As such, it's extremely hot around God's throne.

Because of the radiance of the heat, the fervency of the light and the intensity of the fire around God's throne, cherubim are portrayed as sparkling like burnished brass and their appearance is portrayed as burning coals of fire. (Eze 1:7, 13). Christ's feet are portrayed as fine brass as if they burned in a furnace. (Rev 1:15).

What I'm saying is that the area (expanse/surface) around God's throne is so fervently hot that it looks like a sea of crystal like glass mingled with fire. (Rev 4:5-6. 15:2). The intensity of the fire surrounding God's throne speaks of God's fiery judgments as the righteous judge of the universe. For our God is indeed a consuming fire. (Heb 12:29).

He rode upon a cherub and did fly—Part X

Having discussed the intensity of the consuming fire around God's throne, it leads us to His righteous judgments.

In a vision, Ezekiel saw cherubim in the midst of God's Shekinah glory as they held up God's throne-chariot while God moved about the universe meting out justice. (Ezk 1:4-5, 12, 25-28). This shows that cherubim not only support and uphold God's judgments, but they are divinely intertwined with them.

In other words, cherubim uphold God's throne and everything that pertains to it. So, in walking on the blue expanse under God's throne, the ***color blue*** shows that cherubs are intimately, inseparably and divinely intertwined with His judgments.

In this light, the brazen altar was overlaid with brass: Exod 27:1-2 (some Bibles use bronze for brass). It was in the outer court and used to make sacrifices to God. (Lev 1:9, 9:7, 17:11). Without blood sacrifices, there's no remission of sins. (Heb 9:22). So, brass symbolizes God's judgments. (Deut 28:22-23). And, Christ is the righteous judge over us. (Ps 9:8, Rev 19:11).

Lucifer (God's anointed cherub) sparkled like burnished brass. (Eze 1:7). This shows that he not only walked in God's fiery presence upon the stones of fire, but he was divinely associated with God's judgments. That is, Lucifer (God's chief angel) was called to oversee God's judgments against unruly saints.

Having discussed God's righteous judgments, it leads us into confirming that cherubim are called to oversee the execution of God's judgments against unruly saints. This function is important to God. For it speaks of protecting God's throne (i.e., this function speaks of how the cherubim guard against any impurities or defilements that try to come near the holiness of God's throne and His saints).

He rode upon a cherub and did fly—Part XI

In confirming this cherub function, God shows us (without a doubt) that He indeed called them to oversee the execution of His judgments against unruly saints who disobey His word. Let us now take a look at how God clearly confirms this divine truth.

Lucifer walked on the **_blue sapphire_** expanse/surface upon which God's throne sits. That is, in God's presence, he walked up and down in the midst of the stones of fire. (Eze 28:14).

Remember, our goal is to show that cherubim were called to oversee God's judgments against unruly saints in the holy city. This can also be applied to unruly saints around the world. In confirming this cherub function, God provides a vivid illustration of how His cherubim are called to oversee the execution of His righteous judgments against unruly saints.

He rode upon a cherub and did fly—Part XII

God told a man (an angel) clothe in linen to go in between the wheels (in the midst of the cherubs) and take coals of fire and scatter them over Jerusalem—i.e., bring judgment upon unruly saints in Jerusalem. (Eze 9:1-5, 9-10, 10:2).

The angel stood beside the wheels near the cherubim. He didn't have authority to enter into the midst of the coals of fire upon which the cherubim walked. The angel waited for a cherub to give him coals to fire. (Ezk 10:6-7). The angel had to obey God's line of authority. This shows that cherubim are indeed called to oversee the execution of God's judgments upon unruly saints.

As cherubim guard God's dwelling places (in heaven and in Jerusalem) and the saints who dwell therein, they keep any impurities, sacrilege and wickedness from defiling God's holy mountain in heaven and in Jerusalem on earth.

But, Lucifer became so wrapped up in pride that he wanted to be like God. (Isa 14:12-15, Eze 28: 15-16). He convinced 1/3 of the angels to rebel with him. So, he and 1/3 of the angels were kicked out of heaven. (Rev 12:7-9). The cherubim who remained with God carried on with their duty of overseeing God's judgments against unruly saints. For their calling is eternal. (Rom 11:29).

This shows the seventh and final cherub function that we're going to study. They oversee God's judgments against unruly saints. Since they act like God expects us to act, some racial group was created to fulfill this calling like the cherubim.

One of Noah's sons and his offspring are called to fulfill this purpose. Our goal is to show which one of Noah's sons and his descendants are called to oversee God's righteous judgments against unruly saints. I'll do this shortly.

CHAPTER 6

Shem's Descendants Have A Special Purpose To Fulfill—Session 1

Shem's racial calling:
The light bearer—Part I

> Born to be firstborn sons, in Shem they are the head. Born to be the peculiar ones, by them the world is led.
>
> God created Jews to be the embodiment of His word. They spread news about the covenant they heard. Born with the birthright, they're born as the true light.

We've finally come to the moment we've all been looking forward to. So please listen up. It's time for our official (in depth) study of our respective racial group's purpose both on earth and in the new word to come (Paradise). If you have a curious bone in your body about your racial group's purpose on earth, it's time to gear up for an overflowing river of spiritual enlightenment.

We found that one of the key purposes that cherubim were created to fulfill is that they were made to be the embodiment of God's words. We found that they were created in our likeness (i.e., created in the image of man). (Eze 1:5). We also found that cherubim act like we must act. So, we study their functions and duties to pinpoint our racial group's purpose that must be fulfilled on earth before we die.

So, what now? As promised, I'll now show you which one of Noah's sons and his offspring were created to be the very embodiment of God's holy words, like the cherubim. God created Shem's offspring to fulfill this purpose. Let's confirm this truth that Noah prophesied over Shem. Noah said, "Blessed be the Lord God of Shem and Canaan will be his servant (i.e. Shem is blessed because God's words of wisdom, in the form of Christ came through Shem's family line)." (Gen. 9:26).

This confirms that the cherubs' calling to be the embodiment of wisdom was given to Shem and his offspring. God also said, "You (Moses) will tell Pharaoh, that Israel is my firstborn. (Exod 4:22). God chose Jews to be a peculiar people unto Him above all nations. (Deut 14:2). God said, ". . . to the Jews pertain the adoption, glory, covenants, promises, the giving of the law, and the service of God."(Rom 9:4). This truly shows that the Jews are called to spread God's word.

I'm sure that we all have a general idea that God called the Jews to teach His word to all nations. And that's good. But, there's much more involved than just having a general idea. For, there is a wealth of knowledge in the Bible about the nuts and bolts of what God instructed them to reveal to us.

There's a lot involved in what they must reveal to us about God's spiritual truths. Their calling is no simple matter. This book gets into the nitty-gritty details of the numerous spiritual truths they're called to reveal. For true enlightenment, we must get into the specifics of what God called them to reveal to the world.

So God's salvation plan (in the form of Christ) came through Shem's family line. Since Christ came through Shem's lineage, the Jews are the racial group that God chose to be the embodiment of His holy words. As such, Shem's offspring are to teach the four components of God's birthright blessing to all nations. So, God needed a group to spread His word. Of His own free will, He chose the Jews.

Now, based on the Law of the Firstborn Son, the firstborn son receives a double portion of his father's wealth and succeeds him as the family's head. Since Israel is God's spiritual firstborn son (Exod 4:22), Israel is entitled to lead all nations and receive a double portion of God's wealth. (Deut. 21:15-17).

Since Israel is to lead all nations, all nations must serve her. (Isa 60:12-14). As God's leader, it makes Israel the light bearer of God's words of truth. (Rom 9:4, Mal 2:4-7). We'll be studying Shem's purpose on earth in 15 parts.

In this light, Israel's entitlement to receive a double portion confirms that Shem and his descendants are not only called to lead all nations, but they're also called to reflect God's wealth blessing in their calling.

The bottom line is that your father's bloodline traces back to Shem, Ham or Japheth, the progenitors of all racial groups on the face of the earth after the flood. (Gen 9:1, 7). So, if your father's bloodline (ancestry) traces back to Shem, you now know your true identity and racial group's purpose. Your gift and calling is to be the embodiment of God's words of truth and wisdom.

So, Jews really don't have an identity crisis. All they have to do is identify their father's ancestry, roll up their sleeves, and get on with their racial group's calling of teaching the four components of God's birthright blessing to the world.

If they do, they'll be welcomed into the gates of heaven—i.e., the gates of hell shall not prevail against them. (Matt 16:18). But, if they reject their Messiah (Jesus) and His calling, the gates of hell will be their recompense. (Matt 7:13-14).

Shem's racial calling (purpose): The light bearer—Part II

Because of His love for Jews, they're fearfully and wonderfully made. Hence, His love for them will never gradually or eventually fade. Set under His never flawing eye, it's no wonder He's ever drawing them nigh.

When king Cyrus of Persia was in rule, the Jews were set free from their scattering. Then saith Cyrus rather calm and cool, the Jews would get joy from their gathering. Since Jews have a double portion of wealth as their share, they have no reason to ever despair.

God has unconditional love for Shem's family line (the Jews). Even before the foundation of the earth, they were on His mind. Even before He stretched out the heavens and formed the light (Isa 45:12, Gen 1:3), they were on His mind. For, He created them to deliver His gospel message to the world. And they will use their double portion of wealth to accomplish their God given purpose here on earth.

They're fearfully and wonderfully made (Ps 139:14) and endowed with all the gifts and talents they need to fulfill God's purpose for creating them. So, they are perfectly suited to spread God's holy words to all nations. No other racial group but theirs was created specifically for this purpose. Yes, not only were they always on God's mind, but He always loved them unconditionally.

Stop for a minute and think about Jews relative to anti-Semitism and hateful hostilities that some nations and people express toward them. Such haters can be so intrusive. But, God keeps a watchful eye on His chosen people who love Him.

"For, the eyes of the Lord are upon the righteous and His ears are open to their cries. His face is against them who do evil, to cut off the remembrance of them from the face of the earth." (Ps 34:15-16). Hallelujah! That being said, have you ever really thought about unconditional love? I'll show you unconditional love.

God used King Cyrus to show His unconditional love for the Jews who are the apple of His eye. (Zech 2:6). King Cyrus freed God's chosen people from Babylonian captivity so that they could return to their home (i.e., he allowed them to return to the Promised Land). (Deut 27:3, Isa 44:28, 45:13, Ezra 1:1-4).

Babel (Babylon) symbolizes the origin of evil religious systems. (Gen 11:1-9). It has lured people into idol worship for centuries. Christ will return to free all saints from the Babylonian captivity of that day. So, Cyrus prefigures Christ's second coming. He'll free His people from bondage and return them to their land. (Exod 3:8, Lev 20:24). This is significant. For gathering the Jews unto Himself and returning them to their home ultimately points to their real home in Paradise.

So, Jews cannot be selfish by keeping this message to themselves. They must spread it to all nations (for this is their purpose). In this light, Jews are called to comfort Israel and Gentile nations (Ham's and Japheth's descendants).

"Comfort ye my people, says God. Speak comfortably to Jerusalem. Cry to her that her warfare is over and her iniquity is pardoned. God gave her double for her sins. A voice cries in the wilderness, Prepare God's way;

make a straight path in the desert (i.e., get ready for Christ's return to set up His kingdom)." (Isa 40:1-3).

These verses give Jewish people as well as the whole world everlasting consolation. (2 Thess 2:16). Christ will return to rule the earth and reward His people. As noted, Christ's return ultimately points to their real home that God has in store for them in Paradise. God is all powerful. His word shall not only stand forever, but it shall accomplish what He sent it to do. (Isa 40:6-18, 55:11).

So, the warfare between believers and Satan is over (accomplished)— i.e., it will come to an end. (Isa 40:2-5). The calling that God gave to Shem's offspring is of great comfort to the world. Jews must share Christ's imminent return with all nations. It's vital that they do this. Because of His unconditional love for them, He'll reward them mightily.

Shem's racial calling (purpose): The light bearer—Part III

> Christ came through Shem's family tree. God taught His word first to them. Jews must lift Him up for all to see. And He will draw all men unto Him.
>
> It's no easy task to witness as God wants you to. Don't even ask why from God some men flew. Evil people want to be their own gods. But, press on dear witness even if it seems too hard.

Since the Jews are called to spread God's gospel to all nations, Christ came through Shem's bloodline. (Rom 1:3). That is, God passed His coat of many colors to Shem and his descendants. In order for Jewish people to spread the gospel of peace to all nations, Christ had to first minister His gospel to the Jews.

As it is written, "I am not ashamed of the gospel of Christ: for it is the power of God unto salvation to everyone that believeth, to the Jew first, and to the Greek (i.e., the Gentiles)." (Rom 1:16, Lk 24:45-47, Matt 10:5-7).

So, the Jews have their marching orders. It's not an easy task that God called them to fulfill because there are so many selfish people out there who don't give a hoot about God or His salvation plans. They're so into themselves that they want to be their own gods so that they can do things their way. Nevertheless, Shem's descendants must press on and lift up Christ from the earth and Christ will draw all men unto Him. (John 12:32).

Shem's racial calling (purpose): The light bearer—Part IV

I love to read love stories with happy endings. I even love to share heartwarming love stories with others. As you go through the Bible, you'll find that it's brimming with love stories that have very happy endings.

That said, God's purpose for Jews is a great love story with a happy ending. How so? Because of His undying love for them (even before He stretched out the heavens and formed the light: Isa 45:12, Gen 1:3), it was His heart's desire for them to spread His word. They would also love Him. The happy ending of this love story is that He would reward them with an eternal life of peace, happiness and joy in Paradise. Now that's what I call a true love story with a happy ending.

In showing their true love for God (who's going to reward them with eternal life), Shem's offspring must not only teach the four components of God's birthright blessing, but they must also tell all people that God created the earth for them to inhabit. Because of His love for His creation, He stretched out the heavens and formed the light. (Isa 45:12, Gen 1:3).

Shem's offspring must also tell the world that God makes peace. They must witness that God said, "Woe be unto those who strive against Him." (Isa 45:9). Every knee will bow and every tongue will confess that He's God. (Isa 45:23). In God Israel's seeds will be justified and glory in Him. (Isa 45:25).

In showing their true love for God (who's going to reward them with eternal life), Shem's offspring must warn all nations that they're not to worship material things and creatures that God created. They're not to make idols out of iron, gold, trees, etc., and place them in their houses (i.e., men should not worship people or things more than they worship God). (Isa 44:9-20).

For example, they make fires for warmth from the same tree they use to make idols. (Isa 44:9-20). In today's times, if alcohol doesn't give sinners peace, they try harder drugs. If one evil deed doesn't work, they try another.

They try everything but God. So, idol worship was as wild in Isaiah's time as it is today. This is an abomination. Hence, Shem's offspring have a great responsibility to warn sinners that, it's crucial to stay away from idols.

In showing their love for God, Jews must tell sinners to listen to God. He'll not give His glory to another. So, sinners must flee from today's Babylonian den of iniquity. Had they listened to God, they would have had peace like a river long ago. (Isa 48:3-21). So, show your love Israel and speak to all nations.

It's unfortunate that far too many Jewish people have been rejecting Christ for over 2000 years (since the days that Jesus Christ walked the earth). Far too many Jews do not believe that Christ was here on earth, bled and died on the cross for their sins and will soon return to remove those who don't believe in Christ from the face of the earth.

It is written, "He (Jesus) was in the world and the world was made by Him and the world knew Him not. He came unto His own (Jewish people) and His own received Him not." (John 1:10-11).

So, it's vital that Jewish people get on with their calling of teaching God's gospel to the world. Sinners must know that Christ was wounded for our transgressions and bruised for our iniquities. He was despised, afflicted, and rejected. We esteemed Him not, yet He remained silent. The chastisement of our peace was upon Him; and with His stripes we are healed. (Isa 53:1-7).

Shem's racial calling (purpose): The light bearer—Part V

Isaiah Chapters 40-66 cite many of the Jews' duties as God's light bearers. We'll highlight some of the salient verses in these chapters that reveal God's undying love for the Jews and the purpose for which He created them.

As we study Isa 40-66, we'll find that these chapters bless us with a passionate love story with a very happing ending. Words cannot describe how precious Jews are to God. From the foundation of the world, God created them for a divine purpose to fulfill here on earth. They'll continue to fulfill their purpose in Paradise because God's callings are eternal (i.e., they're never ending). (Rom 11:29).

They're God's chosen people. Day and night, He watches over them. (Ps 34:15-16). People are to keep their anti-Semitic hands off of them. They're not only God's pride and joy, but they're the apple of His eye. (Zec 2:8, Deut 32:10).

Although some Jews have been stubborn in fulfilling their calling, God's love for them hasn't changed. ". . . All day long I've stretched my hands unto a stubborn people." (Rom 10:21). But, God hasn't cast them away. (Rom 11:1-2).

Israel's calling is crucial to the world. The world is depending upon Jewish people stepping up to the plate and going forth to enlighten nations about God's plans. So, Shem's descendants are to tell people about the good things that God has given them: everlasting life, peace, wealth and knowledge of God's word.

In showing their true love for God (who's going to reward them with eternal life), Shem's offspring must tell Israel and the world that the Gentiles (Ham's and Japheth's offspring) will rebuild Israel's walls, houses, etc. Not only that, but they must tell the world about the blessings that'll flow to Israel. Jews will be blessed with (1) Gentile forces (i.e., Gentiles' wealth), (2) great forests, (3) great flocks, (4) riches from the seas, and (5) gold, silver, etc. (Isa 60:3-21, 62:1-3).

As such, Israel will be at peace and nations will serve her. (Isa 60:5-7, 10-16, 61:5). Jews must tell the world that God will create a new heaven and earth and the former things will not be remembered or come to mind. (Isa. 65:17). They must also reveal that voices of crying will never be heard in Paradise. (Isa. 65:19).

A key point is that Christ's millennial reign will be like heaven on earth. So, in showing their love for God (who's going to reward them with eternal life), Shem's offspring must (1) prepare the way for Jesus' return: Isa 62:10, (2) tell Jews that before they call, God will answer: Isa 65:24, and (3) reveal that the wolf and the lamb shall feed together and the lion shall eat straw like a bullock. (Isa 65:24-25).

They must tell the world that the leopard, kid, calf, lion, cow, wolf and lamb will lie down together in peace. (Isa 11:6-7). They're to tell the world that the sucking child will play on hole of the asp. (Isa 11:8) That is, no creature, thing or being will hurt or destroy in the millennium. (Isa 11:9, 65:25).

Shem's racial calling (purpose): The light bearer—Part VI

I can't express enough how vital Jews are to God's plans for mankind. Just look around you. Crime and violence are on the rise. People are dying in the streets. Different racial groups are bickering and clawing at one another. Jews must teach salvation and peace to people. Many Jews are so busy denying the Messiah that they can't see the forest for the trees. They have yet to come into the knowledge of their racial group's calling and purpose for which God created them.

As noted, God called His cherubim to be the embodiment of wisdom. Knowing God's word verbatim, cherubim know what God considers to be fair, just and true. As discerners of God's word, cherubim know when people are being treated properly—i.e., they're aware of injustice, inequality and impartiality.

In showing their love for God, Jews must realize that their racial group is to rightly divide and discern God's word like the cherubim. Jews are to be the discerners of God's word who know when people are treated with justice and equality. Jews cannot reject their Messiah on the one hand and at the same time teach God's word. (2 Tim 2:15). They're to see that His truth, justice and peace permeate the earth. Christ shall bring forth justice and peace on earth.

"A bruised reed (branch) shall He (Jesus) not break. He won't quench a smoking flax (wick): He'll bring forth judgment unto truth and not be discouraged or fail until He has set Judgment (justice and peace) in the earth . . ." (Isa 42:3-4).

Jews are to follow Jesus: God's servant who came to spread truth and establish peace. He came to promote equality, justice and peace and to bind up those who are like bruised reeds. He came not to quench the smoking flax (glimmering wicks) of the weak and feeble. He came to fan their wicks and set them on fire for the Lord.

Shem's offspring are to do the same as Christ did. As they spread the gospel, they're to promote equality, justice and peace. They're to build up those who are like bruised reeds (i.e., they're to bind up those who are weak and feeble by fanning their spiritual wicks). That is, they are to set them on fire for the Lord. So, they must show their love for God as He shows His undying love for them by rewarding them with an eternal life of peace, happiness and unspeakable joy.

CHAPTER 7

Shem's Descendants Have A Special Purpose To Fulfill—Session 2

Shem's racial calling (purpose): The light bearer—Part VII

> Shem's line must stand in judgment of the Jews, but in love. They walk on stones of fire as He views from above.
>
> Stones of fire are symbolic of God's presence. In His presence it's so magnificently pleasant.
>
> God's love, eternal love to Shem's line He gives. In the hearts, sweet hearts of Shem's line He lives.

There's no love like eternal love. As the God of love (2 Cor 13:11), His love is eternal for God is from everlasting to everlasting. (Ps 90:2). His love bears all things, hopes for all things, endures all things and believes all things. (1 Cor 13:7). These are God's emotions for Jews from eternity past; they're always on His mind.

Shem's descendants are not only to bask in God's eternal love, but they are to love God in return. Earlier, we discussed how God's love for Jews is a true love story with a happy ending. God's emotions shown above are all about God's true love story between Him and the Jews with a very happy ending.

In this section we'll show that Jews are called to oversee the execution of God's judgments against unruly saints. Since God is love (1 John 4:8), they must do this with love, for love never fails. (1 Cor 13:8). Love suffereth long, envieth not, vaunteth not itself, is not puffed up and is kind. (1 Cor 13:4). One of the cherubs' key duties is to oversee the execution of God's judgments against unruly saints. (See Chap 5 "He rode upon a cherub and did fly" Part XI-Part XII).

In walking in the role of overseeing chastisements against unruly saints, Jews have to love God and draw on His love. There's no love like it. Some people do not chastise in love. They abuse others unnecessarily. That is, sometimes they overdo it or overstep their boundaries to the point of harming others (some parents do this, some arresting officers do this, some school teachers do this and so on).

Jews are to bask in God's love and love Him in return as they chastise others. They must not misapply God's love when chastising others for that's out of line. Now, as promised, I'll show you which one of Noah's sons and his offspring are called to oversee God's judgments (in love) against unruly saints like the cherubim. We noted earlier that (created in our likeness) cherubim do what we're called to do. So, we study them to find out what we're supposed to do.

In a vision, Ezekiel saw a pavement before 30 chambers in the outer court. (Eze 40:17). Jewish priests walked on it in love for God to do His work. The Greek word for pavement is ritspah (rits-paw). It means hot coals of fire. Hot coals of fire speak of God's presence, His Shekinah glory and His righteous judgments.

So, in walking on the pavement that portrays hot coals of fire, it shows that the Jews are the ones that are called to oversee the execution of His judgments against unruly saints. Thus, like the cherubim who walk up and down in the midst of the stones of fire (Eze 28:14), Shem and his offspring are indeed the racial group that God called to oversee the execution of His judgments against unruly saints.

Jews don't literally oversee God's judgments like cherubim. They only chastise others through God's word (in love) by telling them what is lawful and what is not. By walking on the pavement that portrays coals of fire, they portray the cherubim's function of overseeing the execution of God's judgments against unruly saints. This shows that Shem and his descendants are the racial group that God called to oversee the execution of His judgments against unruly saints like the cherubim.

Shem's racial calling (purpose): The light bearer—Part VIII

A wise man said, "I'll do it today. Tomorrow may be too late. There's no time to play. Sorrow may be my fate."

An unwise man said, "I'll do it in time. I must not hurry. I'll drink my wine. For I must be merry!

These words of wisdom are telling us that today is the day of salvation. (2 Cor 6:2). "Never put off til tomorrow what you can do today." (Thomas Jefferson). That is, do now that which you know you must do.

In this light, Jews must accept their Messiah (Jesus Christ). For, they can't afford to put off until tomorrow what they're called to do today. God loves them unconditionally and He needs them to go forth and spread His gospel unto the world. If they do, they'll receive their reward in heaven.

So, in showing their true love for God, they must go forth and teach the four components of God's birthright blessing. God called them to build His house—i.e., He called them build His kingdom. (Isa 66:1). But, for the past 2000 years, far too many of them have been unwise. They've been drinking their wine and being merry (i.e., they've been slothful).

They have not been wise by doing today what they've been called to do. They have not realized that tomorrow may be too late. Moreover, they've not only been rejecting their Messiah (Jesus Christ), but they've not been building His kingdom.

God wants to know where is His house (His kingdom) that they were supposed to build for Him. (Isa 66:1). Some Jews didn't answer when He called. (Isa 65:12). They chose their own way then and are still choosing their own way today.

That said, Shem's offspring must warn sinners that if they don't reverence God, sorrow may be their fate (i.e., they'll lie down in sorrow). (Isa 50:10-11). Sinners must seek God while He may be found (for today is the day of salvation: 2 Cor 6:2). So, because of His unconditional love, God will pardon them and give them peace. (Isa 55:6-7, 57:19).

Because of His unconditional love for the Jews, He'll bless them with a population explosion. Gentiles will help to bring Jews back to Jerusalem. Kings will worship Jews. People will know that God is real. (Isa 49:17-23). Jews need to be about their Father's business of building His house. Their Father is the God of Abraham, Isaac and Jacob. (Exod 3:15).

Shem's racial calling (purpose): The light bearer—Part IX

Recall that a key duty of God's cherubim is to minister God's wealth blessing. (See Chap 4 "He rode upon a cherub and did fly" Part VII). Also, recall that cherubim were made in our likeness: Eze1:5 (i.e., they do what we're called to do). So, we study them to find out our racial group's purpose.

As promised, I will now show you which one of Noah's sons and his offspring are called to minister God's wealth blessing to the world. God created Shem and his descendants to fulfill this highly crucial purpose. Let's confirm this truth.

Israel is God's spiritual firstborn son. (Exod 4:22). By law, the firstborn son is to receive a double portion of his father's wealth and succeed him as the head of the family. (Deut 21:15-17, 2 Chron 21:3). As God's firstborn son with a double portion of God's wealth, it shows that the Jewish people are called to minister the wealth component of God's birthright blessing, like unto the cherubim.

As noted, the firstborn son's siblings also received a share of their father's wealth. So, Shem's siblings (Japheth and Ham) must also receive a share of their father's wealth. Having noted this fact, we'll find out later that Ham's and Japheth's offspring were also called to minister God's wealth blessing.

Most importantly, all believers need wealth to spread Christ's gospel. Hence, in this light, we're all called to minister the wealth component of God's birthright blessing to everyone who comes into our sphere of influence.

Shem's racial calling (purpose):
The light bearer—Part X

It's absolutely fascinating to see how God confirms His wealth blessing through the creation of black horses. (Ps 86:10). How is this so?

Consider these verses of Scripture. "In the first chariot were red horses and in the second chariot were black horses." (Zech 6:1-2). "The black horses . . . go forth unto the north country . . ." (Zech 6:6). " . . . Behold, these that go toward the north country have quieted (pleased) God's Spirit in the north country." (Zech 6:8).

Now, God's Spirit is quieted when saints obey Him so that He can bless them with wealth. That is, if God's people who're called by His name will humble themselves and pray, and seek His face and repent; He'll hear them from heaven, forgive their sins and heal their land. (2 Chron 7:14, Deut 6:1-3).

So, He'll heal their Promised Land that flows with milk and honey: Lev20:24 (milk and honey is symbolic of a land of wealth overflowing with fertile soils, spiritual and financial blessings, etc.). This quiets (brings peace to) God's Spirit.

But, there's no way that Satan is going to allow God's Spirit to be quieted in the north country without a fight. The north country refers to God's enemies. God had to declare war on Satan. (Gen 3:15). Notice that the chariots speak of war.

Now, who did God send forth to the north country to battle Satan over the wealth of the land. God's Spirit was quieted by none other than God's black horses (who personify God's angels) that went forth unto the north country. (Zech 6:6-8).

These truths confirm, without a doubt, that God's black horses portray His great wealth blessing for believers. For God's black horses (that portray God's angels) are indeed the ones who go forth to the north country to quiet God's Spirit. As noted, God's Spirit is quieted (pleased) when His people obey Him so that He can restore them to the Promised Land of great wealth and abundance.

So, God's black horses ensure that we possess the wealth blessing. As such, black horses portray the wealth component of God's birthright blessing.

Shem's racial calling (purpose): The light bearer—Part XI

> Rain, rain tis such a blessing. Pour out; pour out, the harvest will come. It'll grow, surely grow, no need for obsessing. Our God, our God is where it comes from.
>
> As a rain, lovely rain, the Spirit pours its power on us. Teach; now teach how it pours on sinners and the just. Teaching is the calling of the Jews. Rejecting it shall bring them an eternal bruise.

If you believe nothing else in your life, please believe that God loves Jewish people. For, they are His chosen people. Because of His undying love for them, He gave them two rains: the **early rain** and the **latter rain**.

Now, this is what I call a true love story with a very happy ending. Allow me to elaborate. In Israel, there is an **early rain** in the fall that softens the ground for sowing (planting) seeds. There is also a **latter rain** in the spring that ripens the crops for the harvest.

The **early rain** is symbolic of God's Holy Spirit. God's Spirit rained (poured out) on the Jewish people in the upper room at Pentecost. (Acts 1:13-16, 2:1-5). This is the time when God filled the Jewish people with the power of His Holy Spirit (Acts 1:8) so that they could to go forth to spread His gospel to the world.

This out pouring brought in the church age in which we now live. (Acts 2:1-17). Empowered by the Holy Spirit, Peter (a Jewish disciple) preached the gospel to a crowd and about 3,000 people got saved that day. (Acts 2:14-42).

So, spiritually speaking, the **early rain** refers to the out pouring of God's Holy Spirit in the church age. So, all people have the opportunity of a lifetime to get saved now. In this light, God needs the Jews to (1) accept Christ (their Messiah), (2) stop rebelling, and (3) roll up their sleeves and help God win souls for His heavenly harvest. For, unsaved Jews and Gentiles are dying by the dozens every day. God, however, wants them to get save and join Him in Paradise. (2 Pet 3:9).

If you're a Jewish believer, you have it made. You're passionately involved in a great love story with Christ that has a very happy ending. Because of His undying love for Jews, He has called them to be His light bearers. Jews are to show their love for Him in fulfilling this service.

The happy ending of this love story is that saved Jews will never see hell. They are heaven bound. As their reward, there'll be no sorrows, tears or dying. (Rev 21:4). What a life! They'll bask in heaven in the midst of love, peace and joy. What a love story! Jews should thank and praise God for the **early rain**.

When the church age (i.e., the **early rain**) is finished, Christ will raise up the bodies of saints who passed away to meet Him in the air (He'll not set His feet on earth; He'll meet them in the clouds). They'll be raised with new bodies like Christ's glorious body. (Phil 3:21). Saints who are alive at His coming will also receive new bodies and be caught up in the air with believers who were raised from their graves. Christ will take all of them to heaven with Him. (1 Thess 4:15-18).

So, Jews must teach these truths to all nations. They must warn sinners that after the rapture, the only thing that'll stand between them and hell is the **latter rain**. People cannot afford to miss the **latter rain**. So, let's study the **latter rain**.

Shem's racial calling (purpose): The light bearer—Part XII

Jews are to teach people about the two rainy seasons in Israel. These two rainy seasons show us great truths about the outpouring of God's Spirit that'll save people. The **early rain** refers to how God's Spirit rained on the Jews in the upper room at Pentecost. (Acts 1:13-16, 2:1-5). This was the beginning of the church age in which we now live.

The **latter rain** refers to the outpouring of God's Spirit in the tribulation (i.e., the latter rain will start after Christ raptures His saints out of this world). (1 Thess 4:15-18). During the last 3½ years of the tribulation, sinners left behind will suffer the most horrific plagues known to man. God's Spirit will be pouring out on them. (Matt 24:15-22, Rev 6:1-17, 8:1-13, 9:1-21, 11:15-19, 16:1-21).

The outpouring of God's Holy Spirit will be their only way to get saved out of these horrible plagues. Thank God for the **latter rain**.

On that note, when Christ raptures His church age believers, He'll leave (here on earth) 144 thousand Jewish believers from the church age to witness to the sinners left behind so that hopefully the **latter rain** will bring salvation to their souls. (Rev 7:1-4). Hence, some remnant of Jewish believers will always be here on earth to fulfill their calling of teaching God's gospel to all nations.

God dotes on Jewish people. He wants them to join Him in Paradise. He also wants unsaved Gentiles to join Him in Paradise. (2 Pet 3:9). For the **latter rain** is the only thing that stands between sinners left behind and hell.

Jewish and Gentile sinners who get saved in the tribulation period will be a part of the Lord's harvest (i.e., the gathering of His people unto Himself at the end of the tribulation). (Matt 24:31). But, the problem with the world today is that there are far too many people of Jewish descent as well as people from other racial groups who couldn't care less about heaven, hell or their racial group's purpose.

Many of them think that heaven and hell are myths or something to poke fun at. God's word is foolishness to them. (1 Cor 1:18). There is a heaven, hell and a real God. If any Jew rejects Christ instead of rolling up his/her sleeves and witnessing to lost souls, he/she will be severely recompensed when that person stands before God's great white throne on Judgment Day. (Rev 20:11-15).

Jews must tell people that they should not take a chance on missing out on salvation. People should get saved in the church age. There's no guarantee that they'll be alive for the **latter rain** (i.e., they may die before the tribulation begins).

Jewish saints must teach unbelievers that their bodies will be resurrected unto eternal death. They will be raised with the same vile bodies they had when they died. God never promised them new bodies. (Eph 5:5). So, woe be unto sinners who miss the **early** and **latter rains** (i.e., they didn't get it right before they died).

Jews are to witness to sinners about their twisted thoughts. Sinners may think that they don't need Christ because they feel that they're tough enough. Woe be unto them if the great tribulation gets a hold of them. They'll find out just how tough they are without Jesus. It's dangerous to gamble with heaven. Sinners could get wiped out before they know what hit them. Jews must teach about the **early** and **latter rains**. They have no time to waste. They must forge ahead as God holds them ever so close to His bosom and surrounds them with His undying love.

Shem's racial calling (purpose): The light bearer—Part XIII

With the destruction and chaotic state that the world is showing today, Jews must comfort Israel and tell her that when Christ returns, Israel will have no need of the sun, for Christ will be her light. In showing their true love for God (who's going to reward them with eternal life), Shem's offspring must reveal that saints will (1) inherit the Promised Land, (2) suffer no more violence and (3) be holy.

As noted before, far too many Jewish people are not teaching God's gospel of good news. Nevertheless, God's passionate love story with a very happy ending still holds for disobedient Jews.

But Jews who are still stubbornly refusing to accept Christ are as filthy rags. They don't even bother to call on Him. God has hidden His face from them. (Isa 64:6-7). God has shown His great works in the past. (Isa. 63:11-15). He will save them if they'll just repent and return to Him (Isa 44:22, 55:7, 64:5, 9).

Jews are busy rejecting Christ by waiting for Him to come. That is, Christ was rejected by His own people. (Isa 53:3, Lk 4:24, Matt 21:42-43). So, God sought to provoke them to jealously and get them to serve Him. As such, God gave the Gentiles an opportunity to serve as His light bearers. (Rom 10:16-21, Isa. 65:1-5).

If disobedient Jews continue to ignore their calling, sinners' blood will be on their hands. (Eze 33:8-9). Far too many Jews are serving false gods.

Isaiah told them that God is omnipotent and will help them. (Isa 41:8-10, 44:9-22, 46:1-9, Rev 19:6). Jews must get saved and share God's truths with all nations.

Shem's racial calling (purpose):
The light bearer—Part XIV

> His eyes are set so close on me. (Ps 34:15). From sin and death He has set me free. (Rom 8:2). He's good, so good, O taste and see. (Ps 34:8).
>
> Kiss me with your kisses, they're better than wine. (Sol Song 1:2). They looked for His faults, but none did they find. (Lk 23:4). And I love Him with all of my heart, soul and mind. (Matt 22:37).
>
> For uttering idle words, God keeps a score chart. (Matt 12:36). For sitting at Jesus' feet, Mary got the good part. (Lk 10:39-42). For ministering in His service, we're seals on His heart. (Sol Song 8:6).

It's so good to have a dream (well-functioning) relationship with God wherein He's in love with you and doing good things for you. And, you're in love with Him and doing good things for Him. This is a love story with a very happy ending. The loving words above (from the Bible) are what I call a dream (well-functioning) relationship with the Lord.

Some Arabs don't have a dream (well-functioning) relationship with the Lord. With that said, notice that people of the Arab nations and Jews of Israel's 12 tribes (Gen 35:22, 1 Kings 18:30-31) are genetically related, for they're all descendants of Shem and born out of Abraham's loins.

According to my research, some Arabs are descendants of the 12 tribes of Abraham's son Ishmael. (Gen 16:1-16, 25:12-18). Some are descendants of Abraham and his second wife Keturah. (Gen 25:1-4). And some are descendants of Abraham's grandson Esau. So they are indeed genetically related to the Jews.

Sarah's household began to get a little rocky when Abraham's firstborn got a little cocky. It all began when Sarah told Abraham to cast Ishmael and Hagar out of the household (Hagar had given birth to Abraham's firstborn son, Ishmael). Ishmael had mocked Isaac, Abraham's second son. God chose (substituted) Isaac in Ishmael's place to receive the birthright. (Gen 17:15-21, 21:9-11).

By law, the birthright (1) gives the firstborn son a double portion of his father's wealth and (2) entitles him to succeed his father as the head of the family. But God bypassed the law and substituted Isaac in the firstborn's place. This portrays how God substituted Christ in Adam's place (His first created son). For when Adam sinned, his blood became tainted and he couldn't pass pure blood unto us. As such, Adam passed the death penalty to us. (Gen 3:17-19).

Adam's actions resulted in a true love story with a very happy ending. That is, through His undying love, Christ became God's substitute who passed His pure blood to us to pay for our sins. So, the happy ending to this love story is that through Christ's shed blood, we have eternal life. (Rom 5:8-9, Col 3:12-15).

In bypassing Ishmael (the firstborn), God shows us a great spiritual truth. That is, in bypassing the Law of the Firstborn Son, it shows that Christ moved us out from under the curse of the law and placed us under grace. (Gal 3:13, Rom 6:14).

This is true love. But, we must love Christ in return. That said, since Jews and Arabs are both born out of Abraham's loins, they are genetically related. As such, the offspring of Shem and the offspring of the Arabs are called to fulfill the same purpose (i.e., to teach Christ's gospel to all nations).

This truth means that a person of Arab descent whose father's ancestry traces back to Shem, must (like the Jews) roll up his/her sleeves and get on with God's purpose for his/her life. Otherwise, that person is not being set free from the law of sin and death. (Rom 8:2). He/she is not sitting at Jesus' feet getting the good part. (Lk 10:39-42).

Not only that, but that person is not ministering in God's service, so that God can set that person as a seal upon His heart. (Sol Song 8:6). This shows that he/she has not tasted to see that the Lord is good. (Ps 34:8). That person certainly does not love the Lord with his/her heart, soul and mind. (Matt 22:37). In other words, that person doesn't have a dream (well-functioning) relationship with the lord and is suffering from a serious spiritual identity crisis.

To this end, Jewish people must share their common ancestry with the Arab nations. They must witness to them about their common calling of teaching the four components of God's birthright blessing to the world.

Far too many people of Arab descent allow Satan to keep them blinded under a false Muslim or Islamic religion. The growing anti-Semitism, animosity and attacks that some Arab nations hatefully perpetrate against Jewish people are instigated by Satan who comes to steal, kill and destroy. (John 10:10).

Keeping the Arabs and Israelites divided is one of Satan's key strategies. As such, far too many Arabs whose fathers trace back to Shem are not carrying out their racial group's purpose of spreading the gospel to all people.

The Jews must never give up on witnessing to the Arab nations about their common Abrahamic heritage. No matter what, they must continue to fulfill their purpose of witnessing to all people (including Arabs) about God's holy words. The Arabs would then have a dream (well-functioning) relationship with the Lord.

Shem's racial calling (purpose): The light bearer—Part XV

It's absolutely amazing to see how God confirms His purpose for Shem's offspring through white horses. God shows us that white horses symbolize His word blessing. (Zec 6:1-6, Rev 19:11-16). How so? Let's take a look.

"Heaven opened and I (John) saw a white horse. The rider on the white horse is called Faithful and True. In righteousness He judges and makes war. His eyes were as a flame of fire. Many crowns were on His head. He had a name that only He knew. His vesture was dipped in blood. His name (i.e., the name of the rider) is called the Word of God (Jesus Christ is **The Word of God**)." (Rev 19:11-13).

So, Christ is the rider of the white horse. As noted, He is called Faithful and True. He went forth to judge the earth. He not only went forth to fight for justice, but He also went forth to establish righteousness, truth, and victory for believers. Without dispute, this rider symbolizes Christ, the righteous (God's living Word).

The flame in His eyes identifies Him with Christ (the living Word of God: Rev 19:13), for the flame portrays divine judgment. He'll return to earth at the end of the world (i.e., at the end of the tribulation), judge the wicked and cast them into the fires of Hades. (1 Sam 2:10). So, those who reject God's living Word (Christ); will be tormented and punished in the lake of fire for all eternity. (Rev 20:11-15).

So, white horses are associated with God's word blessing. As we can see, both white horses and Shem's offspring deal with the word blessing. When you consider white horses, they're symbolic of the word blessing (as we've shown). When you consider Shem's offspring, they minister the word blessing (as we've shown). Thus, white horses that portray God's word blessing directly reflect God's word blessing that Shem's offspring are called to minister.

So, God's purpose for Shem's offspring to minister His word blessing is shown through His white horses. Thus, it's absolutely fascinating how God reveals unto us His divine will, purpose and plans for Shem's offspring through His magnificent creation of white horses.

In this light, we must always be careful of Satan's deceptions. Forever trying to be like God, he uses the same white horse symbolism to deceive people—i.e., his white horse symbolism is an imitation of God's white horse. He wants to be like God. He's a master imitator of God and Christ. (Isa 14:14). He comes as an angel of light. (2 Cor 11:14). He's a liar and the father of all lies. (John 8:44).

God's white horse symbolism refers to true prophecy (Rev 19:11-16) while Satan's white horse refers to false prophecy. God called the Jews to teach true prophecy. But, Satan strives to disrupt God's plans for the Jews.

Satan (God's enemy) seeks to destroy true prophecy through lies, deceptions and delusions. The white horse of the apocalypse confirms this truth. His goal is to render God's purpose for His Jewish people unfruitful. Consider the following Scriptures that refer to Satan's counterfeit white horse of the apocalypse.

As it is written, "The Lamb (Jesus Christ) opened the 1st seal and I (John) heard thunder. One of the 4 creatures (angelic beings) told me to come and see. I saw a white horse. His rider had a bow and received a crown. He went forth conquering and to conquer (i.e., he went forth to conquer true prophecy)." (Rev 6:1-2).

Notice that the rider has a bow with no arrows. So, his power is limited. Thus, he doesn't personify God. For, God (Christ) is all powerful. (Matt 28:18). Not only that, but Christ is the Lord God omnipotent who reigns. (Rev 19:6).

By these Scriptures, God shows us that Satan (who is limited in power: 1 John 4:4) is the rider on the white horse of the apocalypse. As noted, he's the father of all lies. (John 8:44). So, Satan is the one who went forth to conquer true prophecy.

His crown shows that he's a counterfeit king riding upon a counterfeit white horse who personifies Satan. Jews must avoid Satan's counterfeit prophecies at all costs. Jews who choose to follow Satan and partake of his counterfeit imitation of Christ will be the ultimate losers in the war between good and evil.

So, we've found that God's white horse symbolism in Zech 6:1-6 and in Rev 19:11-16 personifies God's word blessing that's associated with Jewish people. Hence, if your father's ancestry traces back to Shem, you now know your true identity and your racial group's purpose. Your purpose for being here on earth is to be the embodiment of God's words of wisdom.

Thank God for creating such beautiful white horses in the earth. They are indeed symbolic of God's holy word. Jews don't have an identity crisis. They only need to identify their father's ancestry and get on with their racial group's calling.

Shem's descendants are called (1) to teach the four components of God's birthright blessing to the world, and (2) to oversee (in love) the execution of God's judgments against unruly saints by chastising them (through God's word) about what is lawful and what is not.

CHAPTER 8

70 weeks are Determined For Jewish People—Session 1

70 weeks (God's plan of grace and mercy)—Part I

> I decked thee with leaves of green that'll never wither. (Ps 1-3).
> I decked thee with heaps of gold that'll ever glitter. (Eze 16:13).
>
> I planted thee by a river of living water as a tree. (Ps 1-3). This shows, truly shows how much I love thee.
>
> He holds me in His arms. (Deut 33:27). God and I are in a dream relationship. None shall pluck me from His palms. (Jn 10:28). So, God alone I will worship.

We talked about a dream (well-functioning) relationship between Jesus and the Jews. But, far too many Jews don't believe that Christ has come and gone and will return. Because of their rebellion and God's undying love for them, He gave them 70 weeks to partake of a tremendous plan of love, grace and mercy. At the end of 70 weeks, God will give them new hearts that'll make them love and obey Him. We'll study His 70 week plan in 2 sessions. This first session has 2 parts.

For years far too many Jewish people have not been stepping up to the plate and doing what God called them to do. For years, too many of Shem's descendants have been in a state of rebellion and rejecting their Messiah. Simply put, many Jews identify themselves as Jews, but prefer to remain secular or worldly.

God must be wondering what happened to the love affair between Him and the Jews. For years God has been chastising them for rebellion. But, God still loves them dearly. He still stretches out His hand to them. That's why one of the greatest love stories is that God wants to hold them in His everlasting arms (Deut 33:27) and show them that no one can pluck them from His palm. (John 10:28).

That said, there's good news on the horizon for Shem's offspring. God set in motion a tremendous plan of love, grace and mercy that'll make Jews desire and obey His every word. For God is good and His mercy endures forever! (Ps 118:1).

Jewish people must tell all nations that God has given them 70 weeks to accept His tremendous plan of love, grace and mercy whereby those who're alive (in their natural flesh bodies) when Christ returns will receive new hearts and new spirits that'll cause them to obey, walk upright before Him and diligently follow Him.

As it is written, "A new heart also will I give unto you (i.e., unto the Jewish people), and a new spirit will I put within you: and I will take away the stony heart out of your flesh, and I will give you a heart of flesh (i.e., a loving and obedient heart unto the Lord). (Eze 36:26-28, 11:19-20).

A new heart means that God will give them a supernatural desire in their hearts to serve and obey Him and only Him. A new spirit means that God will give them (in their inner beings) the supernatural power they need to refrain from sin. God will bless them with new hearts and new spirits at the end of the tribulation period.

Shem's family line must tell all people that God showed His plan of infinite love, grace and mercy through Daniel's prayer when Israel was steeped in sin. Daniel, a devout Jew, studied the books of Jeremiah. At that time, he was deeply concerned about the Jews being chastised by God. God had banished them from the Promised Land for rebellion. Because of their disobedience, they had to serve Babylon in captivity for 70 years. (Dan 9:1-7, Jer 25:7-11, 29:10-14).

Now, Daniel knew that the Lord was the God of all mercies, comfort and forgiveness. (Dan 9:9-10, 2 Cor 1:3, Ps 103:1-4). He knew the weakness of his racial group and their propensity to fall away and sin against God. (Dan 9:10-14). Even after his people served 70 years in captivity, Daniel was concerned that Jews could wind up in that situation again because of their propensity to sin. So, he prayed to God for forgiveness, love, grace and mercy. (Dan 9:16-19).

Daniel wanted God to plant them by a river of living water as a tree. (Ps 1-3). Daniel wanted God to show His love for them. So, as he was praying, God sent His angel Gabriel to reveal His plan of love, grace and mercy to Daniel. Gabriel said, "70 weeks are fixed for thy people and the holy city, to finish transgressions, make an end of sins, make reconciliation for iniquity, bring in everlasting righteousness, seal up the vision and prophecy, and to anoint the most Holy. (Dan 9:24). The following paragraphs explain God's divine goals for Israel.

(1) Sins, transgressions and iniquities refer to increasing levels of sin. (Exod 34:4-7). Making an end of sins refers to stopping Jewish people from committing offenses against God (i.e., single events or venial sins: like unto misdemeanors). A sin is anything that comes short of the glory of God. (Rom 8:23). Sins are violations of divine commands or violations of whatever is contrary to God's word. Venial sins (like misdemeanors) are the first level of sins. Jewish believers will no longer commit such sins when they receive their new hearts and new spirits.

(2) Finishing transgressions refers to putting an end to all rebellion against God. Rebellion refers to a progression of falling short of God's glory wherein people know that they're disobeying God's laws, but they rebel anyway. This is open rebellion (revolting against God by choice). Repeated sin (deliberate defiance) becomes transgression. This is the second level of sin. Jewish believers will no longer commit such transgressions when they receive new hearts and new spirits.

(3) Iniquities (in the progression of sin) refer to the highest level of sins (i.e., the worst kinds of offenses before God). In the progression of disobedience, iniquities go well beyond transgressions. That is, iniquities are the sins committed by downright reprobates who're deliberately unrepentant. These are sinners who're completely out of control. These types of sins (if continued long enough) will go beyond transgressions and become iniquities (the worst kinds of sins). Jews will no longer commit such sins when they receive their new hearts and new spirits.

So, making reconciliation for iniquity refers to Christ not only dying on the cross for man's venial sins and transgressions of outright rebellion, but it also refers to Christ dying on the cross for man's highest levels of sin (i.e., He died for our iniquities: Isa 53:6). Christ's once and for all atonement (Heb 2:17, 9:26, Eph 2:16) was so complete that it reconciled unto God even the highest levels of sin.

What I'm saying is that Christ's one time sacrifice made reconciliation for man's sins from the lowest levels to the highest levels of sin (however, Christ's sacrifice doesn't cover the unpardonable sin which can never be forgiven). It's the sin of totally rejecting Christ and God's Holy Spirit. (Matt 12:31-32, Mk 3:28-29).

(4) Bringing in everlasting righteousness means that Christ will return to earth to defeat His foes and set up His everlasting kingdom of righteousness and peace for 1,000 years. (Isa 9:6-7, Jer 23:5-6, 1 Sam 2:10, Rev 20:6). Righteousness is defined as upright actions according to God's laws. It refers to being morally good with attributes of equity, justice, integrity and righteousness.

Shem's descendants must teach the world that Christ is our righteousness, which can only be obtained through Him (Phil 3:9, Rom 3:21-26, Jer 33:14-16, 2 Cor 5:21). Thus, God's plan of love, grace and mercy includes Christ's return to earth whereby believing Jews (as well as believing Gentiles) will dwell in Christ's everlasting kingdom of righteousness and peace. Jewish believers will no longer have to exist under an unrighteous world system.

(5) Sealing up prophecy refers to fulfilling the prophecy that Gabriel gave unto Daniel. (Dan 9:24). It refers to God's promised plan of love, grace and mercy wherein Jewish and Gentile believers will be given new hearts and new spirits that'll cause them to obey God. They'll have new spirits in the sense that God will fill their spirits with adequate power to walk upright before Him and no longer sin.

So, when Christ returns to defeat His enemies (1 Sam 2:10) and set up His 1,000 year reign on earth (Isa 9:6-7, Rev 20:6), visions and prophecies of these events will no longer be needed—i.e., these prophecies will have been fulfilled.

(6) Anointing the most Holy speaks of purifying and sanctifying the Holy of Holies of the millennial temple. When Christ returns in the millennium, He'll rebuild the temple and consecrated it for service. (Zech 6:12-15, Acts 15:16-18). Jewish believers will no longer have to be concerned with their temple being defiled or destroyed. The 6 spiritual goals just described will be accomplished at the end of God's 70 week plan of love, grace and mercy.

These truths show that when God showers His plan of love, grace and mercy upon Jews, they'll be decked with leaves of green that'll never wither (Ps 1-3) and decked with heaps of gold that'll ever glitter. (Eze 16:13).

They won't have to worry about freeing themselves from their propensity to sin. By His omnipotent power (Rev 19:6), God will do that for them. God will see to it that they'll have new hearts (i.e., a supernatural desire to obey) and new spirits (i.e., supernatural power that'll cause them to obey Him). (Eze 11:17-20, 36:18-28).

All Jews need to teach these divine truths. It is so crucial that they get on with their God given calling of teaching God's holy words of truth. For like unto God's cherubim, they are the very embodiment of God's divine truths.

In summary, when Christ returns, God will remove from the hearts of Jewish saints (who are alive in their natural bodies) their propensity to fall into sin. They will have new hearts in the sense that He'll cause them to be so spiritually sensitive that their every waking moment will be in pursuit of God's holiness and purity.

The opportunity to receive docile, dedicated hearts that'll make them obey, numbers among God's greatest love stories in the Bible with a very happy ending. Gentile believers who are alive (in their natural bodies) at Christ's second coming will also be blessed with God's tremendous plan of love, grace and mercy.

Jews must warn people that if they're alive when Christ returns, they'll only be under God's tremendous plan of love, grace and mercy if they've accepted Christ as their Messiah by the end of the 70 weeks (i.e., by the end of the tribulation).

70 weeks (God's plan of grace and mercy)—Part II

I know that love does not come easy when Jews are trying to love others as they love themselves. Loving God and loving others are two commandments upon which hang all the law and the prophets. (Matt 22:37-40). So, Jews must get involved in a dream (well-functioning) relationship with Christ to make it happen.

We'll now study the time period of the 70 weeks. Jews need to know when God's 70 week plan began so that they can be on top it as they tell others about it. God's 70 week plan began in 445 B.C., when the Persian king Artaxerexes issued a decree for a group of Jews to go back to Jerusalem and rebuild the city and its walls. (Neh 2:1-8). Jews were in Babylonian captivity at the time when Babylon was overthrown by the Medo-Persians.

The Scripture that reveals God's time frame is found in Daniel 9:25. "Know and understand that from the giving of the command to rebuild Jerusalem until it's rebuilt will be 7 weeks. There'll be threescore and two weeks (20 +20 +20 +2) until Jesus comes." (Dan 9:25). That is, there'll be 62 more weeks after Jerusalem is rebuilt until Jesus rides into Jerusalem on Palm Sunday. (Matt 21:6-11).

I will first give the proper meaning of 7 weeks. Each day of a week represents 7 years. Adding up 7 years for each day of the week would total 49 years (7 years + 7 years + 7 years + 7 years + 7 years + 7 years + 7 years = 49 years). So, Jerusalem was rebuilt 49 years after Artaxerexes issued his decree.

I'll now give the meaning of 62 weeks. 62 weeks total 434 years (7 years for each day of the week x 62 weeks = 434 years). So, 62 weeks or 434 years after the city was rebuilt, Christ rode into Jerusalem on Palm Sunday. (Matt 21:6-9).

So, the 7 weeks + the 62 weeks totals 69 weeks. But, what do we know about the 70th week? Christ will rapture His church before the 70th week begins. (1 Thess 4:16-17). But, no one knows when Christ will rapture His Church.

This gives us a time gap between the end of the 69th week and the beginning of the 70th week (i.e., no one knows when the 70th week will begin). But, there's one thing we know. Immediately after the rapture, the 70th week will begin. The 70th week is the tribulation period (the last 7 years before Christ returns).

Now, when we consider God's whole 70 week plan of love, grace and mercy, it comes to a total of 490 years (7 years for each day of the week x 70 weeks = 490 years). So, God's plan for the Jews will cover 490 years beginning in 445 B.C. and end at the end of the tribulation period.

The tribulation period is the time when the antichrist (the man of sin: 2 Thess 2:3-4) will appear on the scene. He'll make a 7 year peace treaty with Israel and break it after 3½ years. (Dan 9:26). He'll be in power for 42 months—i.e., he'll be in power during the last 3½ years of the tribulation period (called the great tribulation). He'll severely persecute the Jews. (Rev 11:2).

It is written, "The antichrist shall speak great words against God and shall wear out the saints . . . and think to change times and laws. The Jews shall be given into his hands until a time and times and the dividing of times (i.e., he'll rule for 1,260 days or the last 3 ½ years of the tribulation)." (Dan 7:25, 12:7).

Thirty days a month x 12 months equals 360 days. So, the 1,260 days is counted as follows: 360 days (one year) + 360 days (a 2nd year) + 360 days (a 3rd year) + 180 days (½ year) = 1260 days. Thus, at the end of the antichrist's reign of 1,260 days (the last 3½ years of the tribulation period), Christ will return to earth to wipe all of His enemies off of the face of the earth. (1 Sam 2:10, Matt 24:29-30).

Jews who are not involved in God's 70 week plan of love, grace and mercy and are alive when He returns will be cast into the winepress of God's wrath. The slain of the Lord will be many. (Rev 14:18-20, 19:15, Isa 66:16). The unsaved offspring of Gentiles will meet this same fate. So Jews and Gentiles must get involved with Christ in a passionate love story before the end of the tribulation period.

So, at the end of the tribulation, saved Jews (who are alive when Christ returns) will enter the millennium to dwell with Christ (this also includes saved Gentiles). (Matt 25:31-33, 46). Now, this is a true love story with a very happy ending.

CHAPTER 9

70 weeks are Determined For Jewish People—Session 2

Christ's and God's spiritual marriage unions—Part I

> Jews must know their purpose on earth. Nothing compares to its valuable worth. God has a plan of love, grace and mercy with a happy ending. So, He offered men a marriage proposal from the beginning.

> He wants us to be His bride before we pass away. Yes, I accept is right thing to say. Between husband and wife, their marriage shows a dream relationship. Between God, Adam and Eve, their bond showed a dream fellowship.

This is the second session of God's 70 week plan. We'll study it in 10 parts. We'll focus on Christ's and God's spiritual marriage unions. First, we'll study Christ's marriage with the church (Jews and Gentiles of the New Testament). (Eph 5:22-23, Rom 7:4, 2Cor 11:2). Jews need to know God's purpose for them. They need to know about Crist's marriage proposal so that they can tell the world about it. This is why Jews need to study both the marriage covenant between Christ and His church and the marriage covenant between God and the Jews.

These covenants point to a passionate love story between God and His saints with a very happy ending (Gentiles also need to study these covenants). God's purpose is to enjoy with us an eternal covenant of marriage, filled with peace, joy and heavenly bliss. (Hos 2:19-20). He'll offer us a marriage proposal which we must accept. Those who accept it will dwell with Him in Paradise. Those who reject it will dwell in hell. Shem's offspring must teach these truths to all nations.

God created Adam and Eve in His image to show us the concept of marriage. It's a dream relationship between a husband and a wife. We must agree to become Christ's wife before the 70th week begins. God created Adam and Eve as one single unit. Before He formed Eve out of Adam's side, she dwelled in Adam. (Gen 1:26-28, 2:21-23). They were one body.

Their oneness portrays the inseparable bond between Christ and His saints. He desires to have a dream relationship with them—i.e., He wants a close, intimate relationship with them. So, He wants His church to walk with Him in oneness of spirit, mind and purpose. He's a very jealous God over His people. (Exod 20:5).

Christ's and God's marriage unions—Part II

Christ's spiritual marriage to His bride (the church) and God's spiritual marriage to His bride (Israel: the Jewish nation) are like unto Israel's marriage custom of old. That is, a contract (marriage proposal) was made between the bride and groom. The bride was then betrothed to the groom. The groom gave her a dowry and went away to his father's house to prepare a home for them.

The groom came back to take his bride to the wedding at his father's home. That night they consummated the marriage in the bridal chamber. The wedding supper was held at the groom's father's house. The guests were already gathered at the home of the groom's father awaiting the arrival of the bride and groom.

God uses the Jewish marriage custom to show us great spiritual truths about His marriage union. Shem's offspring must tell all people about Christ's marriage proposal for them in the church age. Those who accept it before the rapture are betrothed to Christ. He'll give them a dowry (financial and spiritual blessings) and go away to prepare their home in heaven (at His Father's home). (John 14:1-3).

Shem's family line must tell the world that Christ will return to rapture His church (1 Thess 4:16-17). That is, He'll return to take His bride to His Father's house in heaven for the wedding ceremony and wedding supper. (Rev 19:7-9). But, there will be 144,000 Jewish believers who will not be raptured. They'll be left on earth to witness to the sinners left behind. (Rev 7:4-8, Matt 16:28).

Christ's and God's marriage unions—Part III

God's 70 week plan is amazing. Jews must tell the world that during the tribulation, Christ and His bride will have their wedding and supper at His Father's home in heaven like the Jewish custom. (John 14:1-3). After the rapture (parallel to Jewish custom) on the night of arrival at His Father's home in heaven, Christ and His bride will consummate their marriage by entering into a spiritual union.

Christ's bride (the Church) will then officially become His wife. For eternity He'll be in the midst of a deep, passionate love story with His wife that'll have a very happy ending. They'll be together forever. His wife will be holy, righteous and sinless. She'll never bring shame to Christ's name by committing adultery against Him. This is good news. Jews must share it with all people. These truths about the wedding ceremony and supper are confirmed by the following verses.

"Let us be glad and rejoice and give honor to Christ: for the marriage of the Lamb (Christ) is come and His wife (the Church) hath made herself ready. And to her was granted that she should be arrayed in fine linen, clean and white: for the fine linen is the righteousness of saints." (Rev 19:7-8). ". . . Write blessed are they which are called unto the marriage supper of the Lamb . . ." (Rev 19:9).

What guests are called (invited) to the marriage supper of the Lamb? This is important. So, the Jews must certainly let the world know who will be the guests. Based on Jewish custom, the guests for Christ's and His bride's wedding supper will already be gathered in heaven at the home of the groom's father. They'll be waiting for the arrival of the bride and groom (Christ and His church).

Christ's and God's marriage unions—Part IV

As noted, these benefits are for those who accept their proposals before Christ raptures His church. Not all saints since the beginning of the world belong to the church such as Old Testament saints. So, they'll be guests waiting for Christ and His bride (the church) to arrive in heaven for the marriage supper.

But, when did Old Testament saints arrive in heaven? When Christ rose from the dead, He led to heaven the spirits of saints who existed before His resurrection. (Eph 4:8-10). The church age began after Christ's resurrection. Saints who are not part of the church age will be in heaven waiting for Christ and His bride to arrive at His Father's home in heaven for the marriage ceremony and supper. (Rev 19:9).

Saints who die in the tribulation (including saints who'll be martyred) and Old Testament saints who were resurrected after Christ's resurrection (Matt 27:50-53) will also be guests at the marriage supper. Angels (eager to learn more about God's plans) will also be there as spectators (not as guests). (1 Pet 1:12).

The spirits of all saints who existed before Christ's resurrection that He led to heaven (Eph 4:8-10), will receive resurrected bodies (like Christ's body) near the end of the tribulation. (Phil 3:21, Dan 12:1-2, 13). They'll enjoy the delicious foods, delicacies and fruit juices that'll be served at Christ's supper in heaven.

Accepting Christ's marriage proposal before the 70th week is the only way under the sun to be Christ bride and avoid hell. If you manage to live until the **latter rain** pours out in the tribulation, you may have a chance to get into heaven.

Christ's spiritual marriage proposal is a critical issue of life wherein we must choose eternal life or eternal death during the 70 weeks. (Deut 30:19). Becoming Christ's wife not only affects the Jews, but it affects the whole world. This is yet another reason why Jews must teach God's birthright blessing to all nations.

Even though Jewish and Gentile believers are all going to be God's wife in Paradise (they'll dwell as one happy family), it's important that we discuss both marriage unions for a better understanding of God's undying love for His people.

Christ's and God's marriage unions—Part V

> By hearing comes faith. By fearing I'm safe. Through faith I believe. Through grace I receive.
>
> I show my faith by my deeds, so that He will supply my needs. My faith has been increased. More truth has been released. My faith is true. That's what I do.

The above poem shows that faith is very important in order for the Jews to have a dream (well-defined) relationship with Jesus. Having discussed Christ's marriage to the church, let us now discuss God's marriage to Israel.

I can't stress enough the importance of accepting your proposal during the 70 weeks. God had married Israel at Mount Sinai. Through the Mosaic Covenant, God betrothed Israel to Himself. (Jer2:2, Eze 16:8). After 400 years of bondage in Egypt, He brought them out of Egypt and gave them a marriage proposal. They accepted it by faith and made their marriage vows to God. (Exod 19:5-8, 20:1-3).

God promised His infinite love to Jewish people by telling them that they'll be a peculiar treasure unto Him. (Exod 19:5). God's words must accomplish what He says. (Isa 55:11). So, long before the church age even began, God and Israel had already tied the knot. In other words, long before Christ died to give us a new and better covenant, God and Israel were already (by faith) husband and wife.

So, from the foundation of the world, God intended for Shem's family line (and the world) to be His wife by having faith in Him. And that faith He'll increase so that more truth is released. God set aside 70 weeks for Jews to become His bride. God really loves the Jews. He's a jealous God over them. (Exod 20:5, Deut 6:15).

Based on all the spiritual truths cited above, Shem's family line has no excuse for not having the faith to share this good news with all nations. God created them for this purpose which they must fulfill on earth before they die. The sinners of the world are depending on Shem's family line to teach them God's divine truths.

When God married the Jewish people, He faithfully watched over them. (Isa 62:6). He led them by the way as they journeyed through the wilderness to the land of promise. He faithfully fed them manna from heaven as they traveled. (Exod 13:21-22, 16:14-18). As you can see, God moves by faith. (Heb 11:6).

But, for centuries Jews have been unfaithful. They broke their vows and broke God's heart. (Jer 3:6-7, 20, Eze 16:32-39, Hos 4:12, 7:4, 9:1). They were unfaithful wives. But, God continued to show His faith in them through His undying love. But, when God's patience ran out, He had no choice but to divorce them, but not permanently. For, He was too deeply in love with them.

It is written, "For a small moment I forsook thee (divorced thee); but with great mercies I'll gather thee (i.e., remarry thee). In a little wrath I hid my face for a moment, but with kindness I'll have mercy on thee (He'll restore their marriage)." (Isa 54:7-8, Jer 3:12). "Plead with your mother (Israel), plead: for she's not my wife and I'm not her husband (i.e., we're temporally divorced)." (Hos 2:2, Jer 3:8).

> Through faith they didn't believe.
> Through grace they didn't receive.
> They didn't show their faith by deeds.
> So, God didn't supply their needs.
> O to know the love He has for them.
> O to know He wants them near Him

Christ's and God's marriage unions—Part VI

But, because of their sins, God did divorce them for a while. However, He's not finished with them. He's too much in love with them and too faithful to them. God loves the Jews too much to give up on them. So, He's not finished with them. Even though they chased after idols (i.e., they broke their marriage vows), God gave them a new covenant (i.e., a new marriage union through Christ).

And, because of His new covenant, He's going to remarry His chosen people and make their marriage succeed forevermore. In time, He's going to reconcile (restore) their marriage permanently. So, God is not finished with the Jews.

God told them He'll make a new covenant with them. Not as the first covenant at Mount Sinai. They broke it. But, He's going to put His law in their hearts. (Jer 31:31-33). They'll be called Hephzibah (God's delight). Their land will be called Beulah (the married land). He's going to marry their land to Himself and protect it. (Isa 62:4). Then His people will never again be exiled from their homeland.

Shem's offspring will be married to their homeland. So, they'll cherish it and protect it. (Isa 62:5). So, the Jews and their land will be inseparable for eternity. Now, that's good news that the Jews must proclaim to all Jews and to the world.

So, God will delight in and rejoice over Jerusalem as a groom rejoices over his bride. (Isa 62:5). Words cannot describe God's love for Shem's family line. Thus, God will again betroth Israel to Himself and remarry her. When Christ returns to earth, God will have a wedding feast (banquet) for all Jewish people who have not yet been honored with their own wedding feast such as the Old Testament saints, tribulation saints, and saints resurrected after Christ's resurrection. (Matt 27:50-53).

Christ's and God's marriage unions—Part VII

You must have faith during the 70 weeks. You must walk by faith; not by sight. (Rom 1:17, 2 Cor 5:7). Without faith it's impossible to please God. (Heb 11:6). Many Jews are in doubt about Jesus and will receive nothing. (James 1:8). Faith and doubt cannot coexist. So, by their faith, God will restore their marriage union.

Although God promised to reconcile their marriage, far too many Jews are not living and walking by faith. Through fear and doubt, they're not teaching God's word. Some even devise their own philosophies (e.g., many believe that Christ has not come). Some flat out ignore God's 70 week plan of love, grace and mercy.

But, no matter what man says or does, he can't stop God's 70 week plan of love, grace and mercy from resting upon the Jews. He will restore their marriage union. He still reaches out to Jews and calls them to receive His unlimited love, grace and mercy. (Rom 10:21, Isa 65:2, Prov 1:24). They must receive it by faith.

God is passionately in love with Israel. As noted, God told the Jewish people that He was their maker and their husband. (Isa 54:5). When they were unfaithful, He said, "Turn, O backsliding children, for I am married to you. I will take you one of a city and two of a family and I will bring you to Zion (i.e., He told them that He was going to reconcile their marriage and restore them to their land). (Jer 3:14). But as noted, they must have faith.

The day will come when Israel will by faith repent. (Hos 3:5, 6:1). God will cleanse them (Zech 13:1) and faithfully betroth them to Himself forever through an everlasting marriage covenant. (Hos 2:19-29, Isa 55:3). Israel's marriage to God will indeed be restored and she'll be adorned like a bride. (Isa 61:10).

Christ's and God's marriage unions—Part VIII

As noted, God will have a wedding feast for Old Testament saints. It will be held here on earth. Jews must tell the world about it. Notice, Old Testament saints will be guests at the wedding feast in heaven for Christ and His church. But, as God's official wife, there'll have to be a wedding feast for Old Testament saints (including the Old Testament saints who were resurrected after Christ's resurrection). (Matt 27:50-53).

Also a wedding feast has to be held for (1) saints who died in the tribulation, and (2) saints who survive the tribulation (including the 144,000 Jewish believers from the church age). These saints will be God's wife. So, there has to be a feast. And that feast will take place here on earth.

How and when will these saints officially become God's wife? When Christ rose from the dead, He led to heaven the spirits of saints who existed before His resurrection (Old Testament saints). (Eph 4:8-10). The moment they entered heaven to be in union with God, their marriage/ceremony was consummated. This is when they officially became God's wife. So, by entering heaven, they entered into spiritual union with God which consummated their marriage and ceremony.

Likewise, Old Testament saints who were raised from the dead after Christ was raised entered heaven to be in union with God. (Matt 27:50-53). The moment they entered heaven to be in union with God, their marriage was consummated.

This is when they officially/ceremonially became God's wife. So, by entering heaven, they entered into spiritual union with God which consummated their marriage and marriage ceremony. This also holds true for saints who'll die in the tribulation. When they die, their spirits enter heaven. (2 Cor 5:8). As they enter heaven, they'll enter into spiritual union with God. This will consummate their marriage and marriage ceremony. At that moment, they'll be God's wife.

O the joy of accepting your marriage proposal in the Old Testament or in the church age. Jewish saints who survive the tribulation in their natural bodies will have proven themselves to be worthy to be God's wife (this includes Gentiles and 144,000 Jewish saints from the church age). They'll receive new hearts and new spirits. They'll enter the millennium. (Eze 36:26-28, 11:19-20, Matt 25:46). Their entrance into union with God will consummate their marriage. They'll officially become God's wife.

God will have to have a special wedding feast just for them on earth. The whole world will be invited as guests. "In this mountain (Jesus' dwelling place in the millennium) the Lord will make a feast for all people—i.e., a feast of fat things, of wines on the lees (well refined), and of fat things full of marrow." (Isa 25:6).

Before the millennium begins, all Old Testament saints and tribulation saints' bodies will be resurrected with new bodies like Christ's glorious body. (Phil 3:21). At their wedding feast on earth, they'll be able to enjoy the finest in dining.

That is, their wedding feast will be overflowing with fruits, vegetables, delightful delicacies, crystal clear water and the delicious fruit juices of the vine. God's scrumptious feast will be served in their honor as God's official wife. The guests will include God's church age saints. Since they will have already had their wedding feast in heaven, they'll be guests at God's wedding feast here on earth.

It's vital for Jews and Gentiles that these truths be told. As Christ's or God's wife, you have to know why it's so important for you to stand by your husband, for you are His help mate. So, you cannot afford to be estranged from your husband. For there is so much work to be done in getting lost souls out of Satan's hands so that they can get on the road to Zion (God's heavenly kingdom). This is all the more reason why Shem's family line must proclaim these truths to all nations.

Christ's and God's marriage unions—Part IX

Saints who survive the tribulation will enter the millennium in their natural bodies. (Matt 25:46). When Christ returns, He'll remove evil from earth. (1 Sam 2:10, Rev 19:19-21, Matt 25:33, 41). So, there'll be no unsaved people at the beginning of the millennium; only believers who can still have children.

Some of their offspring will get saved and some won't (this is also what'll happen during the 70 weeks). Those who get saved will receive new hearts and new spirits that'll consummate their marriage unions with God. They'll be God's official wife. They'll be covered by the promises of Dan 9:24 and Eze 36:22-26. In Eze 36:22 this promise covers the house of Israel which covers all believers no matter if they were born before the millennium or born in the millennium.

What about their wedding feast? I submit that the feast of Isa 25:6 will not be a onetime feast. It'll extend (I believe) to saints who're not even in their mothers' wombs. When these saints get saved and come home to the kingdom, there'll be plenty of food (already prepared) for them to eat for their wedding feast.

God will have prepared plenty of food. Throughout the millennium God will see to it that His saints will eat in plenty and be satisfied, for their floors will be full of wheat and their vats will overflow with wine and oil. The mountains will drop down with new wine and the hills will flow with milk. (Joel 2:24-26, 3:18).

Here's an example of how I believe this wedding feast will work. Suppose someone is not home (not yet born) when the family sits down for thanksgiving dinner. When they come home (get saved) their dinner will be waiting for them. They'll still enjoy their feast, but just a little later than their other family members. This is how I believe the wedding feast will work in the millennium for those who're not yet born.

But, there is a problem with being God's wife in the millennium in our natural bodies. It's natural that we have a tendency to sin. If we say we have no sin, we deceive ourselves. All have sinned and come short of God's glory. (1 Jn 1:8, Rom 3:23). But, God can't have His wife walking around with a natural tendency to sin.

God will solve this dilemma when Christ returns. Upon His return, saints who're still in their natural bodies will be blessed with new hearts and new spirits that'll cause them to be holy and obedient unto God. (Eze 36:25-28).

That is, through His omnipotent power, God will remove their propensity to sin. He'll make them so spiritually sensitive that their every waking moment will be in pursuit of His holiness. He'll cleanse their filthiness and create a desire in them to follow Christ and only Christ. They'll eschew evil and obey God's laws like never before. They'll be living epistles of godliness, holiness, sanctity and obedience.

So, even though they'll be in their natural bodies, God will use His omnipotent power to cause them to obey Him. He'll cause them to be faultless. They'll never bring shame to Him. By His power, God will fix it so that they'll be faithful wives. Shem's family line must proclaim these divine truths to all nations.

Christ's and God's marriage unions—Part X

After the rapture, God will severely judge (pour out His plagues upon) Jewish sinners who're left behind for the great tribulation. The tribulation will be their last chance to prove themselves worthy to be God's wife (i.e., the **latter rain** will be pouring out during the tribulation period). If they don't accept God's marriage proposal in the tribulation, they'll suffer eternal punishment in the eternal lake of fire and brimstone.

So, God is not finished with the Jews. Even though this is true, many unsaved Jews (as well as unsaved Gentiles) will suffer the greatest plagues known to man since the beginning of the world. God will pass unsaved Jewish people through the great tribulation (the last 3 ½ years of the 7 year tribulation period) so that they can become as refined as pure gold.

God's word says, "I'll cause Israel to pass under the rod and I'll bring her into the bond of the covenant (marriage covenant)." (Eze 20:37. 22:17-22). In other words, when the trumpet sounds to announce the end of the church age (1 Thess 4:16), it will also announce the beginning of Jacob's trouble.

What I'm saying is that the trumpet will announce the beginning of God's 7 year tribulation period wherein the last 3 ½ years of it will be the great tribulation judgments for apostate Jews and Gentiles. God will pass unsaved Jews through the tribulation so that they can finally prove themselves worthy to be His wife.

Yes, He did divorce them, but His heart still bleeds for the apple of His eye (the Jewish people). Jews and Gentiles who prove themselves worthy to be God's wife and are still alive (in their natural bodies) at the end of the great tribulation, will be given new hearts and new spirits that'll (1) cause them to be perfect wives and (2) keep them from ever breaking their wedding vows with God. They'll bask in God's love, joy and peace forevermore! So, it's a certainty that God is not finished with the Jews.

CHAPTER 10

Preparing For Christ's 1,000 Year Millennial Reign—Session 1

Preparing for Christ's millennial reign—Part I (Sinners' recompense)

> To be born a Jew is to teach the truths of God's word. To be born a Jew is to reach out to those who've not heard. Christ will clean up and dispose of Jews who have torn men. Christ will step up and impose upon Jews who have borne sin.
>
> A Jews' eternal calling is all in God plans: are you ready? A Jews' eternal living is all in God's His hands: are you ready? O line of Shem make haste. For time is too slim to waste. Are you ready?

I can't say it enough how important it is for Jews to teach the world the divine truths that we've been discussing. For, it's vitally important for the world to not only know God's divine truths, but to also know His next moves. Shem's family line must be ready. We'll study preparing for Christ's 1,000 year reign in 8 parts.

Since God's love for Jews is such an undying love, Jews (in turn) should show their love and concern for lost souls. For, to be born a Jew is to teach about the truth in God's word. Also to be born a Jew is to reach out to those who haven't heard. For the recompense of all sinners is definitely on the horizon (i.e., it's soon to come). For, Christ will step up and impose upon those who have borne sin.

That said, when Christ returns to earth (after the last 3½ years of the antichrist's reign), there will be a few matters that Christ will have to take care of before He can begin His 1,000 year reign on earth. That is, there will be a small period of time (i.e., a small transition period) between Christ's return to earth and the official beginning of His millennial reign.

So, Christ will return to earth after the last 1,260 days of the antichrist's rule. It will take 30 days for Christ to take care of some very important matters. Shem's family line must tell all nations that there will be a 30 day transition period for Christ to take care these important matters.

One of these matters is that during the 30 day transition period, Christ will wage the War of Armageddon against unsaved people (including the antichrist and His armies). This will be their recompense for coming against God's chosen people (the Jews). For the Jews' eternal living is in God's hands.

Likewise, the Jews' eternal calling is in God plans. So Jews must warn sinners about the Armageddon war and the 30 day transition period, cited in Daniel 12:11. It is written, "From the time the daily sacrifice is taken away and the abomination that makes desolate is set up, there'll be a thousand two hundred and ninety days (1,290 days)." Let's take a look at Dan 12:11 and examine this truth.

At the beginning of the 7 year tribulation, the antichrist will appear on the scene as a smooth, charming and charismatic world leader. He'll persuade the nations to believe that has the solutions to the world's problem. With his peaceful persona, he'll make a 7 year peace treaty with Israel. After 3½ years he'll break it and take away the daily sacrifice. (Dan 9:27). He'll take over the temple and set up a statue of Himself to be worshipped (this is the abomination that makes desolate).

This is when he'll begin his reign of terror on earth for the last 1,260 days of the tribulation. We also know that Christ will return after the antichrist's reign of terror during the last 1,260 days. Add 1,260 days (for the antichrist's reign) plus 30 extra days and we get a total of 1,290 days. This shows that there'll be a 30 day transition period (the antichrist's reign of 1,260 days + 30 extra days = 1,290 days).

An important matter that Christ will take care of during this 30 day transition period is that He'll wipe all evil beings off the face of the earth. (1 Sam 2:10). He'll clean up and dispose of those who have torn men—i.e., He'll step up and impose on those who have borne sin. Jews must let the world know what's going to happen during this 30 day period. He'll come with vengeance. By fire and the words of His mouth, He'll judge (punish) sinners. Many will be slain. (Isa 66:16).

Even before Christ returns, millions of sinners (and the antichrist's troops) will be slain by cosmic fireballs that'll collide with the earth causing explosions. (Matt 24:29). Fires setting communities, buildings and homes ablaze will break out all over. Engulfed in flames, sinners will scream in agonizing pain as they're burned to a crisp. Millions of unsaved sinners will be slain by these cosmic fireballs.

Preparing for Christ's millennial reign—Part II (Sinners' recompense)

Believers, however, will be protected from these plagues. (1 Thess 5:9). That said, during the 30 day transition period, Christ will wage the war of Armageddon against the antichrist and his armies. When this war ceases, the blood from any battle down through the ages will pale in comparison to the blood bath that'll result from Armageddon. The blood trail from its carnage will stretch 200 miles along the battlefield. (Rev 14:20).

The antichrist and the false profit will be cast alive into the lake of fire and the rest of the antichrist's armies will be slain. (Rev 19:19-21). Satan himself will be chained in the bottomless pit for 1,000 years. (Rev 20:1-3). Birds will be called to God's great supper to feast on the dead bodies of the wicked. (Rev 19:17-18).

During the 30 day transition period, the greatest earthquake known to man will occur. (Rev 16:18). Shem's descendants must warn people that Mountains and islands will fall into the oceans. (Rev 6:12-14, 19:20). Volcanos will kill sinners. Bone crushing hail stones (up to 100 pounds) will fall on them. (Rev 16:21). The magnitude of this earthquake and the plagues associated with it will cause the earth to be unrecognizable.

Jews are born to teach God's words of truth. They must tell the world that God will protect Jewish and Gentile saints from the earthquake and the plagues associated with it (i.e., their eternal living is in God's hands). For, when Christ returns, He'll stand on the Mt of Olives and it'll split toward the east and west and toward the north and south to create a valley of escape for Jewish and Gentile believers. (Zech 14:4-5).

Since Jews are born to teach the truths in God's word, they must warn all unbelievers who survive the carnage that Christ will judge them in the Valley of Jehosaphat (i.e., in the valley of decision). This is another matter that Christ will take care of during the 30 day transition period.

So, when Christ returns, His angels will gather saints and unbelievers to stand before Christ. Christ's sheep (saints) will be set on His right. Goats (unbelievers) will be set on His left. (Matt 25:31-33, Joel 3:2, 9-14).

It's not feasible for all the people to fit into the valley of decision. Most likely, the saints and sinners there will be a sampling of the population. Christ will judge sinners (goats) and give them an eternal death sentence for rejecting Christ and mistreating Jews. This will be their recompense. (Joel 3:2, Matt 25:46).

His sheep (Jewish and Gentile saints) will be welcomed into the millennium prepared for them before the world began. For they accepted Christ's marriage proposal, loved others as they loved themselves and treated the Jews properly. (Matt 25:34, 46). Jews can't afford to (1) not love others as they love themselves or (2) not treat Jews properly. For Christ will clean up and dispose of Jews who have torn men (i.e., Christ will step up and impose on Jews who have borne sin).

So, these are very important truths that Jews must teach to all nations. They are called to be the embodiment of God's words of wisdom. This is the purpose for which God created them to fulfill on earth. Thus, the words of wisdom that need to be said to the Jews are, "O line of Shem make haste! Time is too slim to waste. Against you, don't make Him turn His face.

Preparing for Christ's millennial reign—Part III (The time of purging)

As noted, when Christ returns to earth there will be a 30 day transition period during which He will defeat His foes. As a result, the earth will be left in ruins. So, there'll be an extra 45 day transition period for the time of purging.

That is, it'll take Christ an additional 45 day transition period to (1) clean up things, (2) rebuild things, (3) teach necessary rituals, and (4) restore the earth from its ruinous state. These matters must be handled before Christ can begin His 1,000 year reign on earth.

Daniel 12:12 mentions the extra 45 day transition period. "Blessed is he who waits and comes to the thousand three hundred and thirty-five days (1,335 days)." Shem's offspring must tell all nations that saints are blessed because the 45 day transition period is the restoration time that Christ will use to prepare for and usher in His millennial kingdom.

Let's study the 1,335 days. We know that the antichrist's reign of terror will be for 1,260 days. At the end of the antichrist's 1,260 day reign, Christ will return to conduct a 30 day transition period to defeat His foes. After that, it'll take 45 more days for Christ to restore all things before He ushers in His millennial kingdom. If we add an additional 45 day transition period for the time of purging, we get 1,335 days (1,260 days + 30 days + 45 days for cleaning up totals 1,335 days). This explains the thousand three hundred and thirty-five days (or 1,335 days).

So, as noted, the Jews must let all nations know that believers are blessed. For, believers of all ages (since the foundation of the earth) will not only be Christ's wife, but they'll dwell in peace with Him on earth in the millennium. (Rev 20:4-6).

Today, the earth's population is around 6 ½ to 7 billion people. Saints from all ages are upwards of 70 to 80 billion people (maybe more). Wow! That's a lot of people for the earth to handle. Will there be enough room on earth for them? Yes, Christ will use the 45 day transition period to make enough room for His saints of all ages to dwell on earth with Him in the millennium. How will He do this?

To begin with, mountains, valleys, deserts and waste places are not conducive to human habitation. Mountains are too high and rocky. Valleys are too low and unstable for houses. Deserts are too hot and dry or too cold for reasonable human habitation. Likewise, waste places around the world are much too uninhabitable.

Jewish people must tell all nations that during Christ's 1,000 year reign on earth, the earth's curse of Gen 3:17 will be significantly lifted. For during the 45 day transition period, Christ will undergo a lot of renovations to the earth's surface to make enough room on earth to accommodate and sustain saints from all ages.

Mountains cover about 1/5 of the earth and are rather uninhabitable. Valleys and canyons are rather uninhabitable. Many rough and rugged surfaces on earth are so uninhabitable that they need to be leveled and made smooth enough for human habitation.

Christ will make more living space on earth by lowering the mountains to inhabitable levels, raising the valleys and canyons to inhabitable levels, and smoothing out the rough and rugged places for human habitation. This will make plenty of extra space for the saints of all ages. So, this is what Christ will do during the 45 day transition period.

It is written, "Valleys will be exalted (many will be raised up). Every mountain and hill (i.e., many mountains and hills) will be lowered. Crooked terrain shall be made straight (i.e., improved for human habitation) and the rugged places will be made a plain (i.e., smoothed out for farming and habitation)." (Isa 40:4). So, renovating the earth's surface in this manner will make enough room for Christ's saints from all ages to dwell on earth with Him in the millennium.

But, that's not all of the renovations that Christ will make during the 45 day transition period to make room for His saints of all ages. Let's go to the next chapter and examine some more of Christ's renovations.

CHAPTER 11

Preparing For Christ's 1,000 Year Millennial Reign—Session 2

Preparing for Christ's millennial reign—Part IV (The time of purging)

> Make room, plenty room for my saints of all ages. I've written their names in my book of pages. I have saints who've gone through some rough stages.

> I'll build a temple in time for my 1,000 year reign. I'll rule with a rod of iron in my holy name. They'll walk the line for all will be tame.

> I'll restore the deserts; they'll blossom like a rose. It'll be like the Garden of Eden where peace like a river flows. The lion and sheep shall lie in peace as the gentle wind blows.

Notice that hot and dry or cold deserts cover about 20% of the earth's surface. They're not that conducive to or suitable for human habitation. Hence, during the 45 day transition period, Christ will restore the deserts and waste places like unto the Garden of Eden. (Eze 36:34-35, Isa 35:6-7). This will make plenty of room available for about 70 to 80 billion saints from all ages.

Shem's descendants must inform all nations that during the 45 day transition period, Christ will make the deserts spring forth with plenty of water and greenery. It is written, "I'll open rivers in high places and water fountains in the midst of the valleys. I'll make the dry land springs of water." (Isa 41:18).

"The wilderness and solitary places will be glad and the desert will rejoice and blossom as a rose (i.e., the desert will have greenery) . . . the glory of

Lebanon's trees will be given to it. The excellence of Carmel and Sharon will see God's glory (there'll be beautiful flowers and fertile plains in the desert) . . ." (Isa 35:1-2).

"The parched land shall become a pool and the thirsty land shall become springs of water (i.e., water will gush forth in the wilderness and streams of water will gush forth in the desert). There'll be grass with reeds and rushes (the desert will have an abundance of greenery)." (Isa 35:5-7).

So, Christ will make the deserts inhabitable for saints of all ages. There'll be enough room for them. He's also going provide enough food for all people. After Christ levels the mountains, raises the valleys and makes the rough places like unto habitable plains, there will be more than enough farming space for crops.

It is written, "Behold, the day will come said the Lord that the plowman will overtake the reaper (i.e., farm lands will be fertile and productive) and the grape treaders will overtake the sowers (i.e., there'll be so many grapes to reap that there'll barely be enough time to plant more) . . ." (Amos 9:13). "You'll eat in plenty and be satisfied and praise the name of the Lord your God . . ." (Joel 2:26).

In sharing God's 70 week plan for Jewish people (Gentiles included), one of the most important messages that Shem's offspring must broadcast to all nations is that at the end of the 70 week period, Christ will anoint the most Holy. (See Dan 9:24). This is the time that Jewish people have been waiting for down through the ages.

Anointing the most Holy speaks of purifying and sanctifying the Holy of Holies of the millennial temple. During the 45 day period, Christ will rebuild the temple and consecrate it. (Zech 6:12-15, Acts 15:16-18, Amos 9:11-15). When He returns and rebuilds the temple, saved Jews will no longer have to worry about their temple being defiled or destroyed again. Jesus will be ruling with a rod of iron from David's throne in Jerusalem. (Lk 1:30-33, Isa 9:7, Rev 2:27). This is the moment that Jews have been waiting for down through the ages. Praise the Lord!

In summary, God's purpose for Shem's family line is crucial to God's plans for salvation. They cannot afford to be silent when it comes to Christ's 45 day transition period. For during the 45 day transition period, Christ will restore the earth to a point wherein the millennium will be like heaven on earth. So, the calling of Shem's racial group is vital. For, the world needs to know these truths.

The 45 day transition period will be a time of refreshing and restoration of all things (including the lands and seas). (Acts 3:19-21). There'll be more than enough room on earth in the millennium for saints of all ages to dwell with Christ. Abundant waters, plenty of milk producing cows, many trees producing fruit and fruit juices will flow to the Jews (Gentiles will also have access to these blessings).

It is written, "And it shall come to pass in that day (i.e., in the millennium) that the mountains shall drop down new wine (fruit juices) and the hills shall flow with milk. All rivers of Judah shall flow with waters and a fountain shall come forth of the house of the Lord and it shall water the valley of Shittim. (Joel 3:16).

During Christ's 1,000 year reign, peace will flow like a river. (Isa 26:3, 48:18, 66:12). Even the vicious and ferocious animals will be at peace. The wolf will dwell in peace with the lamb, the leopard will lie down with the kid (baby goat), the lion will eat straw like an ox and a little child shall lead them. The Lord said, "They'll neither hurt nor destroy in my holy mountain." (Isa 11:6-7, 65:25).

So, God uses the millennium to give us a foretaste of the eternal state that saints will enjoy. The millennium will be like heaven on earth. The same as there'll be plenty of room and food in heaven (John 14:1-3, Rev 7:16), Christ will make sure that there'll be plenty of room and food in the millennium for His saints of all ages.

As it is written, "But they shall sit every man under his vine and under his fig tree; and none shall make them afraid: for the mouth of the Lord of hosts hath spoken it." (Micah 4:4).

Moreover, resurrected saints of all ages will have new bodies like Christ's body. (Phil 3:21). Just as Christ ate food when His body was resurrected (Lk 24:36-44), saints will also eat food when their bodies are resurrected. As they dwell in the millennium with Christ, they'll enjoy the finest in dining: lavish feasts and banquets, overflowing with fruits, vegetables, crystal clear water and the delicious juices of the vine. So, the millennium will indeed be like heaven on earth.

And Shem's family line must share these divine truths with all nations. Jews cannot afford to allow anything or anyone to stand in their way when it comes to fulfilling their God given purpose here on earth. They've been called to spread God's gospel. Jews are the nuts and bolts of God's salvation plans for mankind. For like unto the cherubim, they are the very embodiment of God's words of truth.

God loves them dearly and needs them to get busy doing what He called them to do! They must never give up. Of course, they'll face challenges, but in spite of that, they need to stand strong against the wiles of the devil. God has given them power to succeed and He's counting on them to help Him win soles for Christ.

Preparing for Christ's millennial reign—Part V (dwelling with Christ)

> In the millennium saints will dwell for 1,000 years. On His right side, He'll set him who truly adheres.
>
> On His left side, He'll set him who never reveres. And saints will neither taste of death nor tears.
>
> Sinners will not inherit God's kingdom; for their flesh is corrupted. But, saints will inherit God's kingdom; for their flesh is uncorrupted.

Saints, who survive the tribulation, will live in the millennium with Christ for 1,000 years in their natural bodies. When was the last time you heard of people living for 1,000 years in their natural bodies? In the days of old, Methuselah lived for 969 years. (Gen 5:27). No man has ever lived that long since Methuselah. Nevertheless, believers will live throughout Christ's 1,000 year reign on earth. That is, during Christ's 1,000 year reign on earth (the millennium); saints, who survive the tribulation, will never taste of death in a grave.

The unsaved will die and have funerals in the millennium; but not saints. God keeps saints alive in their natural bodies throughout Christ's 1,000 year reign on earth. God does this to foreshadow the fact that in heaven saints will never die; they'll live throughout all eternity for God gives them the gift of eternal life.

We know saints live eternally in heaven, but can they really live 1,000 years on earth in their natural bodies? That's a long, long time. If this is at all possible, how can we be absolutely certain that saints will never taste of death in a grave in the millennium? What Biblical proof did God provide?

First of all, Christ's 1,000 year reign begins after the tribulation and the first resurrection have been completed. There're no more resurrections for saints after the first one. The only other one will be the second one for sinners at the end of Christ's 1,000 year reign. (Rev 20:7-15). Secondly, in the millennium, saints' lives will be as the days of a tree. They'll long enjoy their work. (Isa 65:22).

Thirdly, as noted, there's only one resurrection for saints with several phases. It'll be completed in all of its phases by the end of the tribulation. (Rev 20:4-6). After it's completed, there'll be no more resurrections for saints. That is, saints won't be able to die because there won't be another resurrection for their bodies to rise up from their graves. God is certainly not going to leave His saints in a grave without a resurrection.

Think about it. If there are no more resurrections for saints, then there won't be any more deaths for saints. God revealed that the spirit that raised Christ body will raise saints' bodies. So, a saint cannot die unless there is a resurrection for his/her body. So, since there'll be no more resurrections for saints after the first one, there'll be no more deaths for saints. For if they die, there must be a resurrection for their bodies. But after the first resurrection there aren't any more for saints.

This is why it's impossible for saints to die after the first resurrection. So, we can be sure that saints will not taste of death in a grave in the millennium.

Fourthly, when Christ returns, He'll set His sheep (saints) on His right and lost sinners (goats) on His left. Saints will inherit the kingdom prepared for them, for He'll welcome them into **life eternal**. (Matt 25:34, 46). Since saints are already saved, **life eternal** doesn't mean that He's giving them the gift of eternal life—they already have that. **Life eternal** means that they're going to live throughout the millennium and on into eternity.

As such, they'll never experience death in a grave. Their only taste of death will be an instantaneous change of their natural bodies to heavenly bodies (as shown by 1 Cor 15:52-55).

For, at the end of the millennium, their natural bodies will be changed—in a moment—in preparation for heaven. It is written, "I (God) will cleanse their blood that I have not cleansed: for the Lord dwells in Zion." (Joel 3:21). So, God will change their tainted blood to pure blood so that they can dwell in heaven.

In this light, God revealed that our flesh and blood must put on incorruption (i.e., we must put on uncorrupted flesh and uncorrupted blood). And, this mortal (earthly body) must put on immortality—i.e., a heavenly body. (1 Cor 15:53).

What I'm saying is that whether you're in your natural body or in a heavenly body, you cannot live without blood flowing through your arteries. For the life of the flesh is in the blood (i.e., no blood, no life). (Lev 17:11).

I'm aware that there is a phrase in the bible that states that "flesh and blood cannot inherit the kingdom". (1 Cor 15:50). But this phrase must be interpreted properly. Don't get confused by it. For 1 Cor 15:50 reveals that corrupted flesh and corrupted (tainted) blood cannot inherit heaven. This is true. For, our natural flesh and blood was tainted by Adam's sin. For this reason, we need Christ's pure, untainted blood in order to enter heaven. (1 Cor 15-22, Rom 5:12, 15-19).

So, by shedding His pure, untainted blood on the altar, Christ made atonement for our souls, which made it possible for us to have pure, untainted blood flowing through our new bodies in heaven—no blood, no life. (Lev 17:11). Hence, there's no way that believers are going to dwell in heaven without new flesh on their bodies and pure, untainted blood flowing through their arteries.

Now, if Christ was raised with new flesh and blood, then new flesh and blood can indeed inherit the kingdom of heaven. But, it cannot be corrupted flesh and corrupted (tainted) blood. That said; let's take a look at Christ's resurrected body.

Preparing for Christ's millennial reign—Part VI (dwelling with Christ)

After His resurrection, Jesus stood on the shore watching (looking at) His disciples returning from an all-night fishing trip. He asked them if they had caught any fish. He heard them say, "No". He told them to cast their nets on the right side of their ships. Observing with His eyes the many fish that they caught, He told them to bring Him some fish. (John 21:1-12).

This reveals that Jesus' heavenly body has eyes to see and ears to hear. His ability to see reveals that He has eyeballs with tiny blood vessels that supply blood to His eyeballs. Now if Christ has blood in His resurrected body, then blood can indeed inherit the kingdom of heaven as long as it is untainted blood as Christ has.

After His resurrection, Christ appeared before His disciples and told them to touch His hands and feet (for spirits don't have flesh and bones as Christ had). (Lk 24:39). His flesh flat-out proves that flesh can indeed inherit God's kingdom if it is uncorrupted flesh as Christ has. For Christ is now sitting on the right side of God in heaven. (Heb 10:12). Since saints' new bodies will be fashioned like Christ's body, their new bodies will have new flesh. (Phil 3:21). So, corruptible flesh cannot inherit God's kingdom, but new flesh can certainly inherit the kingdom.

Think about it! How can you believe that flesh and blood cannot inherit God's kingdom when Christ stood before His disciples with new flesh on His body and new blood flowing through His arteries? Christ is living proof that new flesh and new blood can indeed inherit the kingdom of God, if it's a new body resurrected with new flesh and new blood made like unto Christ's glorious body. (Phil 3:21).

When God says, "I'll cleanse their blood that I haven't cleansed" (Joel 3:21), He's referring to changing their natural bodies to heavenly bodies that'll have new blood. So, at the end of the millennium in preparation for the eternal state, God will change their natural bodies to heavenly bodies with new flesh and new blood.

Shem's offspring must tell these truths to the world. As I speak, there's plenty of work to be done on God's battlefield. They're fearfully and wonderfully made to handle their calling. That calling is to spread the gospel of Christ to all nations. Jewish people are precious to God. He needs them to be His loyal soldiers in His army. There is nothing that He wouldn't do for them to bring them success.

He has stored up in heaven for us more treasures than we could ever hope for, dream of or imagine. (1 Cor 2:9). Shem's offspring need to share this good news with all nations. God's undying love for the Jewish people is everlasting. All He wants them to do is love Him, serve Him and roll up their sleeves to help Him get people saved by lifting up the name of the Messiah (Jesus Christ). (John 12:32).

Time is short. There's no time to waste. Christ is coming soon. So, we must first discover our personal callings. Then, we must operate our personal callings within the framework of our respective racial group's calling. Then, we can be confident that we are serving God completely.

But, Satan doesn't want Shem's family line (or any other racial group for that matter) to fulfill its purpose here on earth. That's why Satan has launched a three pronged attack against all racial groups to keep people in the dark about their respective purposes and callings on earth. With that said, let's take a closer look at Satan's battlefront offensive against the Jewish racial group.

Preparing for Christ's millennial reign—Part VII (beware of Satan)

Satan has launched a three pronged attack against all racial groups. So, you need to beware of him. Thank God you won't have to concern yourself with him in the millennium because God will chain him in the bottomless pit throughout the millennium (i.e., for 1,000 years). (Rev 20:1-3).

Satan is the culprit behind man's blindness. He deludes men into walking in darkness and dying before they find out their racial group's calling. So, he's launched a three pronged attack against all racial groups consisting of three battlefront offensives: his Shemitic, Japhetic and Hamitic battlefront offensives.

Preparing for Christ's millennial reign—Part VIII (beware of Satan)

Although Satan won't be around in the millennium, a man's will is still the only force that can stop him from fulfilling his purpose. (See Chap 1; Prelude to God's racial callings: The Anointing—Part VII). Satan strives to keep the Jewish nation and Arab nations from teaching God's word.

He knows that if they find out that Christ is the Messiah, no force in the universe can stop them from accomplishing God's work that they set their minds to do. (Gen 11:6).

Satan also strives to exterminate Shem's offspring from the earth. He comes to steal, kill and destroy. (John 10:10). He uses people as pawns of aggression against the Jews. Dring World War II, he used Adolf Hitler as one of his pawns to murder over 6,000,000 Jews (1.5 million of these innocent victims were children).

Hitler and his Nazi party devised a plan: "The Final Solution". It was a plan to systematically exterminate Shem's family line. Possessed by Satan, he slaughtered Shem's offspring for nearly five years. His genocide of Jews (i.e., the Holocaust) reached an all-time low in terms of human degradation and depravity.

Even as I speak, Satan is using some of the Arab nations to militate against Israel. Mind you, the Israelites and the Arabs are genetically related, for they are both from the loins of Abraham. Satan's Shemitic battlefront offensive is not only a vicious campaign to exterminate Shem's family line, but it's a strategic plot to take away their peace. Even as I speak, some hostile Arab nations and pockets of terrorists are either attacking or threatening to attack the Israelites' Promised Land.

Satan's Shemitic battlefront offensive is designed to keep the Jews and Arab nations from teaching the four components of God's birthright blessing—i.e., Satan wants to keep them in the dark about their identities and true racial group's calling. In no way does Satan want them to know that as Abraham's offspring, they are called to lead the world to the light. God warns Shem's family line, in particular (i.e., Israel and the Arab nations), that they are to accept Christ as their Messiah.

For when they do, no force in the universe can stop them from successfully fulfilling their purpose of being light bearers. That said, Satan and Israel's foes (including hostile Arabs) will be recompensed for their ungodly deeds. (Isa 60:12).

So, God created Shem's offspring to preach the gospel of peace so that all racial groups would be reconciled to God in peace. Even so, racial strife in our societies is still plaguing us today. This is why it's so important for Shem's descendants to spread the gospel of peace. When people of different racial groups hear, accept and follow their God given racial group's purpose, our racial strife would cease. That is, our racial problems would be solved—i.e., they would go away.

This concludes our study of the purpose for which God created the Jews to fulfill on earth. Let us now officially study the purpose for which God created Japheth (Noah's oldest son) and his descendants to fulfill here on earth.

CHAPTER 12

Japheth's Descendants Have A Special Purpose To Fulfill—Session 1

Japheth's racial calling: The Guardian—Part I

Guarding God's throne (like the cherubim) sounds like a simple task, but it's not. There's a lot involved with it. We'll show that God gave this calling to Japheth. We can't do justice to Japheth's calling unless we delve into the minute details of it. This we'll do for optimum understanding of Japheth's calling.

> Make ready; make ready for Japheth to guard His throne. To guard and support it, Japheth must stand like a stone.
>
> So, unsecure is Shem's land of temporary tents. But, God will give Shem a sturdy land of sound defense.
>
> God gave Shem's offspring the Promised Land. Japheth shall defend it by his own hand. Japheth shall minister eternal life to Shem's offspring. Japheth shall minister even though sinners will be scoffing.

God has a great love story with a very happy ending for Japheth's offspring. It was in His heart to create them to protect Shem's offspring. He wanted Japheth's offspring to love Him. The happy ending of this love story is that He would reward them with an eternal life of peace, happiness and joy in Paradise.

Recall that the cherubim were called to guard God's throne and all things that pertain to it. We'll show that Japheth was given this same calling. God patterned His cherubim's behavior after our expected behavior. (Eze 1:5). We study them to find out our racial groups' calling. As such, we'll find out that Japheth and his offspring were called to guard God's throne and everything pertaining thereto like the cherubim. We'll study Japheth's calling in 12 parts.

God gave each of Noah's sons a specific birthright component to minister in fulfilling his calling. As such, God not only called Japheth to guard His throne, but He also called him to minister the eternal life component of God's birthright blessing (like unto the cherubim).

That said, God's covenant of life and peace was given to Israel's priests. God gave them the laws of His covenant because they feared Him (i.e., they revered Him). They also feared His name (i.e., they respected His name)." (Mal 2:1-7).

These verses refer to Israel's calling to teach God's word to all nations. (Exod 25:16-22). As Israel teaches God's word, cherubim stand guard over God's throne and His chosen people. Cherubim guard God's throne, His throne room, His kingdom, His sacred Ark and His saints. (Eze 28:14, Gen 3:22-24). And, God called Japheth's offspring to perform these same duties like unto God's cherubim.

In guarding the way unto the tree of life (Gen 3:22-24), cherubim help God to keep the unworthy from entering unto the tree of life. For God's throne and kingdom are the very sources of eternal life and peace. But, cherubim give access to the tree of life to the worthy. So, they help God convert the unworthy to be worthy. In this way, they minister God's eternal life blessing. We'll show that Japheth's offspring are also called to minister this calling (like the cherubim).

As noted, God rides upon a throne-chariot that speaks of how He moves about the universe to oversee His creation. (Eze 1:25-26). Cherubs are humbled below His throne-chariot. This shows that they support and uphold all things that pertain to God's throne and kingdom. As guardians of God's throne, Japheth's offspring must also support and uphold all things that pertain to God's throne and kingdom.

Now, God needed a faithful group (like unto His cherubim) to guard His throne, His throne room, His sacred Ark, His kingdom, His saints and the entryway to the tree of life. Of His own free will He chose Japheth's racial group to guard His throne and everything that pertains to it (like the cherubim).

Noah prophesied this calling over Japheth and his family line. Let's take a look at this divine truth. It is written, "God will enlarge Japheth, and he (Japheth) shall dwell in the tents of Shem. And Canaan will be his servant." (Gen 9:27). "God will enlarge Japheth" means that He'll make room for the Gentiles in Paradise.

Some Jews in Abraham's good olive tree were in a state of apostasy. So, God grafted Gentiles from a wild olive tree into the good olive tree. (Rom 11:11-19). Gentiles would then partake of the same blessings that God gave unto Abraham and his seeds. (Gen 13:14-15, 17:7-9, Exod 3:8, Jer 11:5). For God so loved the world that He gave His only begotten Son, Jesus Christ, so that whosoever believes in Him shall not perish, but have everlasting life. (John 3:16).

Recall that my goal is to show that Japheth's family line is the group that God called to guard His throne and everything that pertains to it (like unto His cherubs). That said, once Japheth's offspring are grafted into God's good olive tree, they're to (1) guard the Jews' lives, (2) minister God's eternal life blessing, and (3) guard everything that pertains to God's throne (like the cherubs). Japheth's descendants are very dear to God for He entrusted them with an extremely important calling.

Let us now study and confirm how Japheth's offspring are called to (1) guard God's throne and (2) guard the Jews' lives. Shem's tents portray God's kingdom of eternal life. For Christ (the giver of life: John 17:2) came through Shem's lineage. (Gen 9:26). Because Christ (the life giver) came through Shem's lineage, Shem's tents represent the source from which eternal life flows. (John 4:22, Rom 1:16, Gen 9:26, 12:3). Japheth's offspring will be dwelling in Shem's tents.

Dwelling in Shem's tents means that Japheth's offspring are free to partake of the eternal life that flows forth from Shem's tents. Shem's tents refer to temporary dwellings (i.e., temporary places as you dwell in God's kingdom). In Shem's temporary tents, Jews are constantly being afflicted by their foes. Their tents are not secure enough to protect their lives and keep them safe. So, their lives are threatened by their enemies. But, God promised them that He would give them a secure and permanent dwelling place.

". . . I (God) will appoint a place for my people (Shem's family line) and will plant them, that they may dwell in a permanent place of their own and move no more; neither shall the children of wickedness afflict them anymore . . ." (2 Sam 7:10; see also Jer 30:16-19 and Deut 33:26-29).

Remember, Noah prophesied that Japheth shall dwell in the tents of Shem. (Gen 9:26). Spiritually, when Japheth's offspring choose to dwell in Shem's tents (i.e., get saved), they'll have to (1) guard Shem's temporary tents, (2) guard the Jews' lives, and (3) protect their own lives. For, they'll be dwelling side by side with the Jews until God provides a permanent place for the Jews. (2 Sam 7:10).

Recall that Shem's tents (that Japheth's offspring must guard) refer to God's kingdom of life. So, God needed a racial group to guard His throne and the lives of the Jews. As noted, of His own free will, He chose Japheth's offspring to guard His throne, His kingdom and the Jews. As you can see, Japheth and his offspring are very special to God.

That said, if Japheth's offspring choose to dwell in the tents of Shem (i.e., if they choose eternal life that flows forth from Shem's tents) they've chosen to jump into Israel's fray and will have to be soldiers of stone in God's army to protect Shem's temporary tents where Japheth's descendants now dwell.

That is, when Japheth and his descendants choose to get on the Jews' side and dwell in their temporary tents (i.e., choose to get saved), the Jews' enemies will become the enemies of Japheth's descendants. They'll be attacked. Their homes, cities, buildings and many innocent lives will be destroyed.

They'll have to put up a fight to guard the lives of the Jews as well as their own lives. They'll have to battle to protect Israel's temporary tents in which they now dwell. So, spiritually speaking, the phrase "Japheth shall dwell in the tents of Shem" means that Japheth's offspring are the ones that are called to guard God's kingdom and the Jews. As noted, they have to guard and protect the tents of Shem.

So, the believing descendants of Japheth will be hated by the world because of Christ. (Matt 24:9). But, greater is He who is in believers than he (Satan) who is in the world. (1 John 4:4).

The above truths confirm that Japheth and his offspring were called to guard the lives of the Jews, His throne, His kingdom and everything that pertains thereto, like the cherubim. Recall that Japheth's family line is also called to minister the eternal life component of God's birthright blessing. Let's confirm this truth.

Whoever guards God's throne is responsible for guarding the way unto the tree of life. Cherubim guard God's throne. So, they're responsible for guarding the tree of life. (Gen 3:22-24). They keep the unworthy out and allow the worthy to have access to the tree of life. As such, they help God to convert the unworthy to be worthy through Christ. In this sense, they minister God's eternal life blessing.

Since Japheth's offspring are the ones that God called to guard His throne, they're responsible for guarding the way unto the tree of life. As guardians of the tree of life, they must keep the unworthy out and allow the worthy to have access to the tree of life. In this way they minister God's eternal life blessing.

Japheth's offspring guard God's throne and the tree of life by not allowing any impurities to come near or touch the sacred things of God. Only saved people can preach, teach or handle God's words. That is, Japheth's offspring are to keep sin from tainting their ministries and homes. Only the worthy (saved) can partake of Holy Communion or baptism. Only the worthy are supposed to be ushers, elders, deacons, choir members, etc.

They are to do all that they can to protect the lives of the Jews (and all other people for that matter). They must support, uphold and follow everything that God says in the Bible. Likewise, they must try to convert the unworthy to become worthy through Christ. In this sense, they minister God's eternal life blessing.

Simply stated, God called Japheth's descendants to guard His throne and the Jews as they minister the eternal life component of God's birthright blessing. So, Japheth's descendants' work is cut out for them. But, God is faithful! He's their refuge and everlasting arms. (Deut 33:27).

Japheth's racial calling: The Guardian—Part II

God further confirms that He gave Japheth's family line the leadership role in guarding His throne, His kingdom, the Jews and the entryway unto the tree of life. Let's take a closer look at the leadership role that God gave Japheth's family line.

It is written, "I have set watchmen (Jews and Gentiles) on thy walls, O Jerusalem, they'll never hold their peace . . . ye that make mention of the Lord, keep not silence." (Isa 62:6). So, God called Jewish people as well as Gentiles to be watchmen upon Israel's walls. In Hebrew, the term "watchmen" is shamar (shaw-mar). It means to hedge about, guard, watch over and protect.

Herein, God confirms that He gave the Gentiles the calling of guarding His kingdom and the Jewish people. But the leadership role in guarding God's kingdom and His chosen people (the Jews) was given to Japheth's family line. Let us confirm this divine truth.

It is written, ". . . and he (Japheth) shall dwell in the tents of Shem and Canaan (who portrays Ham's descendants) shall be his servant." (Gen 9:27). That is, Ham's family line will support, backup and help Japheth's offspring as they take the leadership role in guarding God's throne and everything pertaining thereto.

Be aware of the word "servant" in Gen 9:27. Some Bible scholars would have you to believe that the word "servant" means that Ham's offspring are called to be lowly slaves unto men. This is not the correct interpretation of this verse. Servant in this verse means to be a servant like Christ wherein He helps, supports, and looks out for us. Servant is a very fitting description of the relationship of man to God. In Gen 9:27, servant is the description of those who're called of God.

So, Japheth's offspring were called to take the leadership role in guarding God's throne while Ham's offspring were called to back up and support Japheth's offspring. What I'm saying is that as Ham's son, Canaan portrays Ham's offspring. Ham's offspring are called to serve Japheth's offspring. (Gen 9:27). That is, Ham's offspring are called to support and help cover the flanks of Japheth's offspring as they take the leadership role in guarding the Jews.

So, in Gen 9:27, God confirms (irrefutably) that in calling the Gentiles to guard His kingdom and the Jews, God gave Japheth—**not Ham**—the leadership role. God called Ham's offspring to cover the flanks of Japheth's offspring while Japheth's offspring take the leadership role in guarding

God's throne and everything that pertains thereto. Likewise, Japheth's offspring are to take the leadership role in ministering God's eternal life blessing.

The bottom line is that Gentiles (wherein Japheth has the leadership role) are not only to watch over God's kingdom, His throne and the Jews, but they're also to fervently intercede for Jews as they minister God's eternal life blessing unto them (and to the world for that matter).

So, no matter what color you are or what you look like, if your father's bloodline (ancestry) traces back to Japheth, your true identity and racial groups' calling is to guard, protect, intercede for, support, and evangelize the Jewish people while dwelling in their temporary tents (symbolic of God's kingdom).

Japheth's offspring who do this (i.e., please God) will enter Paradise. The gates of hell shall not prevail against them. (Matt 16:18). Those who don't will enter the gates of hell to suffer eternal punishment in the lake of fire. (Matt 7:13-14).

Japheth's racial calling: The Guardian—Part III

God is the God of love and peace. (2 Cor 13:11). There is no greater love for Japheth's offspring than God's love for them. Because of His infinite love for and thoughts of them, He created them for a special purpose—i.e., He created them to take the leadership role in watching over and protecting His throne, His kingdom and His chosen people. This is their calling like unto the cherubim.

Before God created the earth, He knew exactly what He was doing when He created Japheth's offspring. He knew the purpose that He designed for them to fulfill. They're fearfully and wonderfully made (Ps 139:14) and fully equipped with everything they need to guard the lives of the Jewish people and to minister unto them the eternal life component of God's birthright blessing.

Relative to His birthright blessing, God wants saints to enjoy life while they're on earth. No matter what storms come across their paths: God wants them to give their cares to Him so that they can have joy in their hearts (Ps 55:22, 1 Pet 5:7, Phil 4:6-7). Christ also said, ". . . I am come that they might have life, and that they might have it more abundantly." (John 10:10). Saints will indeed enjoy eternal life in heaven, but God also wants them to enjoy their lives while they're here on earth.

For this purpose, Japheth's offspring were called to minister God's eternal life blessing to the Jews (as well as the world). Not only that, but they're called to help God's chosen people live better lives on earth.

Isaiah Chapters 60-61 show an abundance of blessings that God will bestow upon Jews in the millennium to help them enjoy their lives. These future blessings show Japheth's offspring what they're to do now to help Shem's descendants improve and enjoy their lives on earth. That is, as the guardians of Jewish lives, Japheth's offspring are to help the Jews partake of the oil of joy. (Isa 61:3).

Japheth's offspring are well prepared to help the Jews enjoy their lives on earth. Consider one of the great blessing that God will bestow upon the Jews in the millennium to help them enjoy their lives here on earth.

". . . thy gates shall be open continually. They shall not be shut day or night; that men may bring unto thee the forces (wealth and strength) of the Gentiles and that their kings may be brought to thee." (Isa 60:11).

The phrase "thy gates shall be open" speaks of the millennium when the Jews' foes will not come against them. Their days of mourning will be over. (Isa 60:20). They'll be restored to their Promised Land flowing with milk and honey. (Exod 3:8). The sun will no longer set and the moon will no longer withdraw.

That is, they'll no longer need these lights, for the Lord will be their everlasting light. (Isa 60:20, Rev 21:23). Oh happy days will come again to the Jews. These blessings ensure the Jews that they'll enjoy their lives in the millennium. Today, Japheth's offspring must help the Jews actualize these happy days as much as possible. The gates that are open in the millennium speak of an eternal life of peace in Paradise.

In the millennium, strangers (Gentiles) shall feed the flock of Shem's people. Strangers shall be their plowmen and vinedressers. (Isa 61:5). Shem's offspring shall be named the Priests of the Lord. They shall eat the riches of the Gentiles. For their shame, they'll receive a double blessing. Everlasting joy shall be theirs. These blessings will bring happiness to the lives of Shem's descendants. Japheth's offspring must help the Jews actualize these future blessings as much as possible.

Japheth's racial calling: The Guardian—Part IV

Let's consider more of the millennial blessings that Japheth's offspring are to help the Jews actualize in their lives today as much as possible. Japheth's offspring are to help the Jews partake of, benefit from and enjoy the four components of God's birthright blessing: the eternal life blessing, peace blessing, word blessing and the wealth blessing.

Let us first discuss how Japheth's offspring are to help the Jews partake of and enjoy God's eternal life blessing. God entrusted Japheth's offspring with the leadership role of ministering God's eternal life blessing to the Jews as well as the Gentiles. I can't stress this truth enough.

It's fascinating how God knew exactly what He wanted Japheth's offspring to do before He created them. Before they were born, He sanctified them as guardians. (Jer 1:5). So, even before the world began, God chose Japheth's family line to guard His throne, His kingdom and His chosen people (the Jews).

God made Japheth's offspring perfect for their calling and trusted them to fulfill it. By putting His trust in Japheth's offspring, it shows how much He loves them. God promised Jews that their days of sorrow will be ended. (Isa 60:20). The ending of sorrow is the beginning of enjoying eternal life. Japheth's offspring must help the Jews actualize as much as possible God's eternal life blessing. They are to (1) help keep violence away from Israel and (2) help keep her borders safe. Jews will enjoy these blessings in the millennium. (Isa 60:18, 62:8, 65:19-23).

So, in todays' times, Japheth's offspring (as much as possible) must help the Jews enjoy their eternal life blessing by protecting them from their foes.

Isaiah 58:11 reveals how God will guide Israel and make her become as a watered garden like a spring that never fails. Even today, as the ministers of God's eternal life blessing, Japheth's descendants are to help Israel improve her land and waterways. In this light, it's incumbent upon Japheth's descendants to help the Jews improve and enjoy their lives. Jews, in turn, must intercede for and speak life to everyone who comes into their sphere of influence. Jews are to speak life to their families, neighbors, relationships and interactions with mankind.

Jews are to touch the world in such a way that nations become desirous of eternal life. Japheth's offspring must help Jews bring this to fruition. By telling us that Jews will enjoy their lives in the millennium, God gives Japheth's offspring a close-up view of what they're to do today. They must protect the Jews' lives so that the Jews can enjoy their eternal life blessing that begins here on earth.

In the millennium, Japheth's offspring will help Jews build walls of protection. (Isa 60:10). Today, they're to build walls of protection by providing Israel with military armaments to protect her from her foes. As guardians upon Israel's walls (Isa 62:6), they're to stand by Israel's side with enough force to repel any foe that comes against her. These blessings help Jews enjoy God's eternal life blessing while they're on earth today. These truths confirm that Japheth's offspring are called to help Jews partake of, benefit from and enjoy God's eternal life blessing.

Japheth's racial calling: The Guardian—Part V

Yes, in spite of the trials and tribulations that come our way, God wants us to be happy and enjoy our lives in peace. That said, Japheth's offspring are called to help God's chosen people enjoy their lives in peace.

The word of God says, "Rejoice in the Lord always and again I say Rejoice." (Phil 4:4). "Peace I leave with you . . . not as the world gives . . . let not your hearts be troubled . . ." (John 14:27).

God wants our lives to be filled with joy and peace (this includes both Jews and Gentiles). He even anoints us with the oil of joy (gladness). (Heb 1:9). Japheth's offspring must have this mind set (i.e., they must have joy in their hearts) as they minister God's peace blessing unto Shem's family line.

In the previous section, we discussed how Japheth's descendants are to help the Jewish people partake of, benefit from and enjoy the **eternal life** component of God's birthright blessing. In this section we will discuss how Japheth's offspring are to help the Jewish people partake of, benefit from and enjoy the **peace** component of God's birthright blessing.

Isaiah Chap 60 shows how Israel will be blessed with peace in the millennium. But, to bring peace to the Jews in todays' times, Japheth's offspring must help the Jews actualize peace in their lives as much as possible. That is, Japheth's offspring are to help Israel partake of, benefit from and enjoy the peace component of God's birthright blessing. Let's examine some of the future, millennial blessings that pertain to peace. This will show Japheth's offspring what they're to do today.

". . . thy gates will always be open. They'll not be shut day or night; that men may bring the forces (wealth) of the Gentiles and their kings unto thee." (Isa 60:11). This prefigures New Jerusalem's gates in Paradise that'll always be open which refers to eternal peace. For there'll be no foes in Paradise. Only those who're written in the Lamb's book of life will be there. (Rev 21:25-27). Thus, the open gates in the millennium speak of an eternal life of peace in Paradise.

So, Israel will enjoy God's peace blessing in the millennium. In todays' times Japheth's offspring must help the Jews bring God's peace blessing to fruition (as much as possible). Isaiah 60:10 reveals that in the millennium, the Gentiles will build Israel's walls. The building of her walls is symbolic of dwelling in peace. The walls of ancient cities were built for the citizen's safety and peace. The walls (built like a fortress) kept out the city's enemies so that they could dwell in peace.

If God puts a wall of protection around Israel for peace (Isa 26:1-3), then, Japheth's offspring are to do the same to keep her in peace. Since Ham's offspring are to help Japheth's offspring (Gen 9:27), they play a pivotal role in ministering peace to Jews and Gentiles (we'll study this truth later).

In the millennium, Israel's officers and exactors (overseers) will be men of peace. (Isa 60:17). So, in the millennium Jews will be treated justly and not suffer persecution or anti-Semitism. As the ones who were given the leadership role as guardians over God's kingdom, Japheth's descendants (in todays' times) must help Israel bring these peace blessings to fruition (as much as possible).

So, through the eyes of the millennium, we can see that peace is the order of the day for the Jewish people. As the ones who were given the leadership role as guardians, Japheth's descendants are to help the Israelites maintain peace with the world. That is, they are to help the Israelites maintain peace in such a way that every nation that comes into

Israel's sphere of influence is touched by her peaceful endeavors. Not only that, but Japheth's descendants are to help the Israelites keep peace in their homes, relationships, work places and interactions with mankind.

God is counting on Japheth's offspring to guard His throne, His throne room, His sacred Ark, His kingdom and His chosen people. Guarding His throne, His throne room, His sacred Ark and His kingdom is vitally important to God for they are the very sources of life and peace.

Protecting God's throne and Ark speaks of protecting Israel to whom God gave His covenant of life and peace. This is so vital to God's purpose, that Japheth's offspring cannot afford to allow Satan (God's Archenemy) to distract them from what God called them to do which is to minister life and peace to the Israelites or any other racial group for that matter. Japheth's descendants must not allow Satan to derail their calling. But, he will if they allow him.

So, by confirming that Israel will dwell in peace, God gives Japheth's offspring a close-up view of what they're to do today. They're called to help Israel partake of, benefit from and enjoy the peace component of God's birthright blessing.

CHAPTER 13

Japheth's Descendants Have A Special Purpose To Fulfill—Session 2

Japheth's racial calling: The Guardian—Part VI

> Tis the Lord that makes thee rise and shine His holy light. Tis the Lord's glory on thee that is so very bright.
>
> His word blessing is for Shem to reveal. His word blessing is for us to be healed.
>
> Japheth must remove obstacles out of Shem's way. Shem has to teach the gospel without delay.
>
> Then kings can serve Shem's offspring loyally. Those who do, God will bless them royally.

In the previous 2 sections I discussed how Japheth's offspring are called to help the Jews partake of, benefit from and enjoy God's eternal life blessing and God's peace blessing. In this section, I'll discuss how Japheth's offspring are called to help the Jews partake of, benefit from and enjoy God's word blessing. If Japheth's descendants are not experiencing God's word blessing in their lives, they can't help Jews partake of, benefit from and enjoy God's word blessing.

God equipped Japheth's offspring with everything they need. So, they must roll up their sleeves and get busy with what God called them to do. Christ (endowed with all the power of the Godhead) is the anointed one who defeated Satan. (Acts 10:36-40). This same anointing is upon Japheth's offspring. (2 Cor 1:21, Ps 20:6).

Just as cherubim support and uphold everything that pertains to God's throne and kingdom, Japheth's offspring must also support and uphold everything that pertains to God's throne and kingdom. That said, Isaiah Chap 60 shows many millennium blessings that Israel will receive pertaining to the word blessing. Let's examine some of them to see what Japheth's offspring are to do in todays' times.

God said to Israel, "Arise, shine, the light is come and the Lord's glory is risen upon thee. Behold, darkness will cover the earth and gross darkness the people, but the Lord will arise on thee and His glory will be seen on thee." (Isa 60:1-2).

When Christ returns, God's glory will be seen on the Jews—i.e., they'll rise and shine and teach God's word like never before. The glory of God will be upon them. (Isa 60:1). This is a future blessing of the millennium. So, in today's times, Japheth's offspring must support and backup the Jews as they go forth to shine by ministering the word component of God's birthright blessing unto all nations.

Moreover, in todays' times, Japheth's offspring are to prepare the way for the Jews to spread God's word by removing stumbling blocks and obstacles out of their way. (Isa. 40:3, 57:14, 62:10). They are to remove all obstacles that would prevent the Jews from going forth to teach God's word to all nations.

This is what Japheth's descendants are to do today. But it won't be a cake walk because many Jewish people are as stubborn today as they were in the days of old. (Isa 59:6-20). Many Jewish people don't believe that the Messiah (Christ) has come and gone. Hence, Japheth's offspring are called to help evangelize Israel and help her partake of the word component of God's birthright blessing.

So, in todays' times, Japheth's descendants are to help the Jewish people get into a position of honor and recognition as God's source of light so that kings and their nations can serve Israel. (Isa 60:14). Gentiles who fail to serve Israel today will eventually perish. (Isa 60:12). But, God will bless those kings and nations who minister unto Israel. (Gen 12:3).

My point is that Japheth's offspring must take the leadership role in helping Israel to arise to be the light of God's word and shine in His glory. (Isa 60:1).

So, the millennial blessings about God's word show Japheth's descendants how they are to support, uphold and backup Israel today as she goes forth to teach God's holy words to the world. Thus, Japheth's descendants are called to help the Jews partake of, benefit from and enjoy the word component of God's birthright blessing.

Japheth's racial calling: The Guardian—Part VII

> Japheth will bring his wealth to Shem's offspring. For this blessing Shem unto God will cling.
>
> Japheth was born to guard. So, the Jews he'll defend. It'll be a bit hard. But, on him Jews will depend. Japheth was born for God to caress. He was born for God to possess.
>
> He's born for the blessings of God's eternal wife. He's born for the possessing of God's eternal life.

In the previous three (3) sections I discussed how Japheth's offspring are to help the Jews partake of, benefit from and enjoy the eternal life, peace and word blessings. Finally, in this section, I'll discuss how Japheth's offspring are called to help the Jews partake of, benefit from and enjoy God's wealth blessing.

There is one thing that can bring happiness into your life here on earth. That one thing is money if it's used properly. In the first place, you must realize that all of your wealth and money belong to God. (1 Cor 10:26, Col 1:16, Ps 24:1, 50:10).

Using God's wealth properly means that you can't serve God and money. (Matt 6:24). You must serve God with all of your wealth. (Prov 3:9). And do it to God's glory. (1 Cor 10:31). In this light, Japheth's descendants must use their wealth properly to support, uphold and backup the Jewish people as they go forth to teach the four components of God's birthright blessing to all nations.

Isaiah Chap 60 shows how Israel will be blessed with wealth. This shows what Japheth's offspring are to do today to bring this to fruition as much as possible. We'll see that (in supporting Israel as she goes forth) Japheth's offspring are to bless Israel with wealth. For, as God's spiritual firstborn son (Exod 4:22), Israel is to receive a double portion of God's wealth. (Deut 21:16-17).

Let us now study some of the millennial wealth blessings for Jews to see how Japheth's offspring are to support the Jews today. Consider the following verses.

"You'll see and flow together, they'll come to you (i.e., Israel will see her people coming home and Gentile nations coming to Jerusalem). Israel will be filled with the fear of God (i.e., reverence for God). For, the abundance of the sea and the forces (wealth) of the Gentiles shall flow to her." (Isa 60:5-9).

The abundance of the sea will convert to Israel. The sea has plant and fish life. The Mediterranean Sea has oil reserves off shore. Israel's land has oil reserves (untapped) that'll convert to Israel. (Isa 60:5). For God's word reveals that Asher (a tribe of Israel) will dip his foot in oil. (Deut 33:24).

In the millennium, God will also bless Israel with gold, silver, camels, and flocks. Lebanon's trees will flow to her. (Isa 60:6-9, 13). Israel will suck the milk of the Gentiles (i.e., like a mother, the Gentiles will give Israel her spiritual and physical provisions). (Isa 60:16).

In today's times, Japheth's offspring must help to facilitate the flow of these types of blessings to Israel as much as possible. Because of God's anointing that rests upon Japheth's offspring, they're well equipped to handle the task at hand. Based on the help and support given to the Jews by Japheth's descendants, the Jews can enjoy their lives here on earth as God desires. Another wealth blessing that'll flow to the Jews in the millennium is found in the following verse.

"The sons of strangers (i.e., the sons of the Gentiles) will build up thy walls (they'll use their wealth for this) and their kings will minister unto thee: for in my wrath I smote thee, but in my favor (grace) I have had mercy on thee." (Isa 60:10).

So, Japheth's offspring (in their leadership role of supporting Israel) will use their wealth to help the Jews build new infrastructure, hospitals, schools, housing, and business districts. They are to give Israel financial support for projects to improve their communication, radar, satellite, and transportation systems.

Japheth's racial calling: The Guardian—Part VIII

Japheth's offspring must also use their wealth to help bring Jewish people home to Jerusalem. For the Israelites are scattered around the world.

This wealth that Japheth's offspring will give to the Jewish people to help them return home, will be a blessing that'll put smiles on Jewish faces (Ham's family line will help Japheth's offspring in this effort). (Gen 9:27). This wealth blessing that'll help bring Jewish people back home is found in the following verse.

". . . I'll lift up my hands to the Gentiles and set up my standard to the people. They'll bring thy sons in their arms and carry thy daughters upon their shoulders." (Deut 30:3-5, Isa 49:22, Eze 11:16-20).

These verses refer to how God will return the Jews to their homeland. As the anointed guardians over God's chosen people, Japheth's descendants will have to bless the Israelites with their wealth to help them return to their homeland.

The Hebrew word Aliyah (al-ee-yaw) best depicts Israel's return to their homeland. Aliyah refers to the ascension or going up to Jerusalem. That is, Aliyah is the immigration of the Israelites to Jerusalem—called making Aliyah. As noted, Japheth's offspring will use their wealth to help the Israelites make Aliyah.

In helping and supporting the Jews as they make Aliyah, Japheth's descendants must make sure that they provide information and financial support to the Israelites who're returning to their homeland. Japheth's descendants are to work hand in hand with the Israeli government in helping the Israelites have a smooth transition into Israeli life and culture (i.e., they're to help them have a successful Aliyah).

In helping the Jews to make Aliyah (Isa 49:22, 60:9), Japheth's offspring must also use their wealth to assist the Israelites in finding housing, medical coverage, job training, employment, business opportunities and education for their families.

Japheth's offspring must use wealth to (1) buy Israeli products to help bolster her economy, (2) buy emergency equipment for attacks by Israel's foes: fire trucks, ambulances, etc., and (3) hire lawyers to fight anti-Semitism around the world.

In the millennium, Jews will receive many financial blessings. Their future financial blessings show Japheth's offspring how they're to give Jews financial support today. These financial blessings will help Jews enjoy their lives on earth. Japheth's descendants will be blessed because of it. God says, "I (the Lord) will bless them that bless thee (Israel) and curse them that curse thee . . ." (Gen 12:3).

Japheth's offspring are to raise the awareness of the world that all nations are to help the Jews make Aliyah. They're also to donate funds for the transportation that'll be used to make Aliyah: airplanes, ships, trains, cars, trucks, busses, etc. They are to finance workshops, seminars, etc., to give Jews Hebrew language lessons, culture lessons, counseling and information on making Aliyah. They're to show the Israelites God's love.

Japheth's offspring (who have been given the leadership role in ministering life and peace unto Israel) are to pray that Israel realizes that the Messiah has come and gone and will soon return. They're to pray for Israel's peace and safety. They're to also make donations to needy Israelites (e.g., children, families and senior citizens) who're in the midst of the perils of war, violence and terrorism.

Moreover, as God leads them, Japheth's offspring are to help finance programs that provide funds to (1) assist the Israelites who are victims of terrorists, and (2) help poverty stricken Israelites receive the care they need throughout the world.

As a Gentile (i.e., as a descendant of Japheth or Ham), if your church does not have an outreach program to support, uphold and backup Israel as she goes forth to make Aliyah and carry out her calling, you can ask your church to start one. You can even start one yourself. You can also join or support one that already exists.

So then, through the eyes of the millennium, God gives Japheth's offspring a close-up view of their calling to use their wealth to support, uphold and backup Israel until she becomes a nation of economic stability and prosperity. Israel needs wealth to teach the four components of God's birthright blessing to the world.

This confirms that Japheth's offspring are called to help Israel partake of, benefit from and enjoy the wealth component of God's birthright blessing.

So, Japheth's descendants have their work cut out for them. But, God created them with everything they would need to handle the task at hand. (Ps 139:14). Thus, they have no time to waste. They must roll up their sleeves and get on with their racial group's purpose. This concludes our study of how Japheth's family line is called to help the Jews partake of, benefit from and enjoy the four components of God's birthright blessing.

Japheth's racial calling: The Guardian—Part IX

As noted previously, it is absolutely fascinating to see how God confirms His purpose for each racial group through his magnificent creation. As for Japheth's offspring, God confirms that He called Japheth's offspring to minister the eternal life blessing through His grisled colored, bay colored and speckled colored horses.

My goal in this section is to confirm (without doubt) that God did indeed call Japheth's offspring to minister eternal life. God shows this through His creation of grisled colored, bay colored and speckled colored horses. (Zech 1:8, 6:3, 6-7).

We'll see that God reveals that these horses are symbolic of His eternal life blessing. Japheth's offspring are not only called to guard God's throne— the source of eternal life—and everything that pertains to it, but they're also called to minister God's eternal life blessing to the Jews (and all other racial groups). Let us now examine the symbolism associated with these horses to confirm these divine truths.

As we study these horses, we'll appreciate how amazing it is to see how God confirms His purpose for Japheth's offspring through the creation of His grisle, bay and spekle colored horses. We'll study God's grisle colored horses first.

The word grisled in Hebrew is barod (baw-rode). It means spotted. It refers to a horse's coat (fur) that's spotted with gray hairs. Some translators use the word dapple in place of grisled which also means a horse's coat that's spotted with gray hairs. A grisled (dapple gray) horse has a gray color gene that causes some of its hairs to go through a process of color loss (i.e., pigment loss) whereby its coat becomes spotted with gray hairs over time.

The graying process is like humans whose hair roots are surrounded by tissues (follicles) with pigment cells that produce the melanin that gives their hair its color. The pigment cells in our follicles gradually die and our hair turns gray. So, the grisled horse's gray hairs speak of death (i.e., the act of dying). And its colorful hairs speak of life. So, God's grisle colored horses speak of our choice to die and go to hell or accept Christ and go to heaven. (Deut 30:19).

Let us now confirm through two verses of Scripture that God's grisled horses symbolize God's eternal life blessing (the very blessing that God called Japheth's offspring to minister).

"And in the third chariot there were white horses; and in the fourth chariot there were grisled and bay horses." (Zech 6:3). God's grisled horses (symbolic of God's angels) go forth toward the south country. (Zech 6:6).

In Zech 6:6, the south country portrays the land of Egypt (south of Jerusalem). God cursed the land of Egypt (Exod 9:13-16) the same as he cursed the earth. (Gen 3:17-19). The south country (Egypt) represents the world that's under God's curse. Now, Israel was saved from bondage in Egypt. This portrays how people are saved from bondage in the world unto eternal life. (Exod 20:2, 3:7-8, Gal 3:13).

So, the symbolism behind the grisled horse speaks of our freedom to choose eternal life (the horse's colorful hairs) or eternal death (the horses gray hairs). God wants us to choose its colorful hairs that speak of eternal life. (Deut 30:19).

Thus, God's grisled horses and Japheth's descendants are both associated with God's eternal life blessing. Herein, we see that God does indeed confirm (through the creation of His grisled horses) that Japheth's descendants are called to guard God's throne of eternal life as they minister God's eternal life blessing. God is so amazing. Let us now study God's bay colored horses.

"I (Zechariah) looked up . . . 4 chariots came from between two brass mountains . . . in the 4th chariot were grisled and bay horses." (Zech 6:1-3).

God sent His bay horses (that personify angels) to walk to and fro in the earth. (Zech 6:7).

Bay in Hebrew is amots (aw-mohts). It's a strong red color. As such, a bay horse has reddish-brown hair. Because of certain genes, its hair color may vary. But, the basic color of a bay horse's hair coat is reddish-brown.

The bay horse's reddish-brown hair portrays how Christ left glory, came to earth and died for our sins. Its red hairs speak of blood. Its brown hairs speak of the earth. Christ's body was of the earth. (Heb 10:5, Phil 2:5-8). He was 100% man, yet perfectly divine (His pure blood is portrayed by the horse's red hairs).

Christ was raised from the dead on the 3rd day. So, the bay horse's brown hairs speak of His crucified body and His new body that was raised on the 3rd day. Its brown hairs also speak of saints' old bodies that'll be raised like Christ's glorious body. (Phil 3:21). The bay horse's red hairs speak of Christ's shed blood that wrought eternal life for us.

God sent His bay horses (that personify angels) to walk to and fro in the earth to minister unto us about God's gospel of eternal life. (Zech 6:7, Heb 1:14, Rev 1:1, Acts 7:53, Gal 3:19). So, God's bay colored horses speak of the joys, pleasures and quality of eternal life in New Jerusalem (in the eternal state).

We can now see that God's bay horses and Japheth's offspring are both associated with God's eternal life blessing. This shows that God indeed confirms (through the creation of His bay horses) that Japheth's descendants are called to guard God's throne of eternal life as they minister God's eternal life blessing.

Japheth's racial calling: The Guardian—Part X

Finally, let's study God's speckled horses. "I (Zechariah) saw by night a man riding on a red horse . . . and behind him stood red, **speckled** and white horses." (Zech 1:8). Zechariah wanted to know the meaning of these horses. He was told that the red, **speckled** and white horses are they whom the Lord sent to walk through the earth. (Zech 1:9-10). These horses personify God's angels sent forth to carry out God's missions.

The **speckled** horses reveal unto us a great spiritual truth about eternal life. Because of His undying love for us, God sent His only begotten Son, Jesus Christ to the cross to shed His blood and die for our sins so that we might have eternal life. That is, Christ redeemed us from our death penalties with His blood. By His blood, Christ gifted us with eternal life. (1 Peter 1:18-19, Gal 3:13, Rev 1:5, 5:9).

The word **speckled** in Hebrew is saruq (saw-rook). It means bright red (piercing to the sight). **Speckled** horses are reddish-brown or yellowish red such as chestnuts and sorrels. The blood in our arteries is full of oxygen and free of waste materials. As such, the blood in our arteries is bright red (the blood in our veins is dark red, for it carries away the waste materials of our cells and tissues).

Now, when Christ was resurrected, He had a new body with bright red blood flowing through His arteries (this truth was covered in Chap 11 Part VI : Dwelling with Christ").

Spiritually speaking, the red in the **speckled** horse's fur refers to the bright red blood flowing through the arteries of Christ's resurrected body. The horse's brown fur refers to Christ's body (Christ body was of the earth: Heb 10:5). Hence, saints' bodies that are resurrected unto eternal life will be like Christ's glorious body. (Rom 8:11, Phil 3:21). Thus, when saints are resurrected unto eternal life, they'll have new bodies with bright red blood flowing through their arteries.

Therefore, the red coats (fur) of God's **speckled** horses speak of the bright red blood that'll flow through saints' arteries as they enjoy eternal life in Paradise.

These facts plainly show that God's **speckled** horses and Japheth's descendants are both associated with God's eternal life blessing. Thus, through these facts, God confirms without doubt that (through the creation of His **speckled** horses) Japheth's descendants are called to guard God's throne of eternal life as they minister God's eternal life blessing to the Jews and the Gentiles.

Our goal was to show how amazing it is to see how God confirms His purpose for Japheth's offspring through His magnificent creation. We have shown (without a doubt) that through His grisled colored, bay colored and speckle colored horses, that God indeed shows that Japheth's offspring are called to minister His eternal life blessing. Yes! God is so amazing.

Hence, our goal was to not only to confirm that God called Japheth's offspring to minister eternal life, but it was also to show this truth through God's creation of grisled colored, bay colored and speckle colored horses. Our goal has been met.

CHAPTER 14

The Times of the Gentiles—Session 1

Japheth's racial calling: The golden opportunity-Part XI

Jews, as firstborn sons, succeed their fathers and become the ones who lead. But, many Jews have gone astray and are no longer the ones who heed.

So, God grafted Japheth into the good olive tree. This blessing gave Japheth a golden opportunity.

They'll walk as firstborn sons who God called to bear His light. They'll use their wealth to build for Jews who had foes left and right.

Japheth's family line was always on God's mind. Even from eternity past there was not a moment that God was not thinking of Japheth's descendants. (Jer 1:5). This truly shows God's infinite love for Japheth's descendants.

As you know, God is from everlasting to everlasting. (Ps 90:2). That is to say, even in eternity past He knew that He would graft Japheth's descendants into the good olive tree (God's kingdom of eternal life). He knew that he would create them to fulfill one of the most crucial callings in His salvation plans for mankind.

That is, He knew from eternity past that He would create Japheth's offspring to take the leadership role in guarding His throne, His throne room, His eternal kingdom, His chosen people and the tree of eternal life. God also knew that He would choose Japheth's descendants to minister the eternal life component of His birthright blessing.

Allow me to elaborate on God's thoughts of Japheth's descendants from eternity past. Israel represents the good olive tree (Rom 11:11-27). That is, Israel speaks of the source from which eternal life flows.

What I'm saying is that the Israelites are God's chosen people that He sent forth to teach all nations about His kingdom of eternal life. (Deut 14:2, Rom 9:4). God chose Israel to be His spiritual firstborn son. (Exod 4:22). The firstborn son succeeds his father as the leader of the family. (Deut 21:15-17, 2 Chron 21:3).

Thus, as God's spiritual firstborn son, Israel is the leader of all nations. For Israel must lead all nations to salvation by lifting up Jesus Christ. (John 12:32).

Over the years far too many Jews have gone astray and wandered off the path that leads to Zion (i.e., the path that leads to heaven). God was not pleased. (Isa 1:4). So, He gave Japheth's and Ham's offspring a golden opportunity to walk in the footsteps of firstborn sons as His light bearers.

In giving the Gentiles (Japheth and Ham's offspring) a golden opportunity to walk in the footsteps of firstborn sons, God would provoke the Jews to get on with their calling of teaching God's gospel to the world. (Rom 10:19-21,).

God knew from eternity pass that He would graft Gentiles into the good olive tree. The period of time that Gentiles will serve as first born sons is called the times of the Gentiles. (Lk 21:24, Rom 11:25). This period extends from King Nebuchadnezzar's reign to the end of the antichrist's 7 year reign in the tribulation.

So, walking in the footsteps of firstborn sons (Rom 10:16-21, Isa 65:1), obligates Japheth's offspring (as the ones who have been given the leadership role) to stand guard over and protect the lives and wellbeing of Shem's descendants.

Hence, along with our previous discussions about supporting and upholding the Jews, Japheth's descendants are also to use their wealth to help Israel rebuild her cities and land areas that the terrorists, hostile nations and antagonists have maliciously ruined or destroyed. So, while dwelling in Israel's temporary tents, Japheth's offspring are to help Israel maintain her stability until Christ comes.

In a sense, you can say that during the times of the Gentiles, the tables are somewhat turned (i.e., during the times of the Gentiles, non-Jewish people have a golden opportunity to be God's light bearers). So, Japheth's offspring don't have an identity crisis. All they have to do is trace their father's ancestry, roll up their sleeves, and get on with their calling.

Japheth's racial calling: points of caution-Part XII

Yes, Japheth and his descendants have been given a golden opportunity to walk in the footsteps of firstborn sons as God's light bearers. But, the first point that needs to be highlighted is that Japheth's offspring should never mistreat people of other racial groups unto whom they've been called to minister eternal life. This would be a strange paradox if they would mistreat other racial groups while at the same time they're supposed to minister eternal life and peace unto them.

Like the cherubim, Japheth's offspring must concentrate on preventing any form of impurity or defilement from coming anywhere near God's throne, His throne room, His kingdom, His chosen people and the tree of eternal life.

The second point that needs to be highlighted is that Japheth's descendants should never show hatred, prejudice, or anti-Semitism toward the Jews (or any other racial group for that matter). This type of behavior should never be found in the hearts of Japheth's offspring, for they are God's ministers of eternal life and peace. Japheth's descendants must seriously guard their hearts in this area.

The third point that needs to be highlighted is that Japheth's descendants should never allow violence, bloodshed or destruction to come near the Jewish people or any other people who're trying to enjoy their lives and live in peace. For, God called Japheth's descendants to be His ministers of eternal life and peace.

The fourth and final point that needs to be highlighted is that far too many of Japheth's descendants allow themselves to be influenced by Satan who'll delude them into doing the opposite of what God called them to do. Influenced by Satan, some of them harbor hate. That is, they've been in the closet about it for years.

You don't always know if one of Japheth's offspring is in the closet about harboring hate against a racial group unless he/she shows it by his/her actions. God, however, sees in secret and knows what's going on in the hearts of those who harbor hate. (Lk 8:17, Jer 23:24). So, that person must repent before it's too late.

Japheth's offspring must heed these cautions and get busy with God's purpose. God wants us to have peace while we enjoy our lives on earth. For Japheth's offspring must not allow Satan to distract them from their calling. Satan has set up a battlefront offensive against Japheth's offspring to prevent them from ministering God's eternal life blessing. Let us now go to the next chapter and study Satan's battlefront offensive against Japheth's descendants.

CHAPTER 15

Satan's Battlefront Against Japheth's Descendants—Session 1

Satan's Japhetic battlefront—Part I

Guardians of the throne are those of Japheth's offspring. But, many of them are against Shem and doing nothing.

They must get saved and meet the test. Nations who help Shem will be blessed.

On his Japhetic battlefront, their purpose Satan tries to derail. Whatever scheme Satan brings against them, they must not fail.

Because of His infinite love for them, God created Japheth's descendants to not only guard, support and uphold His throne, His throne room, His eternal kingdom and His chosen people, but to also minister God's eternal life blessing. This is one of the most crucial parts of God's salvation plans for mankind. If Japheth's descendants fail in fulfilling their purpose, we would all be most miserable. For, Satan would be deluding far too many people into joining him in hell.

Satan and God are opposite each other. Satan does everything he can to keep Japheth's descendants from fulfilling their purpose. There is no way in the world that Satan is going to allow Japheth's descendants to minister God's eternal life blessing. Satan wants people to suffer eternal death in the lake of fire.

Because of Satan's Japhetic battlefront and satanic pressure, he has far too many of Japheth's offspring doing the opposite of what God called them to do. The only force that can stop them from fulfilling their purpose is their own free wills to disobey God. We're going to study Satan's Japhetic battlefront in 7 parts.

To illustrate my point, millions of Japheth's descendants are serving false gods and not carrying out their racial group's calling. Japheth's descendants are called to take the leadership role in watching over Israel's walls. (Isa 62:6). Thus, they're to protect the lives of the Israelites, help them to dwell in peace, intercede for them and help them to make Aliyah.

Instead of protecting the Jewish people and keeping them in peace, some of Japheth's descendants have been attacking, persecuting and killing them down through the ages. They have been attacked, persecuted and killed by many nations: the Romans, Russians and Germans to name a few. They've also been attacked by Egyptians, Arab nations and the Canaanites of old.

But, the nations that help and bless the Israelites will be blessed by God as confirmed by His word. "I will bless them that bless thee (Israel), and curse him that curses thee: and in thee shall all families of the earth be blessed." (Gen 12:3).

God warns Japheth's offspring (whom He loves dearly) that they are to accept Christ and their purpose. They cannot get to heaven in their own power (as portrayed by Japheth's son, Magog: explained later). Nevertheless, multiple millions of Japheth's offspring either don't know their racial group's purpose or ignore it altogether. Day by day their disobedience is getting progressively worse. Satan is very active and quite busy on his Japhetic battlefront.

Satan's Japhetic battlefront—Part II

In studying Satan's Japhetic battlefront, a wealth of knowledge can be gained by studying the principles of the firstborn son. Through Japheth (Noah's firstborn son), we can get a panoramic view of Satan's death plan for mankind and his goal to keep men under the curse of the law (i.e., under the curse of death). So, the principles of the firstborn son are pivotal in Japheth's descendants knowing what they have to do to guard against Satan's Japhetic battlefront offensive.

I'm aware that there is controversy among Bible scholars about who was Noah's firstborn son. In order to avoid the confusion, let's confirm that Japheth was indeed Noah's oldest son. This is important because Japheth plays a key role in understanding why Satan uses Gog of Magog to wage war against the Jews. Japheth's descendants are called to guard the Jews' lives. Japheth's offspring need to know what Satan is up to. We'll now confirm that Japheth was the oldest son.

Noah entered the Ark at 600. (Gen 7:11-13). Two years later, he was 602. Two years after entering the Ark, Shem was 100. (Gen 11:10). So Noah was 602 when Shem was 100. If you count back 100 years, Noah was 502 when he had Shem.

Noah had his first child when he was 500. (Gen 5:32). So, it wasn't Shem that Noah had at 500. For, Noah had Shem when he was 502. Ham was Noah's youngest son. (Gen 9:24). So, it was Japheth that Noah had at 500 when he started having children. Japheth, therefore, was Noah's firstborn son—the oldest.

Satan's Japhetic battlefront—Part III

Once Japheth's offspring know why Satan uses Gog of Magog to wage war against Israel, they'll not only know what Satan is up to, but they'll also know how to guard against his wicked plans. Ultimately, Satan and his imps will be defeated.

Many examples show how God will cut off Satan and all wicked beings from the face of the earth: (1) the death of Egypt's firstborn sons: Exod 12:29, (2) the great flood of Noah's day: Gen 7:11-24, (3) the pale horse of the apocalypse: Rev 6:7-8, (4) the war of the northern army: Eze Chap 38-39, (5) the War of Armageddon upon Christ's return to earth: Rev 16:12-17, 19:19-21, and (6) the final war against Satan and his army at the end of the millennium. (Rev 20:7-10).

Armageddon foreshadows God's final war at the end of the millennium against Satan and all wicked beings. (Rev 20:7-10). In order to peer deeper into why Satan uses Gog of Magog to wage war against the Jewish people, we need to study the war of the northern army. Let us now focus on the war of the northern army.

Satan's Japhetic battlefront—Part IV

> An army shall enter Shem's land one day. It'll come one route and flee another way.
>
> It's nobler to stand than to flee; my God stands close to me. His right hand is over me; my foes flee to yonder sea.
>
> Their great leader is Gog of Magog. In Satan's wheel he's a mighty cog. All around you they will encamp. But, under God's foot they will be stamped.

By studying the war of the northern army, we gain valuable knowledge about what Satan is up to relative to his Japhetic battlefront. We'll find that Satan's objective is to derail Japheth's calling of ministering God's eternal life blessing.

At all costs, Satan strives to prevent mankind from receiving God's eternal life blessing. For Satan wants all racial groups to join him in hell.

Slightly before the beginning of the tribulation (i.e., before the antichrist comes on the scene), Gog of Magog (led by Satan) will lead his northern army against the Jews to annihilate them. But, it's impossible for a Satan led army to win a war of annihilation against God and His chosen people (the Jews). That is, no matter what force Satan brings against Jerusalem, God and His believers will be the ultimate victors of the war between good and evil.

Nevertheless, an evil thought will come into Gog's mind to attack Israel. (Eze 38:10-12). The Jews will not be at war. They'll be at rest and living safely (i.e., they'll think that they can protect their land). (Eze 38:11). Even so, they'll not really be prepared for a colossal war. Their guards will be down. Gog of Magog will think that this is the perfect time to annihilate them. The Jews will think that they're in this battle alone against all odds. But, God will use this battle to show His glory and that He's the true God who reigns. (Eze 38:16, 23, Rev 19:6).

Daniel 9:27 warns sinners and fallen angels—in advance—what will be the end of those who dare to come against God's chosen people (the Jews). God is going to use the war of the northern army to prove to the world that

Satan is already defeated and that Jews (God's chosen people) will never be annihilated.

"Thou (Gog) shall come against my people as a cloud . . . and I will bring thee against my land that the heathen may know me when I will be sanctified in thee O Gog, before their eyes (i.e., God will be praised for defeating Satan). God will turn Gog back and put hooks into his jaws as he comes forth with his army." (Eze 38:4, 16). Gog is the title of the ruler of those who dwelled in the land of Magog.

Before we continue with our discussion about Gog of Magog and the war of the northern army, let me pause for a moment to discuss the principles of the firstborn son and a few things about what Satan is up to.

Satan's Japhetic battlefront—Part V

Christ is the firstborn of many brethren. (Rom 8:28-29). So, He's our elder brother with authority to lead us (i.e., lead His church). (Eph 5:23). As our leader, He oversees our welfare and well-being. (Phil 4:19). We're to follow in His footsteps. (1 Pet 2:21). That is, He's the example for firstborn sons to follow.

The following verses confirm the principles of the firstborn son. He is to receive a double share of His father's wealth, succeed his father as the head of the family and oversee their welfare and well-being. (Deut 21:15-17, 2 Chron 21:2-3).

In this light, the principles of the firstborn gives Japheth, the oldest son (1) a double share of his father's wealth and (2) the right to succeed him as the head of the family. This blessing is called the birthright (i.e., the firstborn son's rights).

But, God bypassed Japheth (the firstborn) and gave the birthright to Shem. (Exod 4:22). Shem's offspring are now the leaders of all nations—i.e., God gave the rights of the firstborn to Shem. (Gen 9:26). For Christ (God's living Word) came through Shem's family line. So, all nations are to serve Israel. (Isa 60:12).

In bypassing Japheth, God shows us a great spiritual truth. In the same way that God substituted Shem in Japheth's place, God substituted Jesus in Adam's place. This shows that we need a substitute to do what Adam failed to do. Adam failed to pass on pure blood to us—i.e., he sinned which made his blood tainted. Thus, we're now redeemed by the precious blood of Christ. (1 Pet 1:18-19). The important point is that we needed a substitute for our sins. So, God had to choose another son (Jesus) as Adam's substitute.

Notice that God didn't follow the principles of the firstborn son who was supposed to receive the birthright—i.e., God didn't follow the laws of the firstborn son. In bypassing the law (i.e., the law of the firstborn son), God revealed that Christ is not only our substitute, but that His death moved us out from under the law(i.e., curse of the law) and placed us under His grace. (Gal 3:13, Rom 6:14).

But, while Satan wants us under the curse of the law, God wants us under His new covenant of eternal life through grace. (Eph 2:4-9). God did not place His new covenant under Japheth. He bypassed him and placed it under Shem—the substituted son. Thus, we must follow the route that God provided for salvation. If we don't (i.e. if we don't accept Christ as our substitute) we'll be under the curse of the law, which is exactly what Satan wants so that we can join him hell.

Christ said, "I am the way, the truth, and the life: no man cometh unto the Father, but by me." (Jn 14:6). God did this to show us that we need a substitute (Jesus Christ) to get to heaven.

But, Satan, God's opposite, bypassed Shem (the route to heaven) and chose to work his death plan through Japheth. Satan bypassed the only path to eternal life. (John 14:6). Satan can't help his backward moves, that's just who he is.

Satan (as we'll see) chose to work his death plan through Gog of Magog (Gog refers to Japheth's lost offspring for Japheth had a son named Magog: Gen 10:2).

What I'm saying is that Satan wants us to work out our salvation the wrong way so that he can keep us under the curse of the law. That's why he bypassed Shem to work his death plan through Japheth. He doesn't really want us to believe that God provided us with a substitute (Jesus Christ). So, in no way does Satan want Japheth's descendants to know that he chose them as his pawns to derail God's eternal life blessing.

Not only does Satan want us to seek salvation on a route that God bypassed, but he also knows that Japheth's offspring are called to minister eternal life. So, the last thing that he (the minister of death) wants is for Japheth's offspring to succeed in ministering eternal life to Israel or anyone else for that matter. So he has to work his death plan through Japheth's descendants to stop them in their tracks.

For this reason, Satan seeks to pervert and derail the purpose for which God created Japheth's offspring. Satan is determined to stop Japheth's offspring from ministering eternal life to Israel. Thus, as noted, a wealth of knowledge can be gained by studying Noah's firstborn son, Japheth. Having discussed the principles of the firstborn son and a few things about what Satan is up to, let's continue with our discussion about Gog of Magog and the war of the northern army.

Satan's Japhetic battlefront—Part VI

Let us now study the lands that comprise Gog's northern army. Japheth's son Magog and his offspring settled in an area north of the Caucasus Mountains stretching from the Black Sea to the Caspian Sea. Some historians report that he founded the Magogites (Scythians) who inhabited Central Asia near the southern part of ancient Russia.

Tubal and Meshech (Japheth's offspring: Genesis 10:2) will be united with Gog as part of the northern army. (Eze 38:3). Tubal is located in the area of central to western Turkey. Meshech's land area is south of the Black Sea and north of Israel. It's in the geographical area of Armenia and Turkey.

Gomer and Togarmah (Japheth's offspring: Gen 10:2-3) and their bands will join Gog's army. (Eze 38:6). Gomer's offspring (Cimmerians) settled north of the Black and Caspian Seas. They migrated to Eastern Turkey in Asia Minor near Armenia—south of the Black Sea and Caucasus Mountains. Germans descended from Gomer's son Ashkenaz. Togarmar was located in Asia Minor on the upper Euphrates river between the Black and Caspian Seas—modern Turkey of today.

The northern army will be comprised of multiple nations. As such, Persia (today's Iran) from the east, Libya (Phut) from the southwest and Ethiopia (Cush) from the south will also join the northern army. (Ezk 38:5). Thus, the northern army will invade Israel from all directions: north, east, south and southwest. These different compass directions prefigure the final war at the end of the millennium when Satan's forces (led by Gog of Magog of that day) will come from the four corners of the earth to attack Jerusalem—i.e., it'll be a global war. (Rev 20:8).

I know there is controversy about the location of the lands of the northern army. Some scholars teach that Russia is the northern army. But, it's more accurate to say that Russia is the catalyst nation that gathered the northern army (for Russia is only one nation and the northern army will consist of many nations).

My research is ongoing in this area. For now, I believe that we should say that Russia will be the catalyst that'll gather these nations for war. I won't belabor the point. I know the identity of these lands is significant; but my goal is to focus on a panoramic view of what God is revealing to us by the war of the northern army.

God uses the northern army war to show how deceitful Satan is. God wants us to know about Satan's death plan wherein he'll work through Japheth's offspring. Ever the perverted one, Satan bypassed Shem and chose Japheth. His plan has led many of Japheth's offspring to Hades for ignoring their calling (i.e., Satan's goal is to prevent Japheth's offspring from ministering God's eternal life blessing).

God uses the war of the northern army to show us ahead of time that Satan will try his best to defeat Japheth's offspring s and their calling, but he'll fail. God also uses this war to show us His omnipotent power and how He protects His saints against all odds. For Christ and His saints will be the ultimate victors of the war between good and evil.

Satan's Japhetic battlefront—Part VII

Led by Gog (who portrays Japheth's unsaved offspring), the northern army will be soundly defeated: God will slay 94% of them. (Eze 39:2). It'll take 7 years to burn their weapons and seven months to bury their bodies and stray bones in the valley of Hammon-gog (7 is a number of completion). (Eze 39:8-15). This huge clean up prefigures how God will cleanse the earth of all evil beings at the end of the millennium—i.e., the earth will be cleansed before the eternal state begins.

So, after the northern army war, the next major war will be Armageddon when God brings this world to an end. Armageddon will take place immediately after the 7 year tribulation period. (Matt 24:29-30). The war of the northern army foreshadows Armageddon. We need to know what God is up to so that we can keep ourselves ever ready. So, how does the war of the northern army prefigure Armageddon?

To begin with, many of the events associated with the war of the northern army are also associated with Armageddon. For example, relative to the war of the northern army, the birds will be called to partake of God's sacrifice. They'll eat of the dead bodies of Gog's army. (Eze 39:4, 17-20). At the end of Armageddon, the birds will also eat the bodies of the antichrist's army. (Rev 19:17-18).

God will confuse the northern army. Their weapons will go berserk and kill each other. (Eze 38:21). This will also occur at Armageddon. (Zech 12:4, 14:13). The northern army will have a horde of kings and their allies. (Eze 38:4-6). The antichrist's army will also be a horde of kings and their allies. (Rev 16:12-16).

God will devastate the northern army with an earthquake. (Eze 38:19-20). God will do the same thing during the war of Armageddon. (Rev16:18-21). These events show that the war of the northern army points to the war of Armageddon.

Both Gog of the northern army and the antichrist of the war of Armageddon will gather their armies to invade Jerusalem. (Eze 38:15-16, Rev 16:16). God will defeat both of them and their armies. (Eze 39:2-4, Rev 19:19-21). So, the war of the northern army prefigures Armageddon.

God will rain hailstones upon the northern army. (Eze 38:22). Relative to Armageddon, God will also rain hailstones upon the antichrist's armies. (Rev 16:21). There will be a period of peace following the war of the northern army. (Dan 9:27). There will also be a period of peace following the war of Armageddon. (Rev 19:19-21, 20:1-6).

The above truths are more than sufficient to confirm that the war of the northern army does indeed foreshadow Armageddon. As noted, Satan's Japhetic battlefront reveals his death plan. As such, studying Japheth (Noah's firstborn son) provided us with valuable knowledge about why

Satan uses Gog of Magog to wage his death plan against Israel. (Eze 38:2-4).

Satan uses Gog of Magog (who portrays Japheth's offspring) to stop Japheth's offspring in their tracks. That is, he wants to stop them from ministering the eternal life blessing to the Jews as well as the Gentiles. Satan wants mankind to seek salvation on a route that God bypassed.

Thus, God gives Japheth's family line a panoramic view of how the war of the northern army impacts them. Since they're called to minister eternal life to Israel, Satan is after them. For Satan wants mankind to suffer eternal death. He wants to defeat Japheth's descendants at all costs.

So, studying the northern army gives Japheth's offspring wisdom to know what Satan is up to and wisdom to know what to do about it. The northern army's defeat shows that Satan is already defeated. So, as noted earlier, Christ and His saints will be the ultimate victors of the war between good and evil. Praise God!

Thus, Japheth's descendants must get on with their purpose of ministering eternal life unto the world. Eternal life reconciles people of all racial groups unto God in peace. But when it comes to people of different racial groups today, far too many of them are not following peace as God has commanded them. (Heb 12:14).

Even when Jesus walked the earth, there were people of one racial group who frowned upon and hated people of other racial groups. Satan is the culprit behind the racial tension in our societies.

But, as this book points out, if people study their racial group's purpose and follow it, our racial problems would be solved—i.e., they would go away and we would live in peace. God needs Japheth's offspring to be fully functional. Far too many people are not walking in peace and God's eternal life blessing. Not only that, but far too many people don't even know their racial group's purpose.

This completes our study of the purpose and calling of Japheth's racial group. Let us now officially study the purpose and calling of Ham's racial group.

CHAPTER 16

Ham's Descendants Have A Special Purpose To Fulfill—Session 1

Ham's racial calling: God's special servants of servants—Part I

> Ham's calling is to reconcile unto peace God and man. Noah said that Ham's offspring were given this plan.
>
> Ham's offspring are God's peacekeepers. For, they're born to be peace leaders. We know who wins in the end. It's Jesus who was cursed for our sins.

God created Ham's offspring for an amazing calling which we'll study in 11 parts. As noted, a man's will is the only force that can stop him from fulfilling his calling. In carrying out their racial group's calling, Ham's descendants have all the power of the Godhead at their disposal. No force in the universe can stop them from fulfilling their racial groups' purpose.

God gave each of Noah's sons a particular component of His birthright blessing to minister in fulfilling God's purpose. As we'll see, God called Ham to minister the peace component of His birthright blessing. We'll use Chapters 16 and 17 to identify how Ham's family line is called to minister peace unto all people.

To begin with, God called His cherubim to carry out a special ministry of reconciliation between God and man unto peace—i.e., cherubim are God's special peacekeepers. Which one of Noah's sons identifies with this cherubim function?

Ham's offspring were created to carry out a special ministry of reconciliation between God and man unto peace (like the cherubim). That is (like cherubim); they're God's special peacekeepers. Let us now study this divine truth.

The inner walls of Ezekiel's temple were carved with cherubim positioned between a man's face looking toward a palm tree on one side and a lion's face (symbolic of Christ, the Lion of Judah: Rev 5:5) looking toward a palm tree on the other side. Palm trees portray victory and peace. (Eze 41:18-19). So, the fact that the man's face is looking toward a palm tree of victory and peace while the lion's face is doing the same thing reveals that man and the Lion of Judah (Christ) have the victory of peace between them.

The fact that the cherub's body is positioned between a man's face and a lion's face reveals that cherubs have a special ministry of reconciliation between God and man unto the victory of peace. So, cherubs are God's special peacekeepers. As noted, cherubim act like God expects us to act for they have the likeness of a man. (Eze 1:5). So, we study their calling to identify our racial group's calling.

In studying to see which one of Noah's sons is called to a special ministry of reconciliation between God and man unto peace (like the cherubim), notice that Noah prophesied this divine calling over Ham's descendants.

Noah said, "Cursed be Canaan; a servant of servants shall he be unto his brethren." (Gen 9:25).

This divine truth shows that just as Christ was cursed for our sins (Gal 3:13), Canaan was cursed for Ham's sin. So, like Christ, Canaan (who portrays Ham's descendants) was a sacrificial curse (substitution) for Ham. This is the proper interpretation of this verse. Canaan, therefore, portrays Christ's substitutionary death for our sins whereby He (Christ) reconciled us unto God in peace. (Rom 5:10). Like the cherubim, Christ is God's special peacekeeper.

So, Canaan being cursed for Ham's sin portrays Christ being cursed for our sins whereby Christ reconciled us to God in peace. Thus, in order to interpret Gen 9:25 properly, we must know that Canaan portrays Ham's offspring as well as Christ being cursed for our sins.

That is, Christ was cursed (substituted) for our sins. Canaan was cursed (substituted) for Ham's sin. Canaan's curse portrays how Christ was cursed for our sins to reconcile us to God in peace. So, Christ and Canaan reflect suffering under a curse for another which brings reconciliation unto peace. Thus, (without doubt) like Christ and His cherubim, Ham's offspring are the ones that God called to a special ministry of reconciliation between God and man unto peace. Like Chris and His cherubim, Ham's offspring are God's special peacekeepers.

Unfortunately, some Bible scholars innocently or purposely teach another meaning for Gen 9:25. They misinterpret the word servant by teaching that Ham's descendants are called to be lowly slaves unto men. Their theories are erroneous. It was shown that Canaan's curse in Ham's place symbolizes Christ's curse in our place. Hence, their myths are not the proper interpretation of Gen 9:25.

So, as I said earlier, no matter what racial group you belong to, your father's bloodline traces back to Ham, Shem or Japheth (the progenitors of all racial groups after the flood). (Gen 9:1, 7). That said, no matter what color you are or what features you have, if your father's ancestry traces back to Ham, your racial group's calling is to minister to all racial groups your special gift of reconciliation between God and man unto peace. Like the cherubim, you're God's special peacekeeper.

I know that all saints have a ministry of reconciliation. (2 Cor 5:18). But, Ham's offspring have a special ministry in this area. (Gen 9:25). So, they really don't have an identity crisis. All they have to do is identify their father's ancestry, roll up their sleeves, and get on with their racial groups' calling of ministering unto all people their special gift of reconciliation between God and man unto peace. Like God's cherubim, they're called to be God's special peacekeepers.

If they do, they'll be welcomed into Paradise with an eternal life of peace and heavenly bliss. And the gates of hell shall not prevail against them. (Matt 16:18). But, if they reject God's birthright blessing and their racial groups' purpose, the gates of hell will be their recompense. (Matt 7:13-14).

Ham's racial calling: God's special servants of servants—Part II

> In the land of Canaan, Abraham had a great victory. This battle is one that went down in history.
>
> Melchisedec was God's King of peace. Made like Christ his peace shall never cease.
>
> Under him, in comfort and peace Ham's offspring did dwell. So, Ham's descendants show us how conflict is repelled.

Recall that our goal in Chapters 16 and 17 is to identify how Ham's offspring are called to minister peace unto all people. We've shown how God has given Ham's descendants a special gift of reconciliation between God and man unto peace—i.e., like the cherubim, they're God's special peacekeepers.

That said, as noted before, God made a covenant of life and peace with Shem's descendants. (Mal 2:4-7). For God intends for Jews to dwell with Him (throughout eternity) in His kingdom of righteousness and peace. (Rom 14:17). Not only that, but God called Japheth's offspring to take the leadership role in guarding God's covenant of life and peace with Shem's descendants while they're here on earth.

So, Ham's offspring are called to support Japheth's offspring (Gen 9:25) as Japheth's offspring guard God's covenant of life and peace with Israel. So, to help Japheth's offspring minister life and peace to Jews, God gave Ham's offspring a special gift of reconciliation between God and man unto peace—i.e., like cherubim, they're God's peacekeepers. God further confirmed that Ham's offspring are His special peacekeepers when He sent Abraham to the land of Canaan.

God told Abraham to leave the land of Ur and go to a land of Ham's offspring called Canaan where God would make him a father of many nations. Canaan is the Promised Land that God gave Abraham and his seeds as an eternal inheritance in His kingdom of righteousness and peace. (Rom 14:17, Gen 12:1-5, 15:5-7, 17:1-9).

In order to show Abraham that He has the power to give this land to him and his seeds, God gave Abraham a great victory in Canaan over a confederacy of kings led by Chedorlaomer. On his way back from his victory, Abraham passed by Salem where he met Melchisedec, God's high priest, the king of Salem.

In Gen 14:17-20, Melchisedec brought forth bread and wine and blessed Abraham. Melchisedec portrays Christ and His kingdom of righteousness and peace. Christ will rule Jerusalem in peace. Melchisedec was an example of how Christ will rule in peace. As such, the citizens of Salem dwelled in peace under Melchisedec. God shows that Salem's citizens lived in peace under Melchisedec.

". . . Melchisedec, King of Salem and God's high priest met Abraham returning from the slaughter . . . and blessed him . . . Melchisedec is interpreted as the King of peace and King of Salem. (Heb 7:1-2). This truth shows that the Canaanites (Ham's offspring) did indeed dwell in peace under King Melchisedec.

The city of Salem eventually became Jerusalem. David had purchased Jebus to build God's temple. (Jud 19:10-11, 2 Sam 5:5-10, 1 Chron 21:18-28). Jebus became Salem and Salem became Jerusalem, God's future city of peace. So, Salem foreshadows New Jerusalem (Rev 21:2) where saints will dwell with the Lord in peace forevermore. (Rom 14:17).

Salem's citizens who dwelled in peace under King Melchisedec were Ham's descendants. Herein, we see that God used Ham's descendants to show us how to dwell in peace. For when Abraham met Melchisedec, Ham's descendants (the Canaanites) were dwelling in peace under him.

Based on God's account, Melchisedec, the King of peace, ruled in Salem over Ham's descendants (the Canaanites). (Heb 7:2). This truth foreshadows how saints will dwell in peace under Christ's kingship in New Jerusalem in the world to come.

So, through Ham's descendants, God showed us that Jerusalem's saints will dwell in peace in the Promised Land. That is, God used Ham's descendants to show us (saved or unsaved) how the inhabitants of Jerusalem will dwell in peace when Christ returns to set up His kingdom of righteousness and peace. (Isa 9:7).

These truths show how God called Ham's descendants to show us how to dwell in peace. Moreover, these truths show that Ham's descendants were called of God to minister the peace component of His birthright blessing.

In Summary, God called Ham's descendants to be models of peace—i.e., they're called to be God's special peacekeepers. For, as noted, God gave them a special ministry of reconciliation between God and man unto peace like the cherubim (God's special peacekeepers).

So, Melchisedec is an example for pastors to follow relative to keeping peace. Likewise, as God's special peacekeepers, Ham's descendants (portrayed by the Canaanites) are to be models of how to dwell in peace. For, as shown above, God created Ham's descendants to minister the peace component of His birthright blessing.

CHAPTER 17

Ham's Descendants Have A Special Purpose To Fulfill—Session 2

Ham's racial calling: God's special servants of servants—Part III

God's high priest Melchisedec is a model for clergymen to follow. The sins of some clergymen are hard pills to swallow. Ham's clergymen must not disgrace God with sinful deeds. They must be like Christ who supplies our needs.

They must avoid sin for God loves them forever. From His eternal truths they must never sever.

God's true peace is to be received under His new government. Ham's pastors must teach that no peace is in His old covenant.

Melchisedec is an example of Christ. For like Christ, he has no beginning or ending of days. Like Christ, he remains a priest continually. (Heb 7:3). The Bible is silent about Melchisedec's genealogy, so, we don't even know his racial group.

Christ (God's High Priest) is the perfect example for all priests to follow. Melchisedec (God's high priest) is a model example in the natural realm for clergymen to follow. So, Ham's offspring who're clergymen, should aspire to be like Melchisedec God's high priest and like Christ (God's High Priest in heaven).

So, when it comes to peace, God placed a great responsibility on Ham's descendants. They can't go around misbehaving. God called them to be special peacekeepers. Everyday people are dying in the streets. Like

Melchisedec, Ham's clergymen must be models of righteousness and peace. So, at all costs, Ham's offspring must get out of bondage to sin.

It's crucial that Ham's descendants of the cloth eschew evil (Mal 2:1-2) and let sinners know that God made them in His image. (Gen 1:27). Made in God's image, sinners are just as eternal as God is. Far too often sinners don't believe that they will continue to exist after death—i.e., they don't believe in the afterlife.

Lost and in need of guidance, sinners need to be shown how to receive eternal peace. But, too many clergymen are looking the other way. Some chase women, steal or misuse funds, drink alcohol, preach when they're not called, etc. So, Ham's clergymen don't have time to be derelict in being role models for other clergymen.

Ham's offspring who're clergymen are to help Shem's offspring who're clergymen spread the gospel. Endowed with a special gift of reconciliation between God and man, Ham's clergymen are to warn sinners that they'll never find peace under the old covenant (i.e., the old Levitical Priesthood) which is no longer valid. God's peace is now under Christ's Priesthood of the new covenant.

Likewise, Ham's descendants who are clergymen must not disgrace God by committing ungodly acts as many of them do today. Instead of seeking the lost, many are being exposed as child molesters, homosexuals, alcoholics, wife abusers, etc. Some are being exposed for their temper tantrums, insatiable appetites, etc.

They must also tell sinners that if they die without receiving Christ's covenant of eternal life (Gal 3:13, Rom 6:14), they'll suffer eternal death. Without Christ, the only way to avoid eternal death is to live perfect lives. No man can do that. For all have sinned and come short of the glory of God. (Rom 3:23).

In conclusion, God loves Ham's offspring dearly (we'll confirm this divine truth later in the Song of Solomon). God gave them a special role in His plans for His colorful racial groups. So, Ham's descendants and Ham's clergymen cannot afford to spend time misbehaving, straying off course, and allowing Satan to distract them from their purpose (calling). They're supposed be like Ham's descendants in Salem whom God used to show the world how to dwell in righteousness and peace.

So, let me say one thing to Ham's offspring, especially Ham's descendants who are clergymen. Lost in spiritual darkness, people are dying in the streets. So, come home Ham's descendants. Return to the way you dwelled in righteousness and peace under King Melchedisec in Salem. For, like unto Christ and His cherubim, peace is your calling. God needs you!

Hence, as God's special peacekeepers, Ham and his descendants have been called to minister the peace component of God's birthright blessing.

Ham's racial calling: God's special servants of servants—Part IV

It's not only amazing, but it's absolutely fascinating to see how God confirms His purpose for Ham's descendants through His creation of red horses, such as the chestnut, liver chestnut, sorrel and bay horses. When you look upon the beautiful red horses in God's creation, you're looking upon God's symbol of peace that Ham's descendants are called to minister on earth and in heaven. (Rom 11:29).

Ham's offspring are the racial group that God called to minister His peace blessing. In studying God's red horses (Zec 1:8-10), God reveals that red horses are symbolic of His peace blessing. How is this so?

First, you must be aware of Satan's counterfeit red horse of the apocalypse. Satan is against God. We must not confuse God's true red horse with Satan's fake red horse of the apocalypse. For Satan and God are as opposite as night and day. God is love. (2 Cor 13:11). Satan is hate. (Lk 21:17, John 15:18). God is truth. (John 14:6). Satan is a liar. (John 8:44). God is holy. (1 Pet 1:18-19). Satan is evil (John 8:44, Eze 28:15) and the list goes on.

So, Ham's offspring can't serve Satan and minister peace—evil and peace don't work together. A fountain doesn't send forth sweet and bitter water. (Jam 3:11). Ham's offspring must be mindful that God and Satan are opposite one another (i.e., morally, ethically, spiritually and emotionally they're as opposite as night and day). Satan wants to be like God. (Isa 14:14). He comes as an angel of light to deceive us. (2 Cor 11:14). He imitates God, but he does it in a perverted way. He can't help being a counterfeit, for that's who he is—corrupt to the core. (Eze 28:17).

Before we discuss God's true red horse that shows how Ham's offspring are God's peacekeepers, let's examine Satan's fake red horse. "There went out a red horse and power was given to its rider to take peace from the earth, and that they should kill one another: and there was given unto him a great sword." (Rev 6:4).

Notice that the rider of the red horse of the apocalypse went forth to wreak havoc on earth and take away peace (portrayed by his sword). He went forth with power to stir up wars and cause murder, bloodshed and destruction. Thus, the rider of the red horse of the apocalypse portrays none other than Satan. (John 10:10).

So, Satan's red horse of the apocalypse is a fake red horse that speaks of a false peace. Don't ever follow Satan's red horse. It's the opposite of Christ's red horse that's symbolic of peace on earth. Satan's red horse of the apocalypse offers the world a counterfeit (fake) peace. Beware!

Recall that the red horses in God's creation symbolize God's true peace blessing that Ham's descendants are called to minister unto the world. So, let's show that God indeed created red horses to represent true heavenly peace.

"I (Zechariah) saw by night a man riding on a red horse. Its rider stood among the myrtle trees in the bottom; and behind him stood red horses, speckled horses, and white horses." (Zech 1:8).

Zechariah wanted to know the meaning of these horses. The man standing among the myrtle trees told him that the red, speckled and white horses are they whom the Lord sent to walk through the earth. (Zech 1:9-10). These verses clearly reveal that God sent forth the true red horses, which personify God's angels.

With respect to God and Satan, we must understand that there is a law of opposites and reciprocals that operates in the world. This law refers to the antithesis of things and situations in life. Opposites and reciprocals do indeed exist in our world. They are facts of life. You can't get around them.

Relative to God's red horses in particular, based on the law of opposites and reciprocals, Satan (the rider of the red horse of the apocalypse) and Christ (the rider of red horse who stood among the myrtle trees) are opposite one another. If Satan's red horse of the apocalypse portrays a counterfeit peace (as we've shown), then God's red horse portrays true peace—the opposite of Satan's red horse.

So, as we can see, God's red horses and Ham's offspring deal with the peace blessing. When you consider red horses, they're symbolic of the peace blessing (as we've shown). When you consider Ham's offspring, they're ministers of God's peace blessing (as we've shown). So, red horses that portray God's peace blessing directly reflect God's peace blessing that Ham's offspring are called to minister.

So, God's purpose for Ham's offspring to be His peacekeepers is shown through His red horses. That is, God not only reveals that red horses symbolize His peace blessing, but that Ham's offspring are called to minister His peace blessing for they're called to a special ministry of reconciliation between God and man unto peace (i.e., God called Ham's offspring to be his special peacekeepers).

So, it's absolutely fascinating how God reveals unto us His divine will, purpose and plans for Ham's family line through His magnificent creation of red horses. Thank God for creating such beautiful red horses in the earth. For, they are indeed symbolic of true heavenly peace. As intended, we've used Chapters 16 and 17 to identify how Ham's offspring are called to minister peace unto all people.

CHAPTER 18

Ham's Descendants Have A Special Purpose To Fulfill—Session 3

Ham's racial calling: God's special servants of servants—Part V

> As servants of servants, cherubim go where the chariot goes
> How the chariot flies upon the wings of the wind no one knows
> As his purpose, Ham shows the peace of God's throne
> As God's special servant of servants, Ham is fitly cloned
> The genes of men trace to Noah's son's blood
> This is how we find our callings after the flood

As noted before, God's angels serve believers—i.e., they're servants of God's believing servants. (Heb 1:14). So, God's angels are servants of servants.

But, cherubim are God's special servants of servants. For they guard the very throne and throne room where God dwells. Humbled under His throne-chariot, they go where it goes and turn not as they go (i.e., they never stray from obedient service unto God). (Eze 1:22-26, 10:11). So, they're special servants of servants unto God as His throne-chariot flies upon the wings of the winds. (Ps 18:10).

Which one of Noah's sons is called to be a special servant of servants, like unto Christ and His cherubim? First of all, Canaan is Ham's son. In this light, Canaan portrays Ham's descendants. That said, Ham is the son who is called to be God's special servant of servants like unto Christ and His cherubim. Can we prove this?

Yes, we can prove it through God's word. God said (through Noah), "Cursed be Canaan; he'll be a servant of servants . . ." (Gen 9:25). Canaan portrays Ham's offspring. So, God personally gave Ham's offspring a special ministry as servants of servants. Does anyone dare dispute what God said out of His own mouth through Noah? So, what else can I say? God said it, I believe it and that's that.

So, based upon what God told Noah to prophesy over Ham's descendants, they are indeed called of God to be special servants of servants.

Thus, no matter what racial group you belong to, your father's blood traces back to Shem, Ham or Japheth, the progenitors of all racial groups after the great flood. (Gen 9:1, 7, 18-19). So, if your father's ancestry traces back to Ham, your racial group's calling is to (1) be God's special servant of servants, like unto the cherubim and (2) be a special minister of reconciliation between God and man unto peace.

Ham's racial calling: God's special servants of servants—Part VI

As God's special servants of servants, Ham's offspring are called to follow in Christ's footsteps (1 Peter 2:21) and show all nations how to be God's faithful servants. Just as God needed a racial group (the Israelites) to show the world His light of truth, God also needed a special racial group to show the world how to be faithful servants of servants unto God. Of His own free will, God chose Ham's offspring to show the world how to be faithful servants of servants like unto Christ.

So, Ham's descendants are called to show all people how to be totally sold out to God. As God's special servants of servants, God called Ham's descendants to show us how to pick up Christ's cross and follow Christ. Let's take a look.

In order for you to be a true disciple and servant of Christ, you must bear your cross as you follow Christ. It is written, ". . . Whosoever doth not bear his cross and come after me cannot be my disciple." (Lk 14:27, 1 Pet 2:21). Thus, so that Christ will not have to bear His cross alone, all people have a cross to bear as they carry out their individual and racial group's callings. Saints will face problems in life, but Christ will be with them every step of the way. (John 15:19-25, 16:33).

That said, God chose Ham's descendants to show all nations how to bear Christ's cross—i.e., He chose Simon of Cyrene (Ham's descendant) to bear His cross. Even though He could have chosen one of Shem's or Japheth's offspring to do this, nevertheless, He chose Simon of Cyrene, one of Ham's descendants.

We know it was by God's divine providence, for Simon had not come to volunteer. He was just passing by; when suddenly some Roman soldiers laid hold of him and compelled him to bear Christ's cross. (Mark 15:21, Luke 23:26). Shem's descendants didn't volunteer, for they rejected Christ. (Matt 27:17-23). Besides, if they touched a criminal's cross, they would be defiled for the Passover.

Roman soldiers could not interfere with Jewish religious practices. Japheth's offspring didn't volunteer, for Romans could not be told to bear a wooden cross. Helping Christ with His cross would make them just as despicable as the criminal.

As you can see, by divine providence, no descendant of Shem or Japheth was compelled to bear Christ's cross. It was one of Ham's offspring (Simon of Cyrene) that God chose (by divine providence) to show us how to bear Christ's cross. Now, Simon was from Cyrene in North Africa. But, some of Japheth's and Shem's descendants also dwelled in Cyrene in North Africa.

So, in order to confirm that God did indeed call Ham's descendants to show us how to bear Christ's cross, we need sufficient evidence to show that Simon of Cyrene was indeed a descendant of Ham.

So, let's travel back in time to the day of Christ's crucifixion. Roman soldiers were leading Christ to Golgotha to be crucified. (Mk 15:22). Christ was struggling to bear His cross. For the Roman soldiers had brutally flogged Christ with whips. Little pieces of sharp bones and little lead balls were attached to the ends of these whips. They beat Christ unmercifully. Their whips cut so deep into His back that you could see His skeletal muscles.

They slapped Him, mocked Him, hit him in His head, spat on Him, and beat Him with their fists. They stuck a crown of thorns so deep into His scalp that His face was dripping with blood. They whipped Him until blood was all over His body. (Mk 14:65, Matt 26:67, 27:28-32, John 19:2, Isa 53:5, Ps 22:14-18).

When the soldiers finished with Christ, His body was so disfigured that He was almost unrecognizable. (Isa 52:14, Ps 22:14-18). Simon was passing by when he saw some Roman soldiers heading his way. Christ was exhausted and could no longer bear His cross alone. He had no help. Spectators were mocking Him. His disciples had deserted Him. (Matt 26:56). The soldiers were seeking someone to carry Jesus' cross. They compelled Simon to bear Christ's cross. (Mark 15:21).

So, the question is, "Was Simon of Cyrene a descendant of Ham?" The Roman soldiers never bothered to determine whether or not Simon was a Roman citizen. They never bothered to determine whether or not Simon was a Jew. They didn't ask him one single question. They just assumed that he wasn't an offspring of Shem or Japheth.

This means that the soldiers went by his skin color. Had they seen pinkish or olive skin, they would have made sure that he wasn't a Roman or a Jew. They asked him no questions. They just snatched him into service without a thought.

Since they didn't ask Simon any questions, it shows that they didn't see pinkish or olive skin. According to their eyesight, they had no reason to question him. This means that Simon neither had pinkish skin nor olive skin. Hence, this gives us strong evidence that Simon was not a descendant of Japheth or Shem.

Ham's racial calling: God's special servants of servants—Part VII

Since our evidence shows that he was neither an offspring of Shem nor Japheth, it shows that he was a man with dark skin—i.e., he was of an African skin tone.

His dark skin gives us strong evidence that Simon of Cyrene was a descendant of Ham. As such, Ham and his descendants are the ones that God chose to show all racial groups how to bear Christ's cross as loyal servants sold out to Christ.

In being role models of how to bear Christ's cross, Ham's descendants are to be models of how to be forgiving, merciful and humble like Christ. They're to show the world how to be compassionate, kind and meek like unto Christ. (Matt 11:29, 20:34, Luke 23:34, Rom 9:15-18, Eph 2:4-7, Jude 1:21,).

In picking up Christ's cross, they're to be model examples of how to be fair and just. (Zeph 3:5). They are to show the world how to eschew evil and pursue peace. (1 Pet 3:11). They're not only to show men how to feed, clothe and house the needy, but they're also to show men how to give water to the thirsty and visit the sick and the prisoners. (Matt 25: 34-36). They're to be model servants of servants.

These examples provide Ham's descendants with many of the works they must do to bear Christ's cross and be God's special servants of servants. That being said, this book reveals the truth about God's undying love for Ham's descendants. This divine truth will be shown later in the Song of Solomon.

Ham's racial calling: God's special servants of servants—Part VIII

As noted, God's angels are servants of God's saints. (Heb 1:14). So, God's angels are servants of servants. But, as shown, cherubim are God's special servants of servants. Recall that cherubs act like, imitate and exhibit the behavior that God expects of man—i.e., they act like humans are supposed (expected) to act, for they have the likeness of a man. (Eze 1:5).

Since cherubim act like we're expected to act, we study their calling to determine our racial group's calling. Ham's, Japheth's and Shem's callings match one or more of the cherubim's callings. Through His cherubim, God shows us our racial group's calling. We just have to pinpoint the particular cherub function that identifies with our particular racial group so that we can serve God completely.

For example, God gives the ministry of praise and worship to His cherubim who are His special servants of servants. God marvelously created His cherubim to be His praise and worship leaders over God's entire heavenly hosts and creation. That is, God created His anointed cherub Lucifer as a walking symphony.

"Thou (Lucifer) hast been in Eden, God's garden . . . the workmanship of thy tabrets (rhythms, percussions, beats) and of thy pipes (vocal chords, voice pipes, ear for music, etc.,) was prepared in thee when thou was created." (Eze 28:13).

So, when God created Lucifer, He gave him perfect voice pipes, pitch, music tones, rhythms, beats, percussions, and so forth. Lucifer was a walking symphony. God's cherubim, therefore, were especially created to be the very embodiment of praise and worship. God created them to be His praise and worship leaders over His entire creation. That being said, which one of Noah's sons did God call to be His special praise and worship leaders over His creation like unto the cherubim?

As noted, God said out of His own mouth (through Noah), "Cursed be Canaan; he'll be a servant of servants . . ." (Gen 9:25). Canaan portrays Ham's offspring. As such, Ham's offspring were indeed given a special ministry as servants of servants. (Gen 9:25).

Thus, without doubt, Ham's offspring are called by God to a special ministry as God's servants of servants—i.e. they're God's special servants of servants like the cherubim. Does anyone dare dispute what God prophesied over Ham's descendants out of His own mouth (through Noah)? No one should dare do that!

Recall that God gave the ministry of praise and worship over His creation to His special servants of servants, His cherubim. Since Ham's descendants are God's special servants of servants, they're the ones that God called (created) to be His walking symphony like unto God's cherubim—i.e., Ham's descendants are God's special praise and worship leaders over His creation of colorful racial groups.

If your father's ancestry traces back to Ham, you now know your true identity and racial group's calling. You have a special ministry of reconciliation between God and man unto peace like cherubs—i.e., you're God's special peacekeeper.

You're God's special servant of servants like unto the cherubim. You are to show the world how to be loyal and faithful servant unto God.

God also called you to be His walking symphony of praise and worship unto His creation of colorful racial groups (like unto His cherubim).

Ham's offspring who get saved and carry out their racial group's calling will enter Paradise. As for those who don't get saved, they'll enter the gates of hell. This will be their eternal recompense. (Matt 7:13-14).

So, Ham's offspring don't have an identity crisis. They need to identify their father's ancestry and get on with their racial group's calling. Just as God created His cherubim to be His walking symphony, He also creates Ham's offspring to be His walking symphony. That is, He creates many of Ham's offspring with an ear for music, unique singing skills, perfect pitch, rhythmic beats, etc. Ham's offspring who're not gifted in music are to use their gifts to help in other ways.

Ham's racial calling: God's special servants of servants—Part IX

In the millennium, nations that don't go to Jerusalem yearly to keep the feast of tabernacles will have no rain. If unbelievers still don't go to the feast, God will smite them (especially Ham's unsaved offspring) with a plague. (Zech 14:16-19).

How do we know this? God singles out Egypt for this plague. Egypt portrays the land of Ham's descendants. (Ps 105:23-27). This shows that God is serious about Ham's offspring being His walking symphony of praise and worship.

This plague will be the one with which God will smite the antichrist's army. (Zech 14:12-15). In the millennium, this plague will fall upon the unsaved who don't go to the feast. Their flesh will consume away as they stand on their feet. Their eyes will consume away in their sockets. Their tongues will consume away in their mouths. God is serious about Ham's offspring being His praise leaders.

God is not pleased with Ham's offspring who're serving Satan with their voices, instruments, dances, rhythms, choreography, etc. God gave them their gifts and talents to serve Him. Those who don't serve God with their gifts need to know that it's a fearful thing to fall into the mighty hands of the living God. (Heb 10:31).

God is longsuffering (Ps 86:15, 2 Peter 3:9) and very patient. (Rom 15:5). Nevertheless, He will still punish Ham's offspring who use their gifts of singing, dancing, playing instruments, etc., to serve Satan in sin and wickedness.

Punishment may hit their doors at any time. Tragedy may strike sooner than later. They're neither called to serve the devil with rock and roll music, ungodly rap songs, demonic, suggestive rhythm and blues songs, etc., nor listen to them. Look around you and see how far too many of Ham's descendants are using their God given gifts and talents to serve Satan in sin and wickedness.

Far too many of Ham's offspring—who are gifted in music, are destroying their bodies with drugs, sexually transmitted diseases and throat cancers from smoking and not caring for their bodies properly. Many live in the fast lanes of life (wild parties, popping pills, etc.,) and get so out of control that they wind up having mental problems, overdosing on drugs or even committing suicide.

The sad thing about many of Ham's offspring who have musical gifts is that they never sing or play a note unto God. They spend their lives serving Satan. When they're 50 or 60 plus years, they become retired celebrities, thinking that they served their purpose. They wasted their years. They need to get saved and do something for God while they're alive, even if it's singing in the church pews.

Ham's offspring are called to influence the world with their musical gifts in such a way that the earth's kings will praise God. (Ps 138:4). They are to influence the world so that people will not only praise God for His mighty acts (Ps 150:2), but that people will also praise God with their trumpets, harps, psalteries, timbrels, organs, strings, loud cymbals, high sounding cymbals, and dances. They're to worship God so that everything that has breath will praise the Lord. (Ps 150:3-6).

Ham's offspring who don't have musical gifts must help in other ways. They can sponsor singers, dancers, actors, etc. They can sponsor concerts and plays. They can procure music equipment, stage props, costumes, dance outfits, etc. They can arrange for transportation or procure vehicles for traveling, and so on. They can use their gifts in photography, computer technology or creative arts and design.

The above skills barely scratch the surface of the gifts that Ham's offspring can contribute to the praise team. As God's servants, they're set to receive exalted positions in Paradise. For whosoever will be chief, let him be a servant, for Christ came not to be served, but to serve. (Matt 20:27-28). So, as servants, heaven's doorway to high, prestigious positions is sitting wide open to Ham's offspring.

Ham's offspring must endure to the end as special peacekeepers, special servants of servants and special praise team. They'll receive exalted positions in Paradise. (Phil 3:13-14). This divine truth also applies to Japheth's and Shem's offspring who carry out their personal and racial group's purpose in life.

CHAPTER 19

Ham's Descendants Have A Special Purpose To Fulfill—Session 4

Ham's racial calling: God's special servants of servants—Part X

> The last shall be first and the first shall be last
> This is a test that Ham's offspring must pass
> To be first a man must be servant of all
> On humble servants His blessings will fall
> Heaven's chiefs are truly theirs for the taking
> These promises, God is never forsaking

As noted, God gives Ham's offspring a golden opportunity to occupy positions of great honor in Paradise. Christ told us that the last will be first and the first will be last: many are called, but few are chosen. (Matt 19:30, 20:16, Mark 9:35).

The term "first" speaks of believers who gain abundant possessions and great prestige in life, but are not inwardly humble and obedient unto the Lord in reaching their plateaus. Many of them even esteem themselves higher than they ought by taking credit for their accomplishments. Outwardly, the world looks upon them with great honor and prestige—i.e., they're first in man's eyes. But, God knows they're not His true servants. Thus, in God's eyes, they're not first, but last.

By the same token, the world may look upon a believer's works as meager or less than noteworthy. That is, outwardly, they may look upon him as last or of low status. But, if that same believer (1) serves the Lord in meekness and humbleness of heart, (2) gives all the glory and honor to God, and (3) remains a faithful servant like unto Christ, then he's esteemed as first in

God's eyes. This is what the phrase "the last shall be first and the first shall be last" means. (Matt 20:1-16).

So, if any man desires to be first in God's eyes, he must be last of all and servant of all. (Mk 9:35). The servants who bear Christ's cross and diligently serve Him will have high, prestigious positions in Paradise. Whoever will be great, let him be a servant and whoever will be a chief let him be a servant. For humble servants in this world will be God's greatest chiefs in the new world. (Matt 20:26-28).

So, as noted earlier, Ham's offspring have a golden opportunity to be high ranking chiefs in Paradise. For as Simon of Cyrene shows, they're called to bear Christ's cross and show all racial groups how to be model servants for God. Thus, as noted, God has set the doors of heavenly prestige wide open to Ham's offspring. High esteem in Paradise is theirs for the taking if they carry out their racial group's calling as God's peacekeepers, special servants of servants and His walking symphony of praise before all nations.

That being said, it's sad that far too many people on the face of the earth, whom God has given this same golden opportunity, neither believe in Christ nor believe that they should serve Him. There are multiple millions of sinners who neither believe that Christ is a divine being, nor believe that He's the Savior. They believe that Christ is just a man like any other man. Some Israelites don't even believe that Christ, the Messiah has already come and gone and will soon return.

Look around you and you'll see that Christ must come soon. Widespread apostasy, chaos, and violence are rampant in the world today. In light of these truths, God chose a racial group to be His models of peace unto the world. Of His own free will, He chose Ham's family line to be His special peacekeepers, models of praise and worship and special servants who show us how to serve the Lord.

Ham's racial calling: God's special servants—Part XI (beware of Satan)

Satan has launched a three pronged attack against all racial groups. So, you need to beware of him. To this end, let us now examine Satan's Hamitic battlefront. Satan is always roaming about seeking whom he may devour (destroy). (1 Pet 5:8). As God's special servants of servants, Ham's offspring have to watch out for their spiritual and psychological states of mind. On his Hamitic battlefront, Satan wages an all-out war against Ham's descendants.

But, Ham's descendants have all of the Godhead's power at their disposal. The power of God's Holy Spirit operates on their behalf. (Matt 28:18-20, 1 John 2:27). No force in the universe can stop them from being God's special servants of servants, role models of peace and embodiment of praise and worship. Setting their wills against God's will is the only force in the universe that can stop them.

Satan knows that if Ham's offspring find out that they're God's special servants of servants, he'll have a powerful force to reckon with. Satan uses every trick, delusion and fiery dart in his arsenal to derail them. He strives to defeat them by getting them to serve him with their talents, musical gifts, wealth and possessions. He wants them to think that they're an afterthought, inferior, and have no purpose.

Ham's offspring must be aware of God's love for them. They're vital to God's plans. Thus, Satan strives to wear them out and derail their racial group's calling. Through it all, they have to abide in Christ and hold on to God's unchanging hands. For no force in the universe can pluck them out of God's hands. (John 10:28-29).

Of utmost importance, Ham's offspring cannot go around committing crimes against their neighbors, parents, spouses and their own racial group. This type of behavior is contrary to their purpose. Their racial group's purpose and calling is to show the world how to dwell in peace. Thus, they cannot go around acting out of character, misbehaving, abusing or abandoning their children and families.

Satan wants them to wind up in jail so that he can keep them from doing what God called them to do. Satan wants them to walk in violence which is the opposite of being God's special peacemakers. He has far too many of Ham's descendants right where he wants them; bringing shame to God's name. They have to roll up their sleeves, pick up Christ's cross and get on with their racial group's calling.

Yes, God indeed called Ham's descendants to show the world how to dwell in peace, for they are God's special peace keepers. But, when you look around the world today, people of different racial groups are not dwelling in peace with other racial groups as God desires. (Heb 12:14). Satan is very busy causing racial disharmony on his Shemitic, Hamitic and Japhetic battle fronts.

Around the world racial animosity is running rampant. We've shown that Ham's descendants have a special ministry of reconciliation between God and man unto peace. As such, their calling is pivotal in God's salvation plans for man. For when people of different racial groups embrace and fulfill their respective purposes for which God created them, our racial problems would go away; just like that our racial problems would be solved.

So, Ham's descendants have no time to waste. Christ is coming soon. Until then, as God's special peacekeepers, they must avoid Satan's attempts to get them to disobey God by disrupting peace. Does God love Ham's descendants? Let's go to the Song of Solomon in the next chapter and find out how deeply God loves them.

CHAPTER 20

Solomon's Song: God's Love For Us (especially people of color) Session 1

<u>The Song of Solomon—Part I</u>

In Christ's love, all things consist. (Col 1:17). In His love, Ham's offspring exist.

In His covenant, He makes life and all things much better. (Heb 8:6). In His loving hands He holds Ham and all things together. (Col 1:17).

In Solomon's love song, Ham's offspring are black and beautiful. Yes, in God's loving eyes, Ham's beauty is irrefutable.

Love is what their God obliges to them. Their beauty, sweet beauty, the enemy tries to condemn

Let us now study the deep, undying love that God expresses in Solomon's Song for His bride (especially people of color). The bride is Christ's church. In Solomon's Song, God shows His love for His church in general, while showing His love for people of color in particular.

We'll study Solomon's Song in 11 parts. Solomon's Song is the greatest love story ever told. It gives us a close-up view of the intensity, passion and fervency of Christ's love for His church and His love for all people of color, which definitely includes Ham's offspring. God's word states that no greater love has a man than one who would lay his life down (as Christ did) for his friends. (John 15:13).

God knew that Ham's offspring (as well as other people of color) would need to know how much He deeply loves them. God knew that Ham's descendants would go through persecution. Solomon's Song gives Ham's descendants (as well as all other people of color) a panoramic view of God's master plans for His colorful racial groups and how they fit into His plans.

God seeks to open the eyes of the church so that it can see the beauty of Ham's offspring. For Ham's offspring are the works of God's hands and creative genius. The church has yet to come into the light about God's purpose for creating the unique skin tones and facial features of Ham's offspring. God wants His churches to love all of His colorful racial groups the same as He does.

In Sol Song, God ensures that Ham's offspring are recognized on equal footing. God ensures that Ham's offspring know that He's no respecter of persons. (Acts 10:34). No matter what racial group you belong to, God's undying love applies to you. So, when it comes walking in God's image and worshipping in His house of prayer for all people (Isa 56:7, Matt 21:13), saints are not to love in word and tongue only. They're to love in deed and in truth. (1 John 3:18).

When God created Ham's offspring (and other people of color), He knew that some people would not see their beauty through His eyes. So, Solomon's Song is a passionate love story between God and believers in general and God and people of color in particular. As we study Sol Song, we'll focus on the following four characters:

1) A dark skinned maiden who portrays saints in general and people of color in particular. Her character represents each believer in general, while at the same time she also represents each believer who is a person of color in particular. That is, her character shows that God deals with us on a one-to-one basis. Each one of us must have our own personal and intimate relationship with God.

(2) A young shepherd boy who portrays Christ the good shepherd who gives His life for His sheep. (John 10:2, 11). He is indeed the great and the chief shepherd who watches over His sheep in general and His people of color in particular. (Heb 13:20, 1 Pet 5:4, Isa 40:11).

The shepherd boy portrays Christ in His humble position as God's sacrificial Lamb. (Zech 9:9, Heb 10:9-12). Yes, though He was rich, He became poor that we might be rich. (2 Cor 8:9).

For Christ humbled Himself, came to earth, shed His precious blood and died on the cross for our sins. Throughout the Song, Christ (as the shepherd) shows His undying love for believers in general and all saints of color in particular.

(3) King Solomon also portrays Christ, but not in His humbled position. That is, he portrays Christ in His exalted position as the King of kings and Lord of Lords. (Rev 19:16). King Solomon portrays Christ the King of kings in that Solomon was the king who had everything. As you know, Christ is the King of kings who owns everything. (1 Cor 10:26, Col 1:16, Ps 50:10, 89:11).

King Solomon's kingdom and government knew a time of unprecedented peace. (1 kings 4:24-25). This prefigures Christ the King whose kingdom, government and peace will never end. (Isa 9:7). No man has ever been nor ever will be as wise as Solomon. (1 kng 3:12). This speaks of God and of Christ the King in whom are hid all the treasures of wisdom and knowledge. (Col 2:3). So, in all of his wisdom and wealth, king Solomon was a type of Chris the King of kings.

Not only that, but King Solomon portrays Christ as the creator of all people and things (which includes people of color). (John 1:3, Col 1:16-18). Christ the creator loves us dearly and is now sitting down (in glory) at the right hand of the throne of God. (Heb 12:2, Ps 110:1). So both the shepherd boy and King Solomon portray Christ, but in His two different positions.

(4) The daughters of Jerusalem portray the church. (Zech 9:9). In this setting, the church still has a lot of growing to do. It's not at the level that God wants it to be. Although the church loves the Lord, it still needs to come into full compliance with God's way of doing things. The church needs to see (1) the beauty of Ham's offspring through God's eyes, (2) His divine truths more clearly, and (3) His love for all people (which includes Ham's descendants and all people of color).

Throughout the Song, the dark-skinned maiden witnesses to the church about the beauty of Ham's offspring and other people of color. Far too many churches are silent about the dark skinned maiden who portrays Ham's offspring and all other people of color.

We'll study some of the salient verses that show how Solomon's Song expresses God's love for His bride (the church) in general, while it makes reference to His love for Ham's descendants and all other people of color in particular.

The dark-skinned maiden desires the kisses of Christ, the King of kings (as portrayed by King Solomon). For Christ (the King of kings) has kisses that are sweeter than wine. (Sol Song 1:1-2). The kisses of Christ the King of kings speak of His sweet communion and intimacy with His saints in general and His saints who are people of color in particular. Wine is sweet and makes one merry, but it doesn't compare to Christ's kisses of unspeakable joy.

Christ the king of kings invites His bride into His private chambers (i.e., He invites saints in general while He invites Ham's offspring in particular). (Sol Song 1:4). His chambers are for His closest and dearest friends. He wants to enter into an intimate and secret place with His believers who have free access to His holiest place—His throne room. (Heb 4:16). For, God loves Shem's, Japheth's and Ham's offspring in general while He emphasizes love for all people of color in particular.

The Song of Solomon—Part II

Throughout Solomon's Song, Christ the King and creator (Col 1:16) expresses the beauty of the maiden's entire body. She portrays all people in general and all people of color in particular. Christ the King focuses on the maiden's beauty because He created her and knew exactly what He was doing when He did. He wants us to see her beauty through His eyes. For, His creation is His masterpiece.

Even though Shem's, Japheth's and Ham's offspring all have beautiful skin tones (for God didn't make any mistakes when He made them: Gen 1:31), in Solomon's Song 1:5, Christ, the creator, is expressing the beauty of the maiden's dark skin in particular.

Moreover, God's plans for colorful racial groups with their beautiful skin tones would not have worked without the mixing of Japheth's, Shem's and Ham's color genes. So, these three primary bloodlines are equally important in creating God's colorful racial groups. Thus, the importance of God's plans for Ham's descendants and all people of color is one of the key themes of Solomon's Song. Far too many churches do not highlight this divine truth when they teach Solomon's Song.

Solomon's Song 1:5-6 reveals that the maiden's skin was black and beautiful. She was as black as the tents of Kedar. The daughters of Jerusalem (i.e., the church) stared at her (for the color of her skin was uniquely different). They made her feel self-conscious. She told them not to stare at her skin because she had been working in the sun. That is, they failed to see her beauty through God's eyes.

Some Bible scholars innocently or purposely fail to teach that the maiden was born black. That is, some scholars use the term "suntan" to skirt around the truth that her skin was black because she was indeed born black. That is, they teach (unknowingly or purposely) that she had a suntan, worked in the sun or anything except that she was born with black skin. Think about it! Usually, people don't deride you about a suntan; they usually complement you.

So, in no way were they staring at her because of a suntan. They were staring at her skin because it was unusually dark from working in the sun all day. Consider the phrase "as black as the tents of Kedar". (Sol Song 1:5). The word Kedar is equivalent to blackness. The tents of Kedar were made of black goatskins.

So, in no way do these tents describe a suntan. You can't describe a suntan by using the phrase "as black as the tents of Kedar". That's a good way to twist a person's mind into a ball of confusion. That is, you can't get tan out of black. In other words, the maiden's skin was not dark because of a suntan; it was dark because she was born with dark skin. Her skin may have even been a shade darker than usual because she had been working in the sun all day.

The sun can turn the pinkish skin to reddish or tanned skin; but not as black as the tents of Kedar. Thus, the dark-skinned maiden's skin color was not tan. It was as black as the tents of Kedar. So, being born with black or dark skin is not the same as acquiring a suntan as some scholars misinterpret her true skin color.

The word black used in Sol Song 1:5 is shachor. According to Strong's Concordance, shachor means dusky and it also means jetty (i.e., black or dark). No matter how you look at it, jetty means black; not tan. A suntan is one thing, but jetty is quite another thing. Hence, the dark-skinned maiden was indeed born black which is the meaning of jetty.

The word black used in Sol Song 1:6 is shecharchoreth (shekh-ar-kho'-reth). According to Strong's Concordance, shecharchoreth means swarthy or black. Swarthy means one who naturally has skin of a dark color or complexion. What I'm saying is that the maiden represents people in general and people of color in particular. In Sol Song, God sees a need to address His undying love for Ham's descendants and all other people of color.

That said, God is the one who told us through His word that the maiden's skin was black. God told us through His word that she was as black as the tents of Kedar. We shouldn't change her black skin to a suntan because God never said that she had a suntan. He said that she was black and beautiful. (Sol Song 1:5-6).

Let us consider whether or not the dark-skinned maiden was a person of color in Solomon's eyes. God's word reveals that (1) Solomon married one of Ham's offspring who was the Pharaoh's daughter (an African Princess: 1 Kngs3:1), and (2) the majority of the women that he fancied were dark complexioned (i.e., they were Ham's descendants or mixed with Ham's genes). They were his preference.

That is, he took many wives of various Canaanite tribes such as the Ammonites, Hittites and the Zidonians. (1 kings 11:1). Suffice it to say that King Solomon had a penchant for dark-skinned, non-Jewish women.

While this truth doesn't necessarily prove that the dark-skinned maiden was a person of color, it does show strong evidence that she was. This gives you some good food for thought. That is, this strong evidence gives you something to seriously think about when it comes to whether or not the dark-skinned maiden was a person of color.

The bottom line is that if you don't think that the dark-skinned maiden was born with dark skin (i.e., if you reject the fact that she was black), you'll never be able to interpret this Song properly. You'll miss God's divine truths in this Song by miles.

The Song of Solomon—Part III

You can see the beauty of ham's offspring through God's eyes.
Some say they can't see their beauty; they must stop their lies.

Some do see God through His creatures, but can't see Him
through Ham's features.

For Ham's descendants society sometimes mistreats. About
their beauty churches must step forward and teach.

The black maiden further states that her mother's children were angry with
her. They made her keep the vineyards wherein she didn't have enough
time to care for her own vineyard. (Sol Song 1:6).

Her mother portrays the church. Her mother's children (who were angry with
her: Sol Song 1:6) portrays church members who are rather disrespectful,
condescending and unfair when it comes to Ham's offspring and other
people of color. Sacrificing herself to serve in other vineyards speaks of
Japheth's, Shem's and Ham's descendants as well as all people of color
who serve God in His vineyard in spite of unfair or harsh treatment from
others.

Serving God while bearing up under unfair and harsh treatment also refers
to Ham's offspring in particular. For while working in God's vineyard, many
of Ham's descendants encounter prejudices because of their skin tones,
lip sizes, nose sizes, hair texture, etc. (Sol Song 1:6). God knew that some
people would have to see the beauty of Ham's descendants through His
eyes. The last three chapters of this book discuss (in great detail) the
beauty of Ham's offspring in particular through God's eyes. It should be
an eye-opener with plenty of food for thought.

In this light, I want to point out an ongoing prejudice against Ham's offspring
in particular. That is, God made humans with two legs. Centipedes have
30 or more legs. Most saints can see God through centipedes that are
different from them, but yet these same saints cannot see God through
Ham's offspring who have different features from them. The Song of
Solomon seeks to open the eyes of those who do not see the beauty of
Ham's descendants through God's eyes.

Consider the beautiful butterflies that are created differently from man.
Some people can see God the creator through beautiful butterflies that are
different from them. By the same token, people can see that the features
of Ham's offspring are created differently from theirs. But yet some of
these same people cannot see God the creator through His beautiful and
ingenious design of Ham's descendants.

Isn't that ironic? Why? The churches have yet to come into the light about God's genius in creating Ham's offspring. The church needs to see the truths in Sol Song so that it can teach the beauty of Ham's descendants through God's eyes.

The Song of Solomon—Part IV

Christ is the rose of Sharon; the lily of the valleys among thorns (wicked people of the church and the world). Christ states that the maiden is a lily among thorns (wicked people of the church and of the world). (Sol Song 2:1-2). Believers are God's lilies among thorns (i.e., they're lilies among lukewarm churches and the wicked world).

In Solomon's Song 2:3-4, the apple tree portrays God's kingdom. Japheth's, Ham's and Shem's descendants are to sit under the apple tree. That is, they're to abide in God's kingdom in spite of the tribulations they encounter from time to time. As they abide in God's kingdom, they're to help God seek and save the lost.

Christ's providential care for them will be delightfully sweet while they wait for Christ to come and take them to His wedding banquet. Christ their Savior consoles them for now and tells them that He'll soon return for them.

Ham's offspring in particular are to sit under the shade of the apple tree (i.e., they're to abide in God's kingdom) and wait for Christ to come and take them to His wedding banquet. As they abide there, Christ consoles and cares for them as they serve as His peacekeepers. They're to seek and save the lost and stand tall through the storms and prejudices of life. They're to know that God created their unique features for a purpose (more details on this are in the last 3 chapters).

As Shem's, Ham's and Japheth's offspring abide under the apple tree, God's left hand is under their heads and His right hand embraces them. (Sol Song 2:6). God always shows His undying love for them. The maiden adjures the church to not stir up nor awake her love until He pleases. (Sol Song 2:7).

Herein, she's telling the church that Christ doesn't want us to pretend that we love Him. He wants us to love Him with all of our hearts, minds and souls. (Mk 12:30). So, why stir up His love if we're not ready to love Him?

We should stir up His love when He's pleased with us—i.e., when we're in love with Him.

For example, when some of the worst backsliders in the church or worst sinners in the world get themselves into deep trouble, the first thing they cry out is, "God help me!" They should have been in love with God before they asked Him for a quick fix. So, don't stir up Christ's love until He pleases. That is, don't stir up God's love until you're ready to love Him properly. Then you can stir Him up.

In Solomon's Song 2:8-9, the roe and her beloved (the shepherd boy) portray Christ in His humbled position as the Savior. Christ (as portrayed by the roe) looks through the lattices of life to see if the church is treating all people with love, especially Ham's descendants (as portrayed by the dark-skinned maiden).

In Solomon's Song 2:10, Christ (as portrayed by the shepherd boy) tells Shem's, Japheth's and Ham's believing descendants to rise and come away with Him. These verses are very comforting to saints, for they speak of the rapture (i.e., saints meeting Christ in the air to go to heaven with Him). (1 Thess 4:16-17).

Sol Song 2:10 does indeed refer to the rapture. How so? The chills and cares of winter will pass. This refers to the rapture in that the world's cares will pass when saints are raised from their graves to meet Christ in the air. Saints who're alive at His coming will be caught up in the air with them. (1 Thess 4:16-17).

The signs of spring certainly refer to the rapture—i.e., spring awakens Mother Nature with new blooms, vines, chirping birds, etc. As you can see spring (the time of new life) refers to the rapture. So then, spring speaks of the resurrection unto new life the same as Aaron's rod that budded. (Sol Song 2:11-13, Num 17:8)

In Sol Song 3:1-4, the dark-skinned maiden seeks Christ with every fiber of her being. This is what all of us should do. Even in her dreams she seeks Him. When she wakes up in the morning she seeks Him. All day long she seeks Him. In her every waking moment her heart and mind are staid on Christ, her Savior.

If we seek Christ, we'll find Him. (Lk 11:9-10). We're to draw near Him and He'll draw near us. (James 4:8). The maiden found her Savior when she sought Him. (Sol Song 3:4). The watchmen in Sol Song 3:3 speak of those who point out the way to find Christ, such as pastors, evangelists and other witnesses for Christ. When we find our beloved Savior as shown in Sol Song 3:4, we have to embrace Him, take Him home with us to our private chambers and hold on to Him until the end—i.e., until we die. For, He is our rock and our salvation. (Ps 62:6).

Relative to Sol Song 3:1-4 God wants us (especially Ham's offspring) to stick close to Him. Christ knows that people who don't see the beauty of Ham's offspring through His eyes will be unfair to them for no cause. The dark-skinned maiden (who portrays people of color) revealed that her mother's children (church members who're unfair to people of color) were angry with her. (Sol Song 1:6).

Saints cannot call themselves upright in one breath and in the next speak against a racial group that God created uniquely different. Sol Song inspires the church to examine itself to see where it stands relative to the beauty of Ham's offspring. Racists and antagonists live in darkness. Churches that are in the light should see the beauty of Ham's offspring and other people of color and love whom God loves.

If you're one of Ham's offspring, pay very close attention to what I'm about to say. God cannot do without you (Chapters 23-25 explain this truth in detail). You have to know who you are and your valuable worth in God's eyes. You're not an afterthought. You're not second class; you're created equal. Thus, how God sees you is all that matters. Never allow society to override what God said about your creative beauty. All things that He made were very good (His masterpiece).

God said it, so, that settles it. These truths are vital to your spiritual, social and psychological well-being. You were born of God; therefore, self-esteem is your divine birthright. You need to know the loving things that God says about you. You're to bind them around your heart, mind and soul as eternal truths. Keep lifting your head and shoulders and walking in the excellence in which God created you. For God is a God of excellence. (Ps 8:1, 148:13, Phil 1:9-10).

You were born; therefore, you exist. Excellence is your birthright. This book shows your first class status with God. Let's go to the next chapter and continue with our study of the truths about Ham's offspring that permeate (run through) Sol Song. God wants Ham's people to really know about His undying love for them.

CHAPTER 21

Solomon's Song: God's Love For Us (especially people of color) Session 2

The Song of Solomon—Part V

> God looked at everything He created and it was very good. To improve upon anything He made, He never could.
>
> In sculpting Ham's flawless skin tone and hair, He was very wise. Fearfully and wonderfully made were Ham's lips, nose and eyes.

In Solomon's Song 4:7, Christ the King of kings and creator of all beings and things: Col 1:16 (as portrayed by King Solomon), directs His attention to the beauty of His creation. He knew exactly what He was doing when He created them. He looked at everything He created and it was very good. In His eyes, His creation was a perfect masterpiece that could not be improved upon. (Gen 1:31).

In this light, Solomon's Song 4:7 reveals that when He created Japheth's offspring their beauty was flawless—i.e., they had absolutely no spots. Their eyes, noses, lips, hair textures, skin tones and so forth were an absolute masterpiece. Likewise, Sol Song 4:7 reveals that when He created Shem's descendants their beauty was flawless—i.e., they had absolutely no spots. Their eyes, noses, lips, hair textures, skin tones and so forth were perfectly sculpted in God's eyes.

Sol Song 4:7 reveals that when He created Ham's descendants and people of color their beauty was flawless—i.e., they had absolutely no spots. Their eyes, noses, lips, hair textures were an absolute masterpiece. Hence, in focusing on Ham's descendants in particular, their lip sizes, nose sizes, hair textures, skin tones and so forth were ingeniously sculpted by God's hands.

That is, the Song of Solomon 4:7 reveals that Shem's, Ham's and Japheth's descendants (including all other people of color) are all fearfully and wonderfully made. (Gen 1:31, Ps 139:14). In order to grasp this truth about Ham's offspring, you must know that (1) the dark-skinned maiden's beauty was flawless and (2) she portrays people in general while portraying Ham's descendants in particular.

The Song of Solomon—Part VI

> She slept, but her heart was awake; she was dreaming. He stood at her door and knocked; His love was beaming.

> He was knocking because He loves her dearly. She was sleeping for sometimes we do grow weary.

> When her love knocked, He left myrrh on her knob. Myrrh is the bitterness of life that makes one sob.

In Solomon's Song 5:2, the Shulamite maiden had a dream wherein she said, "I sleep, but my heart is awake. The voice of my Lord knocks, saying, Open to me my sister, my love, my dove, my undefiled. My head is filled with dew and my curls are filled with the drops of the night."

In this passage, the dark-skinned maiden is talking about Christ the Savior (as portrayed by the shepherd boy). Christ (whose head is filled with dew and the drops of the night) neither sleeps nor slumbers. He stands at our doors 24 hours a day. He gives us our missions for His service. (Matt 28:19-20). He stands at our doors because He wants to come in and sup with us, keep us in peace and give us golden opportunities to serve Him. (Rev 3:20, Rom 15:33, Gal 6:10).

Notice that in Sol Song 5:3, she had taken off her robe and slippers and was already in bed. She was hesitant about getting out of bed to open the door for Christ (her beloved). This shows that sometimes in life—although we love the Lord—we may grow a little weary and not respond to God with love and fervor.

There are times when we may not be as fired up for Him as usual and miss out on some opportunities to serve Him so that we can store up treasures in heaven. (Matt 6:19-20). That is, sometimes we may be a little lukewarm when it comes to serving the Lord or we may find ourselves in some kind of a spiritual slump.

Even though saints may grow a little weary and miss some golden opportunities to serve Him (i.e., the maiden was asleep and reluctant to get out of bed when He knocked: Sol Song 5:2-3), He'll still be there knocking on our doors. In other words, even though we may lose a little fervor sometimes and need a revival, He'll be there to revive us. Lo, He's always with us. (Matt 28:20).

In Sol Song 5:4-6, her love put His hand in her door hole and she was moved by it. She opened the door, but He was gone. He left myrrh on her knob. She sought Him but didn't find Him. Her love wanted to give her an opportunity to serve Him. Because of her self-indulgence, she missed the opportunity.

Sometimes in life we can get so preoccupied with so many things on our agendas that we stop spending good quality time with Jesus. This means that we have left our first love and we must return to Him. (Rev 2:4-5).

Mary's sister Martha is an example of how we can leave our first love (Jesus). Martha was preoccupied with the things of life while Mary spent quality time sitting at Jesus' feet getting the good part (His holy word and sweet communion). (Lk 10:38-42). Let us now consider the myrrh that Jesus left on her door knob.

The Magi brought baby Jesus (1) gold which portrays His divinity, (2) myrrh which portrays His bitter sufferings that He endured for our salvation: Matt 2:9-11, Phil 2:8, Heb 5:8), and (3) frankincense that portrays His truthfulness. Saints will partake of His myrrh. (Phil 3:10-11, 2 Cor 1:5). But, Christ will see them through their storms. The pressures of life may weigh them down and they may want to throw in the towel. But, just as Christ weathered the storms, He'll help us weather our storms. For, He's our refuge, rock and salvation. (Ps 57:1, 18:2, 62:6).

It is written, "But the God of all grace unto His eternal glory through Christ, after you have suffered a while, will make you perfect, established, strengthened and settled." (1 Pet 5:10). That is, we'll go through storms and sufferings, but Christ (who is always with us) will deliver us out of them all. (2 Tim 3:11-12).

The Song of Solomon—Part VII

Pretenders of the cloth are false witnesses for Christ. They use lying doctrines to wound and smite.

Hate groups twist Scriptures to fit their beliefs. They'll take your veil; so get close to God for relief

Stay away, stay away from the evil pretenders of the cloth. Through His pure blood and the veil we'll enter His heavenly loft.

In Solomon's Song 5:7, the watchmen found the dark-skinned maiden and smote her, wounded her and took her veil. Notice that the watchmen in Sol Song 3:3 are God's shepherds who watch over God's sheep and point out the way to Christ (i.e., they are God's pastors, evangelists and other witnesses for Christ). But in Sol Song 5:7, the watchmen wounded and abused her. These watchmen were not sent by God. If God didn't send them, then who do they portray?

They portray the great pretenders of the cloth who're not of God. They're not true shepherds for they don't enter the door of the sheepfold. They, climb in some other way. (John 10:1-4). As for Ham's offspring, if they listen to God, He'll protect them from the great pretenders for He loves them dearly.

Christ said, "Many will come in my name, saying I am Christ; and shall deceive many." (Matt 24:4-5). So, there are many fake preachers, self-made evangelists and false witness for Christ out there. They neither have your interest nor Christ's interest in their hearts. They only have their own private agendas in their hearts.

They'll serve you the myrrh of bitterness. They'll smite and wound you like they did the dark-skinned maiden. They'll smite and wound you spiritually with their false teachings. Some will smite and wound you physically. Consider Jim Jones who was a fake preacher who came in Christ's name. He took his flock to Guyana to a place in the jungles of South America. He named it Jonestown.

In November, 1978, as his own self-made god, he (through his henchmen) strong armed his flock into committing mass suicide by forcing over 900 of his members to drink Kool-Aid laced with poison (potassium cyanide)

or be injected with it. Instead of watching over his flock, he served them the myrrh of suffering unto death. For, he smote them spiritually, mentally and physically (unto death).

In Sol Song 5:7, Christ (through the dark-skinned maiden) is teaching us to stay away from these great pretenders who're not in touch with the gospel. As the dark-skinned maiden found out, they're against Christ's gospel. They hated Christ and they'll hate us. (John 15:18-19). They'll only use you, abuse you, misguide you and do you harm (spiritually, mentally and sometimes physically).

This is why Shem's, Japheth's and Ham's offspring have to hold onto God's undying love for protection. The watchmen also took the maiden's veil. The veil separates the holy place from the most holy place. It speaks of our blood covering that we have because Christ was sacrificed on the cross for us. (Heb 10:19-22). When the veil was rent (Lk 23:45), it signified that through Jesus blood covering, we can now enter into God's presence as long as we're covered by Christ's blood.

Therefore, if you take away one's veil, that person cannot enter into God's presence. That person would not be covered by Christ's blood. As shown by the dark-skinned maiden, the watchmen (pretenders in this case) took away her veil. Herein, God is showing us that great pretenders will try to take away your veil (Christ's blood covering) through their misguided teachings and false doctrines.

They don't care about your salvation. They're in the shepherd con to get what they can out of you. These pretenders don't give a hoot about God's undying love for Ham's offspring. They discriminate against them and other groups. This is why Sol Song must be taught properly for it addresses the mistreatment of people in general and Ham's offspring in particular. Jesus wants us to steer clear of them.

There are many supremacist hate groups who believe that they are the superior racial group and Jews, Blacks and other people of color are inferior to them. They teach that they must separate themselves from inferior racial groups. They commit hate crimes against them to intimidate them in order to keep them away from them. Since supremacists believe that they must gain and maintain power by bringing the myrrh of suffering on minorities, their objective is to terrorize, frighten and hold down Jews, Blacks and other people of color.

Such racial groups are the Ku Klux Klan, skinheads, American Nazi party (a neo-Nazi group based on Adolf Hitler's hateful ideologies), Aryan Resistance (also a neo Nazi group) and the Christian Identity group to name a few. These groups come and go. Some die out and another one forms—i.e., the fabric of our society is still infested with racism, prejudice and discrimination.

Some of these hate groups even believe that they are God's chosen people (the true Jews). They support their separatist beliefs and violence by quoting such verses as Exod 33:16 which says, "So shall we be separated . . . from all the people . . ." They also quote Lev 20:24 which says, "I am thy God which has separated you from other people." So, they feel that they are doing God's will.

Basically, these are great pretenders who twist Scriptures to fit their ungodly beliefs—i.e., they use religion to justify and mask their violent activities against Jews, Blacks and other people of color.

Far too many of these hate groups target Ham's offspring as their foes. Contrary to God's command to love one another (1 John 4:7-8. 11), they hate Ham's offspring with a passion. Many of them believe and teach that based on Gen 9:25, Ham's descendants are cursed. Nothing could be further from the truth.

They twist Scriptures to justify their discrimination, bigotry, violence and abuse against Ham's and Shem's offspring. They have a need to exploit, subjugate and exercise power over them. Christ said, "If the world hates you . . . it hated me first. If you were of the world, the world would love you. But because you're not of the world . . . the world hates you." (John 15:18-19).

These groups mistreat Ham's offspring because of their skin tones and features. So, as shown by the dark-skinned maiden, they'll not only smite and abuse Ham's offspring (mentally, spiritually and physically), but they'll try to take away their veil (Christ's blood covering). (Sol Song 5:7). This is why Solomon's Song comforts believers in general while at the same time it comforts and shows its love for Ham's offspring in particular (as portrayed by the dark-skinned maiden).

Shem's and Ham's offspring (and other people of color) must get close to God, for He's their rock and salvation. (Ps 62:6). If these groups don't repent and alter their behavior, they'll receive their reward. Although the God of patience is slow to anger, He'll pour out His wrath on them in due time. (Rom 15:5, Nahum 1:2-9).

The Song of Solomon—Part VIII

In Sol Son 5:8, the dark-skinned maiden charges (admonishes) the daughters of Jerusalem (the great pretenders in this case who're not sent by God and certain worldly churches who're out of touch with God) that if they find her beloved (Christ, the Savior) tell Him that she is sick of love (i.e., she's telling them how deeply she loves her Lord and admonishes them to follow suit).

In Sol Song 5:9, their response was rather smug, condescending and skeptical. They wanted to know who was this Jesus that she was so in love with and why they should love him instead of any other god. That is, they wanted to know what makes her think that her God is the only one. So, they wanted to know why she was admonishing them.

She responds to them in Sol Song 5:10. She tells them that no one compares to Jesus' spiritual colors: white and ruddy. White portrays Christ's righteousness. (Rev 19:8). Ruddy refers to the blood that Christ shed on the cross to pay for our sins. (1 John 1:7, 1 Pet 1:18-19).

The maiden charges (admonishes) the great pretenders who are not sent by God and certain worldly churches who're out of touch with God that they need to stop smiting, wounding and abusing Ham's descendants, Shem's descends and other people of color. They must start following in Christ's footsteps. (1 Pet 2:21).

Relative to Ham's family line in particular, these hate groups must repent of their ways before Christ returns. They must change their hearts so that they can see the creative beauty of Ham's descendants through God's eyes. The world cannot see this divine truth, for it's in the dark. But, believers have no excuse because they're in the light (i.e., they have eyes to see).

CHAPTER 22

Solomon's Song: God's Love For Us (especially people of color) Session 3

The Song of Solomon—Part IX

Churches do indeed teach us about Solomon's Song and its passionate love story. But, far too many of them do not teach it from the aspect of God's undying love for Ham's descendants. This is crucial information that Ham's offspring need to know. They're not an afterthought. They matter to God. God's undying love for them is right before preachers' eyes. They really can't miss it if they're looking at it through God's eyes.

If the divine truths of Solomon's Song are not taught about Ham's offspring properly, Ham's offspring can suffer from lack of knowledge. This could be quite damaging to their self-worth. This is why this book focuses on the beauty of Ham's offspring that permeates the Song of Solomon.

So, how important are Ham's offspring in God's eyes? Without them, there would be no Adam and Eve, no Jewish people, no colorful racial groups and no olive skin tone on Christ's body. Moreover, without them, God's creation would not have been the creative masterpiece that He desired. So, keep reading for (as we go along) these divine truths will unfold before your very eyes.

> Come seek my love to find where He has gone
> O swoon us Holy Spirit; to Christ we'll be drawn
> He's gone to gather lilies from His aroma filled garden
> He gave us flawless features; but some won't harken
> His creative beauty runs throughout the whole creation
> His genes of beauty are in all people from every nation

"Where is your beloved one gone O fairest among women? Where has your beloved turned aside that we may seek Him with you? My beloved is gone down into His garden, to the beds of spices, to feed in the gardens, and to gather lilies. I am my beloved and He is mine: He feeds among the lilies." (Sol Song 6:1-3).

Recall that in Sol Song 5:8, the maiden told the pretenders of the cloth (as well as worldly churches) how deeply she loves her Lord. They wanted to know why her God was so special; and what makes her think that her God is the only one?

In Sol Song 6:1-3, these same pretenders are now seeking her Lord (i.e., her beloved). It's so amazing how God's Holy Spirit goes to and fro throughout the earth convicting the hearts of men and drawing them to Christ, the Savior (as portrayed by the shepherd boy). These great pretenders who were not interested in Christ have changed their hearts and minds and have become aware that they need a Savior. Thanks be to God's Holy Spirit, it happens all the time.

She told them that her beloved (Jesus Christ) has gone down into His garden (His believers are His garden of sweet aromas). He enjoys feeding on the love of His lilies (i.e., His saints). (Solomon's Song 6:2).

In Sol Song 6:4, Christ the King and creator (as portrayed by King Solomon) is speaking. He tells Japheth's, Shem's and Ham's offspring as well as other people of color (as portrayed by the dark-skinned maiden) that their beauty is not only as impressive as the great cities of Jerusalem and Tirzah, but their beauty is also as awe inspiring as a great army's marching band with its colorful banners.

In Sol Song 6:5-9, Christ told the great pretenders and worldly churches that He created Japheth's, Shem's and Ham's offspring with beautiful teeth and temples. And, when you look upon them, you'll see God's choice in beauty. In God's eyes, their beauty is awe inspiring and incredibly dazzling. Through the dark-skinned maiden, He's referring to the beauty of all people in general and Ham's offspring in particular.

The Song of Solomon—Part X

In Solomon's Song 6:10, Christ the King and creator of all beings (as portrayed by King Solomon) further highlights His creative beauty of Shem's, Japheth's and Ham's descendants. As it is written, "Who is she that looks forth as the morning, fair as the moon, clear as the sun, and terrible as an army with banners?" (Sol Song 6:10).

In this verse, Christ the King and creator (as portrayed by King Solomon) is showing us (through His eyes) the beauty and creative genius of human beings. They are indeed His masterpiece of creation. (Gen 1:31). Moreover, the reality of God's existence and omnipotent power is seen through His creation. (Rom 1:20). God made two great lights: the sun that rules the day and the moon that rules the night. (Gen 1:14-18). God made all things, including the dawn. (Col 1:16).

In God's eyes, the features of Japheth's offspring (eyes, noses, lips, skin tones, hair textures, etc.) are as beautiful as the dawn (morning) that shows before the sun rises (dawn shows that Christ the morning star is on His way back). You can see this truth and God's existence through His creative beauty of Japheth's offspring.

Likewise, the dazzling beauty of their features is as glorious as the moon (the moon is symbolic of God's light shining in a world of darkness). So, you can see the truth of God's existence and the truth of His light shining in a world of darkness through His creative beauty of Japheth's descendants.

Their beauty is also as glorious as the sun (the sun represents the day that Christ, the Sun of righteousness, rules the earth—i.e., the light has come: Mal 4:2, Rev 12:1-5). You can see the truth of God's existence and the truth of Christ dwelling on earth through His creative beauty of Japheth's descendants,

We must also address the beauty of Shem's offspring. Sol Song 6:10, reveals that the features of Shem's offspring (eyes, noses, lips, skin tones, hair textures, etc.) are as breathtakingly beautiful as the morning dawn before sunrise (dawn is symbolic of Christ's imminent return). You can see the truth of God's existence and the truth of Christ's return through His creative beauty of Shem's offspring.

The magnificent beauty of the features of Shem's offspring is as stunning as the moon, which reflects God's light in a world of darkness. So, you can see the truth of God's existence and the truth of His light shining in a world of darkness through His creative beauty Shem's offspring.

Their beauty is also as radiant as the sun (sun refers to the day that Christ, the Sun of righteousness rules in Jerusalem with a rod of iron). (Mal 4:2, Rev 12:5). So, you can see the truth of God's existence and the truth of Christ dwelling on earth through God's creative beauty of Shem's family line.

As noted, the dark-skinned maiden portrays all people in general and Ham's offspring in particular. In Solomon's Song 6:10, God also shows the beauty of Ham's descendants.

Sol Song 6:10, shows that in God's eyes the features of Ham's offspring (eyes, noses, lips, skin tones, hair textures, etc.) are as ravishingly beautiful as the moon, that shines light in darkness. Herein, God shows us through His creative beauty of the flawless features of Ham's offspring that you can not only see the reality of His existence, but you can also see the light of His truth shining in a world of darkness.

Likewise, in God's eyes, Ham's offspring and their features (eyes, noses, lips, skin tones, hair textures, etc.) are as magnificently splendid as the morning dawn. Dawn refers to the light that shines before sunrise. Dawn shows that the sun (i.e., Christ) is soon coming. Through the beauty of Ham's descendants (like unto the morning dawn) you can not only see the reality of God's existence, but you can also see that Christ is definitely on His way back to earth in all of His glory.

Also, the Song of Solomon 6:10 shows that in God's eyes, the beauty of the features of Ham's offspring is as fabulously delightful as the sun. The sun refers to the day that the Son of light (Christ) will reign on the earth. Thus, through God's ingeniously created features of Ham's offspring, you can not only see God's existence, but you can also see His kingdom of light ruling on earth.

So, Ham's offspring are not an afterthought. They matter to God in a vitally important way. God needs their unique features for they're His color reservoir for creating a variety of colorful racial groups. His love for them is an undying love.

The phrase "as terrible (awesome) as an army with banners" refers to God's army of angels. It also refers to His army of saints adorned in white. They'll be seen with Christ in the air from the east as He descends to defeat His enemies. This is when He'll begin His 1,000 year reign of peace on earth. (Sol Song 6:10, Rev 19:14-15, 1 Sam 2:10, Zech 14:5-9). So, when God created our features, we had no spots—i.e., our features were absolutely flawless. (Sol Song 4:7).

God created what and whom He purposed and that settles it. He's our Father and potter. We're the clay and the work of His hands. (Isa 64:8). How then can any man question God's creative genius? His thoughts are not our thoughts and His ways are not our ways. As the heavens are higher than the earth, God's ways are higher than ours and His thoughts are higher than ours. (Isa 55:8-9).

So, all men can see the truth of God's existence through His creation. (Rom 1:20). You can look at the Milky Way and see God's reality and beauty. You can look at the earth's variety of plant life, beautiful forests, mountains, birds, animals and know that no one but God created such earthly beauty.

The Song of Solomon—Part XI

Since Christ is soon to return, the maiden went down to her garden to check its buds to make sure that her garden was in order. (Sol Song 6:11). If you're Shem's descendant, are you being God's light bearer? As God's spiritual firstborn son, are you leading all nations? That is, are you tending to God's garden? For Christ is coming soon.

If you're Ham's offspring are you a special servant of servants and God's peacekeeper? Are you reconciling man and God to peace? Are you being God's praise leader? That is, are you tending to His garden? For Christ is coming soon.

If you're Japheth's descendant, are you watching over Shem's descendants and their covenant of life and peace with God? Are you ministering God's eternal life blessing? Are you supporting Shem's offspring and helping them to make Aliyah? That is, are you tending to God's garden? For Christ is coming soon.

The maiden witnessed to the church over and again about God's love for us. She's a witness to all people in general and a witness to Ham's offspring and all other people of color in particular. Her dark skin in particular is a witness about God's creative beauty of Ham's descendants. How is she a witness?

Throughout the Song she talks over and again about her beloved (Jesus Christ). Some of the worldly churches as well as some great pretenders had a change of heart and sought Christ. (Sol Song 6:1). This shows that the maiden is a strong witness for Christ.

So, God wants us to change our hearts and minds like some of the worldly churches and great pretenders did. They asked the dark-skin maiden to return. They wanted to see her beauty through God's eyes. (Song of Sol 6:13).

So, the question is what will worldly churches and great pretenders see when they look at the beauty of the dark-skinned maiden through God's eyes. She portrays saints in general and Ham's offspring in particular. Up to this point, we've studied the awe inspiring features of people that God created. That said; let us now concentrate on the beautiful features of Ham's descendants in particular.

Looking through God's eyes, we will see why He created their features uniquely different. We'll see how God knew exactly what He was doing when He sculpted their skin tones, eyes, nose sizes, lip sizes, hair textures, etc. So, let's take a look (in 15 parts) and see the beauty of Ham's offspring through God's eyes.

CHAPTER 23

The Beauty Of Ham's Offspring
Through God's Eyes—Session 1

The beauty of Ham's offspring through God's eyes—Part I

> The offspring of Ham are as beautiful as can be. The beauty, sweet beauty in their genes is the key.
>
> So, their design, true design, they'll never shake. A trinity, sweet trinity with God's Spirit they make.
>
> Adam and Eve made up God's entire gene pool. They made people, many people for God to rule.

Do you know what beauty is in God's eyes? In these last 3 chapters, we'll study (in15 parts) beauty in God's eyes. For centuries there has been a lot of negativism about the beauty of Ham's offspring. We'll discuss this issue in detail. But first, we need some key background information about the Holy Trinity.

God gave us an example of His Holy Trinity. He made Adam (Gen 2:7) and formed Eve out of Adam's side. (Gen 2:21-22). Before God formed Eve, she abided in Adam. That is, they were one unit in God's Spirit. Thus, just as God, Christ and the Holy Spirit (i.e., the Holy Trinity) are one divine being; Adam, Eve and God's Spirit were one being (i.e., a trinity joined together as one).

Before Eve was formed out of Adam's side, they were one being operating in three roles (the same as the Trinity operates in three roles: God the Father, Christ the Son and God's Spirit). Eve operated as the mother of all flesh. (Gen 3:20). Adam operated as the father of all flesh (we're all descendants of his blood). They were also one with God's Holy Spirit. (Acts

17:26, 1 Cor 6:17, 15:45). So, they portrayed God's Holy Trinity (as do all godly marriages between men and women).

As the first man created, God endowed Adam with His entire gene pool to procreate all racial groups on earth. God said, "Let us make man in our image, after our likeness: and let **them** have dominion . . ." (Gen 1:26). The word "**them**" reveals that Eve abided in Adam when God gave **them** dominion. So, when Eve was formed out of Adam, her gene pool came from Adam. Thus, together, Adam and Eve made up God's entire gene pool for procreation.

So, a baby receives ½ of its genes from its father and ½ from its mother. Adam and Eve came together and filled the earth with a variety of colorful racial groups. (Gen 1:28). We'll find that God created Ham's offspring to be His reservoir of pigmentation for filling the earth with colorful racial groups. So, Ham's family line plays a pivotal role in filling the earth with a variety of colorful racial groups.

Before God spoke heaven and earth into existence (Gen 1:1), He had a master copy in His mind of His entire creation. The Lord's Prayer confirms this divine truth. For the phrase "Thy will be done in earth as it is in heaven" shows that God used His master copy to replicate on earth things that He had already created in heaven: water, trees, plants, fruits, precious stones, etc. (Matt 6:10).

God's creation is His masterpiece. He put a master copy of His creation in the cells of His species called genes to ensure that His creation reproduces after its kind. (Gen. 1:11-12, 20-28, 31). This ensured that the beauty of His creation would never be altered. For, His masterpiece couldn't be improved upon.

Genes determine the amount of melanin (a dark, brown pigment) that our cells produce. A lot of melanin produces dark skin, a little produces yellowish to pinkish skin and a medium amount produces olive skin. So, God put genes in our cells so that His original design would never be altered. Thus, God knew exactly what He was doing when He created the features of Ham's descendants.

The beauty of Ham's offspring through God's eyes— Part II

As we continue with our background information, we need to know that if we can't see the beauty of Ham's offspring through God's eyes, then we need to pray on these truths that are before us. Ham's offspring and other racial groups don't need to alter their features. God doesn't want Ham's offspring to look like any other racial group. God's perfection (masterpiece) cannot be improved upon.

"And God saw everything that He had made and, behold, it was very good. And the evening and the morning were the sixth day." (Gen 1:31).

In spite of God's perfection, people will alter their noses, lips, skin tones, hair textures, etc. That's their choice. I'll not argue with that. But, the point I'm making is that God knew exactly what He was doing when He created them.

So, no matter how much people alter their features, when they're raised from their graves, they'll have the same genes and features they were created with. All of the changes they made will go right out of the window. The only difference is that although their features will be the same, their bodies will be new and eternal.

The beauty of Ham's offspring through God's eyes— Part III

Let us continue with our background information. God is a God of great variety. Look around you. You'll see butterflies with all sorts of dazzling colors. You'll see blue birds, black birds, red birds, gray birds, etc. You'll see colorful horses: brown, silver, golden, red, mahogany, etc. You'll see green frogs, pink flamingos, and colorful peacocks. You'll also see a great variety of colorful plants.

God created three primary family lines (or bloodlines) that are all descendants of Adam. And, their genes mix together to produce a variety of colorful racial groups. Their offspring continue to do likewise. For God loves great variety.

Ham carried the genes for a lot of melanin (dark skin). Japheth carried the genes for a little melanin (yellowish to pinkish skin). Shem carried the genes for a medium amount of melanin (olive skin). Their gene pools produced all racial groups on earth after the flood of Gen 6:17. God's word confirms this truth.

After the flood (Gen 6:17, 8:13-15), Noah, his wife, his sons (Shem, Ham, and Japheth) and their wives left the Ark. Noah's sons were the ones who overspread (refilled) the earth with colorful racial groups. (Gen 9:1, 7, 18-19). In refilling the earth their gene pools had to mix together. So, God approves of mixed marriages.

For God commanded Japheth, Ham and Shem to be fruitful, multiply and refill (replenish) the earth. Hence, Noah's three sons overspread the whole earth with a variety of colorful racial groups. (Gen 9:1, 18-19).

The beauty of Ham's offspring through God's eyes— Part IV

Satan wants us to think that mixed marriages are prohibited, taboo and immoral. He wants us to think that the mixed children of color from interracial marriages are a bunch of half-breeds with no identity. This is a lie (more on this topic later).

After the flood, God refilled the earth with the racial groups that existed before the flood. This was not possible without the melanin in Shem's genes, Ham's genes and Japheth's genes. The melanin in Ham's genes was pivotal; no dark skin tones for mixing; no colorful racial groups could be produced. We now know how important Ham's offspring are to God's creation.

The beauty of Ham's offspring through God's eyes— Part V

My skin, my skin is O so beautiful. In caring for it, I'm O so dutiful.

By Adam and Eve my smooth and lovely skin was made. God knew exactly what He was doing whatever my shade.

But was Adam's and Eve's skin brown, white or black? God knows the answer as a matter of fact.

I've provided a color chart to show how skin color is determined. Many scholars claim that Adam and Eve had yellowish to pinkish skin. Some claim that they had black or very dark skin. So, what was their true skin color? Skin color involves a number of genes. Color genes have a dominant form that calls for a lot of melanin and a recessive form that calls for a very small amount of melanin.

A person may receive only the dominant form of a gene which calls for a great amount of melanin. This person would have very dark or black skin. A person may receive only the recessive form of a gene which calls for a very little amount of melanin. This person would have high yellowish to pinkish skin.

A person may have perfect balance between the dominant and recessive forms (calling for a lot of melanin and a little melanin at the same time). This person would have medium to light brown skin or olive skin (a mixture of both forms of the gene). This person is called heterozygous—i.e., he/she has both the dominant form and the recessive form of a color gene.

We'll show that Adam and Eve were heterozygous—i.e., because to the amount of melanin they had (i.e., the melanin that Ham's offspring are so richly endowed with), they had medium brown to light brown skin. For simplicity, the chart below shows a hypothetical case of a heterozygous couple where skin color is determined by two genes. One gene's dominant form is EBONY BLACK. **Its recessive form is Cotton Pink**. The other gene's dominant form is NOIR BLACK. Its recessive form is **ROSE PINK.**

COLOR CHART FOR
A HETEROZYGOUS COUPLE'S OFFSPRING

Genes in mother's egg mixed with genes in father's sperm	If the father contributes EBONY BLACK AND NOIR BLACK	If the father contributes EBONY BLACK AND ROSE PINK	If the father contributes NOIR BLACK and COTTON PINK	If the father contributes ROSE PINK and COTTON PINK
If the mother contributes EBONY BLACK and NOIR BLACK	The baby's color will be black or very dark (it has all black dominant genes)	The baby's color will be dark brown (it has 3 black genes and one pink gene)	The baby's color will be dark brown (it has 3 black genes and one pink gene)	The baby's color will be medium brown (½ of its genes are black and ½ are pink)
If the mother contributes EBONY BLACK and ROSE PINK	The baby's color will be dark brown (it has 3 black genes and one pink gene)	The baby's color will be medium brown (½ of its genes are black and ½ are pink)	The baby's color will be medium brown (½ of its genes are black and ½ are pink)	The baby's color will be light brown to olive (it has 3 pink genes and one black gene)
If the mother contributes NOIR BLACK and COTTON PINK	The baby's color will be dark brown (it has 3 black genes and one pink gene)	The baby's color will be medium brown (½ of its genes are black and ½ are pink)	The baby's color will be medium brown (½ of its genes are black and ½ are pink)	The baby's color will be light brown to olive (it has 3 pink genes and one black gene)
If the mother contributes ROSE PINK and COTTON PINK	The baby's color will be medium brown (½ of its genes are black and ½ are pink)	The baby's color will be light brown to olive (it has 3 pink genes and one black gene)	The baby's color will be light brown to olive (it has 3 pink genes and one black gene)	The baby's color will be highly pinkish (all of its genes are pink and recessive)

This chart shows the possible skin colors of the offspring of a heterozygous couple. Since a father contributes ½ of the baby's genes and the mother contributes ½ of its genes, a father can contribute only one form of a color gene, but not both forms. This is also true for the mother.

Take another look at the chart and consider the color gene with EBONY BLACK as its dominant form and **COTTON PINK** as its recessive form. If the father gives the EBONY BLACK form of the gene, he can't give the **COTTON PINK** form—i.e., he can only give half of the color gene, but not both forms of it. This is also true for the mother.

In our chart, the top row shows the gene contributions that a father can give. The first column shows the gene contributions that the mother can give. The intersection of a row and its corresponding column forms a block that shows the outcome of their baby's skin color.

A father could also be homozygous—i.e., he would not have perfect balance between the dominant and recessive forms of a color gene as a heterozygous person would have. That is, both of his color genes could be in totally dominant form such as **EBONY BLACK and NOIR BLACK**.

His wife could also be homozygous wherein both of her color genes could be in totally dominant form such as **EBONY BLACK and NOIR BLACK**. Both of them would have black or dark skin. They would only be able to produce black or dark-skinned offspring (see color chart). They would not have been able to fill the earth with a variety of colorful racial groups. Therefore, Adam and Eve could not have been a black skinned couple.

A wife's two color genes and her husband's two color genes could also be in totally recessive form such as **COTTON PINK** and **ROSE PINK**. They would both have yellowish to high pinkish skin. They would only able to produce pinkish skinned offspring. Hence, they would not have been able to fill the earth with a variety of colorful racial groups. Adam and Eve, therefore, could not have been a highly pinkish skinned couple.

But, a heterozygous couple (with melanin that Ham's offspring are so richly endowed with) has perfect dominant and recessive gene balance. They also have medium to light brown skin. The color chart confirms that a heterozygous couple can produce all skin tones in God's skin color spectrum. A heterozygous couple can produce hues that are dark brown, black, yellowish, pinkish, caramel, cream, olive, golden tan, chocolate, copper, various hues of mulattos, and so on.

So, to fill the earth with a variety of colorful racial groups, a couple would have to be a heterozygous couple with melanin that would make them have medium to light brown skin. Adam and Eve filled the earth with a variety of colorful racial groups. Thus, Adam and Eve was a brown skinned couple. Noah and his wife were also a heterozygous couple with medium to light brown skin.

Noah and his wife had Ham who was very dark, Japheth who had yellowish to high pinkish skin and Shem who had olive skin. So, without the melanin that Ham's family line is so richly endowed with, Adam and Eve would not have been a heterozygous couple that could produce a variety of racial groups.

How important are Ham's offspring to God's creation? God's plan to fill the earth with a variety of colorful racial groups would not be possible without the melanin that Ham's descendants are endowed with—i.e., no melanin; no brown skinned couple named Adam and Eve to fill the earth with colorful racial groups. Thus, Ham's descendants need to realize their vital importance in God's creation.

The beauty of Ham's offspring through God's eyes— Part VI

We noted before that God's DNA principles preserve His creation. God created exactly what He wanted for His own purpose, good will and eternal pleasure. God was well pleased with everything that He created. (Gen 1:31). Everything was created by and for Christ. (Col 1:16).

The hair textures, lip sizes, skin tones and nose sizes of Ham's offspring were created by and for Christ. Everyone that is called by Christ's name was created for Christ's glory. (Isa 43:7). Thus, Ham's descendants were created for Christ's glory.

But, as Satan's pawns, there are evil doers who claim that the wooly hair, large lips, large noses and black skin of some of Ham's offspring are ugly. Some claim that Ham's offspring descended from apes and are not as intelligent as Japheth's or Shem's offspring. Some think that beauty is in the eyes of what society dictates.

But, according to God's own sovereign will, He created Ham's offspring with unique features for His own divine purpose. People should realize that God is the God of the universe. So, they should let God be God. He is indeed the potter.

So, when you see Ham's offspring being persecuted (knowing that they're God's special servants of servants), Jesus' suffering should come to mind. (1 Peter 2:21). Hence, just as we're to help Christ bear His cross, we're to help Ham's offspring bear their crosses should they be abused without cause like Christ was.

The beauty of Ham's offspring through God's eyes—Part VII

We now have enough background information for our study. God uses Ham's offspring to fill the earth with great variety. We must understand that in God's eyes, beauty is in great variety and not in what society thinks. In understanding why God created Ham's offspring with uniquely different features, we must know that in God's eyes, beauty is in great variety. God couldn't have such great variety in His human species without the uniquely different features of Ham's offspring.

So, in God's eyes, the skin tones, hair textures, nose sizes and lip shapes of Ham's offspring create great variety. Variety is the key! For example, in creating skin tones, God chose a color spectrum for skin tones. He used the colors at the opposite ends of the spectrum to create a variety of colorful racial groups—i.e., He blended different skin tones to produce all skin tones in the color spectrum.

God uses the dark tones of Ham's offspring from one end of the color spectrum, the pinkish tones of Japheth's offspring from the other end and the olive tones of Shem's offspring from the middle of the spectrum. Through their color genes, God blends their skin tones to create a variety of colorful racial groups.

God also chose a color spectrum for eye color. He chose black from one end and blue from the other end of the color spectrum. Through procreation, if there is a lot of melanin in the iris, the eyes may be black or brown. If there is very little melanin in the iris, the eyes may be blue: the color at the other end of the spectrum.

Likewise, depending on the amount of melanin in the iris, the eyes could be green, hazel, gray, or varying hues of brown or blue. This occurs when the amount of melanin in the iris varies between the opposite ends of the color spectrum.

God uses this same pattern to fill the earth with great variety in other parts of the body. God used this method after the flood. God used Ham's wide nose, Shem's medium nose and Japheth's thin nose to create a variety of nose shapes and sizes. God used Ham's full lips, Shem's medium lips and Japheth's thin lips to create a variety of lip shapes. Hence, in God's eyes, beauty is in great variety.

God used Ham's wooly hair texture, Shem's frizzy to medium hair texture and Japheth's straight hair texture to create a variety of hair textures. God could not fill the earth with variety without the features of Ham's offspring. So, without the features of Ham's offspring, great variety in God's human species would not be possible. So, Ham's offspring (God's perfectly created design) are indeed a fearfully and wonderfully made group that's very important to GOD. (Ps 139:14).

The beauty of Ham's offspring through God's eyes— Part VIII

We noted that some of Satan's pawns propagate myths that Ham's offspring are not as intelligent as Japheth's or Shem's offspring. Just as Japheth and Shem have intelligent offspring, so does Ham. Work places are filled with Ham's offspring in positions of high intelligence. Given equal opportunity, all men are created equal, no matter what color they are. God is no respecter of persons. (Acts 10:34).

Some of Satan's pawns want us to think that the creation originated with an explosion. Some claim that our racial groups began with the Tower of Babel. Some claim that man descended from birds, fishes and/or apes. Some of Satan's pawns reason that since some apes have slanted foreheads and some of Ham's offspring have slanted foreheads, Ham's offspring must have descended from apes.

This is extremely faulty logic. Nothing could be further from the truth. Satan specializes in faulty logic. His pawns don't realize that you can find people with slanted foreheads in all racial groups. Paul set the record straight about man's true origin. He revealed that God made all nations from Adam's blood and determined their life spans and dwelling places. (Acts 17:26).

So, God is the origin of all life and creator of all life forms. (Col 1:16 Gen 2:7). His gospel is before us. We must seek Him and we'll find Him, though He is not far from every man. For in Him we live, move and have our being. Thus, we are God's offspring—i.e., we all originated from Him. (Acts 17:26-28).

Man has a free will. He'll not be forced to see the beauty of Ham's offspring through God's eyes and love them as God does. We're to love others as we love ourselves. (Matt 22:35-40). We'll not be forced to love Shem's offspring (His chosen people), nor to love Japheth's offspring who guard His chosen people.

That is, even though God commanded us to love one another, we still have our own free wills to disobey God. But, all of our works will be judged. If anyone persecutes Ham's or Shem's offspring or abuses Japheth's offspring, that person will suffer loss of some of his/her heavenly treasures (if he/she is saved).

If our works are unholy or ungodly, they'll burn up like hay and stubble. (1 Cor 3:10-15). We must not fail God's testing of our faith, obedience and love toward Him. Let's proceed to the next chapter and continue with our detailed study of the beauty of Ham's offspring through God's eyes.

CHAPTER 24

The Beauty Of Ham's Offspring Through God's Eyes—Session 2

The beauty of Ham's offspring through God's eyes— Part IX

God's own mouth spoke about the beauty of Ham's offspring. He said that His creation was good and He's the King.

God's creation has more than one form of beauty. Some say Ham's features are ugly and don't suit me.

In God's eyes, beauty is truly seen in great variety. Ugliness was not seen in the creation; only piety.

O man, O man why disagree with God; He is the potter. We are the maker's clay to be formed; He is the plotter.

Now, let me have your undivided attention. Do Ham's offspring really matter to God? Yes, you can't even begin to imagine how important they are to God. Their color pigment is the color reservoir that makes it possible for God to create a variety of colorful racial groups. Their features make it possible for God to create great variety in hair textures, nose sizes, lip shapes, skin tones and so on.

We've provided the background information we need to see the beauty of Ham's descendants through God's eyes. Now it's time to listen to what God said out of His own mouth about the beauty of Ham's descendants. For the Lord giveth wisdom: out of His mouth comes knowledge and understanding. (Prov 2:6).

God saw everything that He had made and said, "Behold, it was very good (i.e., a perfect masterpiece)." (Gen 1:31, 2:1-3). This is what God saw with His own eyes and what He spoke out of His own mouth. The evening and the morning were the 6th day. As noted, God's creation was His best and could not be improved upon. He was well pleased. On the 7th day, He rested, for His ingenious creation was finished. He blessed the 7th day and sanctified it. (Gen 1:31, 2:1-3).

Now, these are God's words out of His own mouth. (Gen 1:31). The features of Ham's offspring that God sculptured, therefore, are very good and not ugly as it seems to some people. It's just that some people may see them that way because they don't understand God and what true beauty is in His creation.

Is the sun more glorious (beautiful) than the moon? No! Is the glory of the moon more beautiful than the glory of the stars? No! In God's creation, the sun has one form of beauty, the moon has another and the stars have yet another. Even within the stars, each star has its own glory (beauty). (See 1 Cor 15:41).

Are Japheth's offspring more beautiful than Shem's? No! Are Japheth's offspring more beautiful than Ham's? No! Just as the sun, moon and stars have different forms of beauty, Japheth's, Shem's and Ham's offspring (as well as all other people of color) have different forms of beauty.

God never saw ugliness in His creation. That was not even a thought on God's mind. It was on Satan's mind. Ever working against God, Satan took what God saw as beauty and twisted it. That is, he twisted the minds of some people to see Ham's offspring as ugly. So, that is Satan's doing; not God's doing.

For everything that God made was perfect (His best). (Gen 1:31). So, in order to see the beauty of God's creation through God's eyes, we have to know (1) what His motives and intentions were in the creation and (2) why did He create man?

Motivated by love, His motives were to (1) create a variety of colorful people (the key is variety), (2) create heaven and earth for His racial groups' habitation, and (3) dwell with them in peace forevermore. (Rev 21:2-3, Isa 9:6-7).

Also, motivated by love, God's intentions for man were to (1) create him in His image: Gen 1:27, (2) crown him with glory and honor (Heb 2:7), (3) bless him with an eternal inheritance (Eph 1:11,1 Ch 28:8, Isa 34:17), and (4) give him dominion over the earth and the works of His hands. (Gen 1:26, Ps 8:5-6).

Knowing God's motives and intentions, we have to understand that He loves variety in His creation. He created all things for His pleasure and glory: mankind, birds, fishes, plants, the firmament, etc. (Ps 19:1, Rev 4:11). And there is great variety in God's creation. So, in God's eyes, beauty is in great variety. Thus, God created man, celestial bodies and all species as His masterpiece of variety.

Furthermore, variety in His creation would not have been possible without wide, thin and medium sized noses. Variety would not havebeen possible without full, thin and medium lips. Variety would not have been possible without a variety of hair textures and skin tones. So God knew exactly what He was doing when He created us. As noted, we have to know God's motives and intentions.

Those who have tunnel vision (those who only see themselves, their racial group or a select class as the standard of beauty) don't comprehend the unlimited beauty that God sculpted in His creation. Stroll through the forest in the fall and observe the variety of leaves, their various shapes and their various colors. Visit the aquarium and observe the beauty of the variety of fish species that God created.

Stroll through the park and observe the variety of skin tones that God created. Observe the great variety of nose sizes that God created: wide, thin, medium, etc. Observe the great variety of lip shapes that God created: full, thin, medium, etc. Observe the great variety of hair textures that God created: wavy, wooly, curly, straight, etc. You'll see just about every shape and style you can imagine that God called very good (perfect) and it's impossible for God to lie. (Gen 1:1, Heb 6:18).

Thus, in God's creation, **there is more than one form of beauty**. As noted, just as each star has its own glory (beauty), each racial group (in God's eyes) has its own glory (beauty). No racial group has cornered the market on beauty. For, as noted, God saw everything that He created and said, "It is very good (perfect)". (Gen 1:31). This is why—in God's eyes— **there is more than one form of beauty.**

Of course, some people disagree with God who told us that everything He made was perfect. Some people see wide noses, full lips, wooly hair and dark skin as ugly. Who is right, God or those who disagree with Him? God is right! We're the clay and the works of His hands. (Isa 64:8). So, we all have a choice to believe what God said out of His own mouth or to believe Satan and our lying eyes.

Those who disagree with God about the beauty of wide noses, full lips, wooly hair and dark skin will never know what God sees as beauty unless they see beauty through His eyes. God's beauty is unlimited. Those who disagree with God have a limited concept of beauty. They only see themselves, their racial groups or a select class as the standard of beauty. Where does their tunnel vision come from? It comes from Satan's perverted influence. His wisdom is corrupted. (Eze 28:17).

What God sees as beauty, Satan (God's Archenemy) influences people to see it as ugly. Satan doesn't want us to see beauty through God's eyes. He wants us to have a limited view of beauty whereby society (instead of God) dictates beauty. But, God never saw discrimination, prejudice or ugliness in His creation. Nothing of the sort was on God's mind. So, if you remove Satan from the equation, you would have the truth; Ham's offspring are God's masterpiece of sheer beauty.

So, Satan is the one who blocks peoples' view of how God sees beauty in variety. I can't say this enough. God created over 30,000 species of birds, over 100,000 species of fish and thousands of plant species. This reveals that God sees beauty in great variety. He made horses such as the Clydesdales, Thoroughbreds and Mustangs. They have great strength, beautiful muscular structure and majestic poise. They're also swift afoot, but yet each one has its own unique beauty.

Likewise, each racial group has its own form of beauty. God could not have created a variety of racial groups without (1) mixing the genes for wide, medium and thin noses, (2) mixing the genes for full, medium and thin lips, (3) mixing the genes for dark, pinkish and olive skin, and (4) mixing the genes for wooly, kinky, straight, wavy and frizzy hair. God's purpose was to create great variety. Blending a variety of genes was the only way that it could be done.

So, God knew exactly what He was doing when He created Ham's, Japheth's and Shem's descendants with uniquely different features. Let's take a look at a few examples of How God produces variety in His creation.

As noted, God loves variety. Think about it. Variety in God's creation would not be possible without the wide noses of some of Ham's offspring. God knew exactly what He was doing in His creation. Without the wide noses of some of Ham's descendants, God could not have produced a variety of nose sizes. So, how important are the wide noses that some of Ham's descendants have? As you can see, wide noses are vitally important to God—no wide noses; no variety of noses.

In God's creation, when the genes for full lips mix with the genes for thin lips, these genes produce medium sized lips. This variety in God's creation would not be possible without the full sized lips of some of Ham's offspring. So, how important are the full lips of some of Ham's offspring? As you can see, full lips are vitally important to God. Without full lips, God would not have been able to produce the variety in lip sizes that He desires—i.e. no full lips; no variety in lips.

In God's creation, when the genes for woolly or kinky hair mix with the genes for straight hair, sometimes these genes produce wavy, curly, frizzy and other sub classes of hair (wavy whirly, wavy fine, curly tight, etc). This variety in God's creation would not be possible without the woolly or kinky hair genes of some of Ham's descendants—i.e., no wooly or kinky hair; no variety in hair textures.

So, how vital is the wooly or kinky hair of some of Ham's offspring? Wooly or kinky hair is vital to God. Without wooly or kinky hair, God could not have produced the variety of hair textures in the world today.

When the genes for dark skin mix with the genes for fair to pinkish skin, they produce medium to olive skin tones. Without the melanin that Ham's offspring are endowed with, God could not have created such skin tones as golden, tan, caramel, dark brown, chocolate, yellowish, black, pinkish, olive, copper, etc. So, how vital is the dark or black skin of some of Ham's offspring? As you can see, dark skin is vital to God—i.e. no dark or black skin; no variety of skin tones.

So, by mixing the gene pools of humans, God created great variety in people: wide noses, thin noses, medium noses, full lips, thin lips, medium lips, curly hair, straight hair, frizzy hair, wooly hair, wavy hair, dark skin, pinkish skin, olive skin, etc. God created every possible size, shape and style of human features imaginable wherein beauty, in God's eyes, is in great variety. So, before you can understand beauty in God's eyes, you must know that God loves great variety in His creation.

The beauty of Ham's offspring through God's eyes—Part X

While some people do not see the beauty of Ham's descendants through God's eyes, the fact remains that God could not have created a variety of racial groups without the melanin in the genes of Ham's descendants.

God used the same color genes with which Ham's descendants are richly endowed to produce Shem's olive skin tones. God also used the same color genes with which Ham's descendants are richly endowed to produce Christ's skin tone.

Christ's skin tone is olive to medium. His skin tone represents all people (more on this topic later). So how important to God is the melanin in the genes of Ham's offspring? No melanin, no Jesus Christ! Ham's descendants must look in the mirror and see how pivotal they are in God's awesome creation. God is so amazing! His works are so wondrous! (Ps 86:10).

Speaking of the melanin that Ham's descendants are so richly endowed with, earlier we found that Adam and Eve was a heterozygous couple with melanin that made them have medium to light brown skin. So how important is melanin?

If Adam and Eve did not have melanin that Ham's offspring are so richly endowed with, they would not have been able to produce a variety of colorful racial groups on earth (i.e., no melanin; no Adam and Eve to produce colorful racial groups).

So how important is the melanin that Ham's offspring are so richly endowed with? Without melanin, Adam and Eve would not exist. Without Adam and Eve, Ham's family line would not exist (no Adam and Eve; no offspring of Ham to be God's reservoir for creating colorful racial groups). So, without the melanin that Ham's family line is so richly endowed with, God could not fulfill His purpose.

At this point, an important note is in order. Ham's skin had the dark tones of one end of God's skin color spectrum and Japheth's skin had the pinkish tones of the other end. Shem's color, therefore, was a blend between

Ham's and Japheth's skin tones (i.e., close to an olive tone). So, Ham's and Japheth's color genes were pivotal in the making of Shem's and Christ's olive skin tones. What I'm saying is that God knew exactly what He was doing when He created the genes of Ham's offspring. They're not an afterthought as Satan would have you believe.

So, Japheth's and Ham's color genes were equally important in the making of the skin tones of Shem's descendants. This is symbolic of God's calling for Japheth's and Ham's offspring—i.e., they are called to work together to support, backup and up hold Shem's descendants as they spread God's gospel to the world.

The beauty of Ham's offspring through God's eyes— Part XI

God's creation in the beginning was not only a divine masterpiece, but it could not be improved upon. Speaking of God's marvelous creation, the believers of all racial groups will have their same features in the world to come, except that their features will reflect heaven's glory and their bodies will not have any frailties, weight problems, abnormalities or sicknesses. Not only will there be no more deaths, but God will wipe away their tears, sorrows, pains and crying. (Rev 21:4).

On that note, God's says, ". . . Some men will say, How are the dead raised? What type of bodies will they have? The body you sow will not have life unless it dies (in Jesus) . . . the body you sow is not the body that'll be . . . But God will give it a body that pleases Him and you'll have your own body." (1 Cor 15:35-38).

The features that God created in the beginning pleased Him; they're His masterpiece. So, these are the features that people will be raised with. For these are the features that pleased God in the beginning. And, just as the sun, moon and stars have different forms of glory (beauty); resurrected bodies will have their own forms of glory (beauty). (1 Cor 15:41). So, saints in each racial group will have their own form of beauty when their bodies are resurrected. (1 Cor 15:37-44).

Like the stars have individual glory (1 Cor 15:41), each racial group will have its own glory (beauty) when it's resurrected on the other side. For, as noted, God gives every seed his/her own body as it pleases Him. (1 Cor 15:35-38).

God's creation was perfect. So, in Paradise, all racial groups will have the same perfect features they were created with, except that they'll reflect heaven's glory. Their bodies will have no imperfections. These are the bodies that please God. This shows that God was well pleased with the features of Ham's offspring when He created them in the beginning. Through the dark-skinned maiden who portrays Ham's offspring and all other people of color, God shows us that there are no spots (flaws) in the features of Ham's offspring.

As Sol Song 4:7 says, "They're fair (beautiful)—i.e., flawless. So, do you believe what God said about Ham's offspring or do you believe Satan's lie that they're ugly? God forbid that anyone should believe Satan, for he's the father of all lies. (John 8:44). He'll have you so blinded that you won't be able to see strait; you'll be as blind as a bat when it comes to seeing the beauty of Ham's offspring through God's eyes.

Those who don't believe that the dark-skinned maiden was born black and portrays Ham's offspring (Sol Song 1:5), will not be able to interpret Sol Song properly. They'll miss God's truths about the beauty of Ham's offspring by miles.

Satan knows the truth, but he doesn't want you to know. He turned what God meant for good (Ham's features) into a lie. (John 8:44). But, God's purpose is for all racial groups to strive to keep the unity of the Spirit in the bond of peace. (Eph 4:3). Fitly joined together, they're to supply the needs of each other. (Eph 4:16).

Satan knows that Ham's, Japheth's and Shem's offspring have a racial calling to fulfill—i.e., they're to work together in carrying out God's great commission. (Matt 28:18-20). That said, thank God that there are pockets in our society where Ham's Shem's and Japheth's offspring bind together to carry out God's purpose.

You'll find that Satan's evil plot to derail their purpose is quite ineffective when they bind together for God—each racial group supplying the needs of the other racial groups. For God is love. Satan is full of hate. (1 John 4:8, John 10:10). Satan is determined to derail God's plan for mankind by any means necessary.

He set himself up as the only god in the universe. (Isa 14:13-14). He strives to have God's racial groups scratching and clawing at each other's throats.

God's saints who listen to Satan and discriminate against Ham's descendants or other racial groups by thinking more highly of themselves than they ought are steadily losing heavenly treasures. They should be storing up heavenly treasures for themselves. (Rom 12:3, 1 Cor 3:10-15, Matt 6:19-20).

The beauty of Ham's offspring through God's eyes— Part XII

Some people think that their racial group has cornered the market on beauty. Those who follow Satan's claim that Ham's descendants are ugly don't realize that it's not about who has straight hair and who has a thin nose. It's what Christ looks like that matters—i.e., having Christ's features is true beauty in God's eyes.

All racial groups emanate from Christ's gene pool for He created all things. (John 1:1-3, Col 1:16). Possessing God's entire gene pool means that Christ's features do not reflect just one racial group. Christ's features are reflected in all racial groups. As such, Christ's features are a perfect blend and a perfect composite of all racial groups.

So, when we see Christ, we'll be like Him (1 John 3:2)—i.e. saints will be conformed to His image; not the image of a certain racial group. (Rom 8:29). We will not look like people from another racial group who think that they've cornered the market on beauty. Instead, each racial group will see its features reflected in Christ who is the perfect blend of all racial groups. The fact that Christ's features reflect your features is all that matters.

In this light, God gives us a full-length portrait of the dark-skinned maiden's body. As noted, she portrays people in general while at the same time she portrays Ham's descendants in particular. God uses the breathtaking splendor of His creation to poetically portray—feature by feature—the captivating beauty of Shem's, Japheth's and Ham's descendants (including all other people of color).

So, let's go to the next chapter and study (through the dark-skinned maiden's body) the details of God's full length portrait of Shem's, Japheth's and Ham's offspring (including all other people of color).

CHAPTER 25

The Beauty Of Ham's Offspring Through God's Eyes—Session 3

The beauty of Ham's offspring through God's eyes— Part XIII

> The people that God made are truly beautiful. Their features, lovely features are delightfully suitable.
>
> He didn't make any mistakes for our noses are His best. Our hair textures, lip shapes and skin tones are flawless.
>
> O how beautiful and pleasant thou art O creation. So joyful will be your heavenly destination.

In this section, Christ the King and creator of all beings: Col 1:16 (as portrayed by King Solomon) is describing—feature by feature—the captivating beauty of Shem's, Japheth's and Ham's descendants (including all other people of color).

The dark-skinned maiden's skin is black and beautiful. (Sol Song 1:5). She represents all people. Thus, all the people that God made are beautiful. As such, the skin tones of Shem's, Japheth's and Ham's offspring (as well as all other people of color) are delightfully beautiful. As for Ham's offspring in particular, this also means that their dark skin tones are delightfully beautiful in God's eyes.

The feet, belly and navel of the maiden are beautiful. Her joints and thighs are like jewels. Her hands are a cunning work. Her neck is as lovely as an ivory tower. Her eyes are as the fish pools in Heshbon. (Sol Song 7:1-4). Christ didn't make any mistakes when He created people. They are His masterpiece.

Christ reveals that the dark-skinned maiden's nose is as beautiful as the Tower of Lebanon. (Sol Song 7:4). She has no flaws in her nose. As for Ham's offspring in particular, God made no mistakes. He created their noses with no imperfections (i.e., their noses are flawless and their nose sizes are delightfully beautiful).

Herein, God shares that He had to create wide noses so that He could have variety in nose sizes (variety is the key). Without wide noses, He couldn't have variety. So, in God's eyes, wide noses are needed for beauty. You have to see it through God's eyes. Otherwise, you'll be blind when it comes to beauty.

Christ (the King and creator of all beings) speaks (through the dark-skinned maiden) about the head and hair textures of people. "Thine head upon thee is like Carmel, and the hair of thine head is like purple." (Sol Song 7:5). Purple speaks of royalty. That is, in God's eyes, the dark-skinned maiden's hair equates with royalty in that it's as majestic as a king. In God's eyes, her hair has no flaws.

As for Ham's descendants in particular, God didn't make any mistakes. Their hair textures are flawless. Many people use the words **good hair** to refer to certain hair textures. But in God's eyes, all people have **good hair**. For when God looked upon our hair textures, He saw that it was very good. (Gen 1:31).

In Sol Song 4:3 Jesus speaks about her lips. Talking through the dark-skinned maiden, Christ, the King and creator of all things said, "Thy lips are not only as beautiful as a thread of scarlet, but they are also as beautiful as a drop of honeycomb." (Sol Song 4:11).

Herein, we see that when God created the lips of Shem's, Japheth's and Ham's descendants (including all other people of color), their lips were not only beautiful, but they had no spots—i.e. their lips were flawless. (Sol Song 4:3, 11).

As for Ham's descendants in particular, God loves their lips. He didn't make any mistakes when He created their lips. In other words, when God created the lips of Ham's descendants, their lips had no flaws or imperfections— i.e., in God's eyes, the fullness of their lips were perfectly created.

Conclusively, in describing the features of Shem's, Japheth's and Ham's descendants (including all other people of color), Christ reveals that their features are without flaws, without spots and delightfully beautiful.

The beauty of Ham's offspring through God's eyes— Part XIV

Christ in His humble position as God's sacrificial Lamb came to earth, shed His precious blood and died on the cross for our sins. Christ in his humble position (as portrayed by the shepherd boy) further speaks to Shem's, Japheth's and Ham's descendants (including all other people of color).

Remember, the dark-skinned maiden portrays Ham's offspring. As such, Chap 8 of Sol Song refers to believers in general while at the same time it refers to Hams descendants in particular.

Japheth's, Shem's and especially Ham's offspring are to take Christ home with them, for His love is sweet and He sticks closer than a brother. They're to kiss Him with love as He embraces them in His arms (for He puts His left hand under their heads while His right hand embraces them). They (especially Ham's offspring) are to feed Him the spiced wine of the juice of their pomegranates. (Sol Song 8:1-3).

Pomegranates have many seeds. Spiritually, they're to feed Christ many seeds of their fruitfulness, righteousness, holiness and joyfulness. Likewise, the many seeds of the pomegranate speak of the many seeds (bodies) of saints that'll be resurrected unto eternal life.

In Sol Song 8:5 the phrase "leaning upon her beloved" portrays the love that Christ desires of His saints (especially Ham's offspring). Saints are to love Christ with all of their hearts. (Mk 12:30). God wants the maiden (who portrays saints in general and Ham's offspring in particular) to lean on His everlasting arms as Israel did when He brought her out of bondage in Egypt. (Ex 20:1-3).

In Sol Song 8:6, the maiden responds to her beloved (Jesus Christ). She says, to Him, "Set me as a seal upon thine heart and upon thine arm." That is, make me your love permanently, protect me with your strength and never let me go. If Japheth's, Shem's and Ham's offspring (as well as all other people of color) receive Christ, He will indeed love them and set them as seals upon His heart.

Death's strength that won't let go isn't as strong as Christ's love for them. His love and jealousy for them is as fervent as the flames of Hades. Even many waters cannot quench His love for them—i.e., floods cannot drown Christ's love for them. So, they are seals upon His heart. (Sol Song 8:6-7). If you're one of Ham's offspring, you must engrave these divine truths in your heart as long as you live.

The beauty of Ham's offspring through God's eyes— Part XV

In Sol Song 8:11-14, Christ, the King of kings and creator of all things (as portrayed by King Solomon) is speaking to Japheth's, Shem's and Ham's offspring (including all other people of color) about the callings of their racial groups.

They must work in God's vineyard (His kingdom: Matt 20:1, 21:33). As light bearers in the vineyard, Shem's offspring are to teach the 4 components of God's birthright blessing. As watchmen in the vineyard, Japheth's offspring are to watch over Israel and the covenant of life and peace that God made with her.

As servants of servants in the vineyard, Ham's offspring are to minister their special gift of reconciliation between God and man unto peace. They're to be God's walking symphony by leading all nations in praise and worship like unto the cherubim. And, they're to be God's special servants of servants who show the world how to serve God faithfully.

In verse 14, the phrase "make haste my love" shows that Shem's, Japheth's and Ham's descendants (and all other people of color) are waiting for Christ to return to earth. As such, Satan strives (by any means necessary) to keep them from knowing the callings of their respective racial groups.

As for Ham's offspring in particular, Satan (on his Hamitic battlefront) strives to make people think that they're an afterthought—i.e., they're insignificant to God. He doesn't want us to see their beauty through God's eyes. He doesn't want us to know how much God loves them and how pivotal they are in God's plans.

So, do Ham's offspring matter to God in an extremely important way? From eternity past, have they always been on God's mind? Are they first class in God's eyes? Yes, a thousand times yes is the answer to all of the above. Here and now and throughout eternity, God has undying love for Ham's offspring.

Therefore, as a descendant of Ham, you must not listen to what society dictates as beauty. As this book clearly shows, you're an ingenious work of art created by and for Christ—i.e., you're God's genius of sheer beauty. So, lift your head and walk in the divine beauty in which you were created.

Most importantly, there are celestial bodies and terrestrial bodies. But, the glory of the celestial is one form of beauty and the terrestrial is another form of beauty. (1 Cor 15:40). Is the sun more beautiful than the moon? No, it is not. Is the moon more beautiful than the stars? No, it is not. Even the stars differ from one another in beauty (1 Cor 15:41).

God loves variety. He purposed to have great variety in His creation. In God's creation, the same as the stars differ in beauty; God's racial groups differ in beauty. So, with respect to beauty, society can think whatever it wants to think. But, God knew what was beautiful when He created all beings and all things. (Col 1:16).

Each time Ham's offspring look in the mirror; they'll see an ingenious form of God's creative beauty. He didn't make any mistakes. (Gen 1:31). Ham's offspring should never let another racial group dictate the standard of beauty for them. They must adhere to what God (the creator) said about their beauty.

They must lift their shoulders, hold their heads up and walk on by any negativism from society about their beauty. As long as they live, Ham's offspring must keep the divine truths that God spoke about their beauty in the inner parts of their souls, hearts and spirits. So, will you listen to what God said about your beauty Ham's descendant (Sol Song 4:7) or will you listen to Satan?

When God created Ham's features, they were very good. (Gen 1:31). Satan took that and ran with it. What God meant for good, Satan influenced people to think that Ham's features are ugly. God forbid, he's such a liar. (John 8:44).

Ham's offspring were always on God's mind. He had no thoughts of ugliness. His thoughts were of beauty and variety. Thoughts of ugliness come from Satan. God's thoughts are of whatsoever is lovely, of a good report, true, pure, honest and just. (Phil 4:8). Once you look beyond Satan, you'll be able to see the beauty of Ham's offspring through God's eyes—i.e., true beauty.

One final question is in order. Why does God love Ham's offspring so much? He loves variety (so, variety is the key)—i.e., variety in creating us would not have been possible without wide noses, full lips, wooly hair and dark skin. The only way God could have great variety was to create Ham's offspring who made it possible for Him to have the variety that He desired in His creation.

Before the world began, God sanctified Ham's offspring to make His desire possible. That is, He chose and predestinated them to make it possible for Him to have a variety of colorful racial groups according to the good pleasure of His will. (Eph 1:4-5,11). Even though they stepped forward like a lamb (as Christ was a lamb) and made it possible for God to have great variety in His creation, God would bestow upon them a mighty blessing and a great reward.

He made them special servants of servants, which is a mighty blessing and a great reward. For whoever will be great, let him be a servant and whoever will be a chief let him be a servant. Servants in this world will be God's greatest chiefs in Paradise. (Matt 20:26-28). Because of this blessing and reward, God made a way for Ham's offspring to have high prestige positions of honor in Paradise. So, with this mighty blessing and great reward, God made it worth their while for serving Him so faithfully in making His desired creation possible.

All Ham's offspring have to do to obtain this reward is to (1) lift their heads and shoulders for all to see their creative beauty, (2) walk on by society's negativism about their beauty, and (3) fulfill their purpose and they'll receive God's mighty reward in heaven for making it possible for a variety of colorful racial groups to be created. Ham's offspring really need to realize their importance in God's creation.

This completes our study of the calling of Ham's racial group. As noted, Ham's offspring must keep these divine truths ever before them. Let's now study God's purpose for mixed children of color both in this world and in the world to come.

Mixed children of color

Special are children from interracial unions
With them God walks in sweet communion
They were born with a truly defined identity
They were born with a truly divine destiny
They were born to honor Jesus' holy divinity
They were born to dwell with Jesus for eternity

Ham's offspring play a pivotal role in God's creation of a great variety of skin colors. They provide the melanin that produces mixed children of color. Their color genes are mixed and blended with the color genes of Japheth's and Shem's color genes to procreate the beautiful mixed children of color around the world.

If you fall under the category of "mixed children of color" from interracial marriages, you are **truly blessed**. All races descended from Adam's blood. (Acts 17:26). All things that were made, such as Adam's genes, were made by and for Christ. (Col 1:16, John 1:3). Since Christ created Adam's gene pool, Christ is the origin and gene source of all mixed children of color.

So, Christ is the origin of all genes. (John 1:1-3). Thus, mixed children of color emanate from His gene pool. All mixed children of color, therefore, are made up of Christ's genes. Hence, all of their features are in Christ. Christ is the perfect blend of all people and mixed children of color. This truth shows that when you see mixed children of color, you see Christ who is the perfect blend of all races.

Mixed marriages and their mixed children of color are **truly blessed**. For their mixed children of color portray Christ, the perfect blend of all racial groups. God's master copy of their genes is coded in their cells. So, in this world and in Paradise, mixed children of color are memorials of the perfect blend of Christ's genes, which refers to the unity of Christ and His saints. Unity in Christ is God's purpose for all racial groups and mixed children of color. (Eph 4:1-6, Col 1:16-20).

So, if you're in an interracial marriage, **you're special**. Your children of color are a special blend of Christ's genes on purpose. For, both on earth and in Paradise, they memorialize Christ who is the perfect blend of all racial groups.

By divine design, they are whoever their fathers are. Satan tries to give them an identity crisis. But, they and their parents now know who they are. They are whoever their fathers are. For, it is his blood and only his blood that flows through their bodies. They do not have an identity crisis. This book has revealed the truth. Lastly, allow me to give you my final thoughts.

> The truth has been told. God has spoken. Ham must be bold and not be broken. God called Ham unto a special ministry of reconciliation. Ham's special ministry is between God and man unto salvation.
>
> Under God, Ham is a special peacekeeper. Under God, Ham is God's praise and worship leader. Under God, Ham's offspring are a walking symphony. Under God, the voices of Ham's offspring are precious gems to me.
>
> Ham shows us how to dwell in peace. As God's special servant it's his motif. God's created beauty in more than one form. For variety in creation is the norm.
>
> Ham's features are God's masterpiece with no flaws. Some say ugly things about Ham without cause. Some may not agree with Ham's creative beauty. Ham must walk on by those who're acting rudely.
>
> The features of Ham's offspring were created as God's best. If through God's eyes you see their beauty, you're truly blessed.
>
> I pray that in sharing God's word, I left no stones unturned. I pray that you enjoyed this book and all the things to be learned. To God be the glory!